MW00843608

CABIN

CABIN

OFF-THE-GRID ADVENTURES
WITH A CLUELESS CRAFTSMAN

PATRICK
HUTCHISON

ST. MARTIN'S PRESS
NEW YORK

First published in the United States by St. Martin's Press,
an imprint of St. Martin's Publishing Group

CABIN. Copyright © 2024 by Patrick Hutchison. All rights reserved. Printed in the
United States of America. For information, address St. Martin's Publishing Group,
120 Broadway, New York, NY 10271.

www.stmartins.com

The Library of Congress Cataloging-in-Publication Data is available upon request.

ISBN 978-1-250-28570-6 (hardcover)
ISBN 978-1-250-28571-3 (ebook)

Our books may be purchased in bulk for promotional, educational, or business use.
Please contact your local bookseller or the Macmillan Corporate and Premium Sales
Department at 1-800-221-7945, extension 5442, or by email at
MacmillanSpecialMarkets@macmillan.com.

First Edition: 2024

10   9   8   7   6   5   4   3   2   1

*Dedicated to all who ever found themselves
at that little cabin on Wit's End.*

That place, and this book, will forever be because of you.

CONTENTS

1

FOUND

bought the cabin for $7,500 from a guy on Craigslist. He was a tugboat captain. His name was Tony.

Here's why.*

I was in my midtwenties and experiencing what felt like a sort of quarter-life crisis. People all around me, people I thought were my friends, were going off and doing ridiculous things like getting careers and advanced degrees, husbands, wives, kids, dogs, and other accoutrements of the heavy-responsibility genre. They knew what Roths and IRAs and 401(k)s were, or at least they knew enough to know that wondering what those things were was something to be concerned about. And here I was, thinking that we had all agreed to get through college, or

---

* Why I bought the cabin, not why Tony was a tugboat captain or why he was named Tony. I assume because he liked tugging boats and because his parents liked the name, but it's anyone's guess. Except for Tony. He probably knows.

at least those years when one might go to college, and then just sort of hang out forever and eat pizza and watch *The Simpsons*. It had seemed like a good plan, but no one else was holding up their end of the bargain. I had no idea what I wanted.

I was living in Seattle, trying to be a writer. But it wasn't working out. I'd gone to college. At one point, there was a plan to become a doctor. Instead, I double majored in anthropology and history. It's hard to imagine an educational shift more perfectly suited to destroying a person's job prospects. After graduating, I wandered. I spent six months in Patagonia, a month in Colombia. Rarely did I receive mail for more than a year at the same address. I worked at random jobs—a bartender, a sandwich delivery person, a sushi busboy. Out of those wanderings and a social science education, I'd landed on a dream of becoming a gonzo journalist travel writer–type person. Think Hunter S. Thompson meets Paul Theroux and Anthony Bourdain. I wanted to hunt down bizarre stories and wild characters, mostly because it seemed like a surefire way to fuel an endlessly intriguing day-to-day life. Apparently, however, those jobs are not easy to come by. Instead, I'd sit at my laptop and fire off story pitches to editors who couldn't have cared less. Jobs were few and far between. The pay was terrible. The reality was a constant, stressful, demoralizing struggle.

I started selling off parts of the writing dream for things like being able to afford rent, health care, and foods that didn't rhyme with Rop Tamen. I stopped chasing the underpaid cool magazine jobs and accepted the desk jockey marketing copy gigs. Years after leaving college with an intent to roam the earth telling the stories of beautiful lunatics, I was in an office creating email templates to sell advertising to plumbers and wondering how I'd ended up here.

It felt like a great secret that I was completely lost. The lack of direction and purpose were embarrassing, like a part of me was missing. When I looked around, it seemed that everyone else was getting on with things, stacking their cards, squirreling away, creating plans for five years, ten years, and beyond. My long-term plans ended at knowing when the leftover Chinese food would go bad.

At first, I really wanted to fix the problem. I wanted to find a new purpose and dive in with everything. But it wasn't happening, or I wasn't looking in the right place, or I was being too lazy about the whole thing. I had no idea. What I did know was that every passing week, month, and year that the aimlessness went on, I was more and more desperate.

Slowly, that desire to find a purpose festered into a simple desperation to at least appear like I had a purpose. If I couldn't find a cure, maybe I could at least find something that worked on the symptoms. I needed a distraction of responsibility, a smoke and mirrors show that I could hold up to the rest of the world while I feverishly figured out what in the hell I was doing.

I knew that there were a few gold-standard, proof-of-responsibility milestones that I could turn to. Things like grad school, marriage, kids, enlisting in the military, maybe. But the idea of going back to school seemed ludicrous, which made the idea of a new career seem pretty unlikely. Getting married was a bit too dependent on the cooperation of others, and having a kid was that same problem multiplied. The military, as far as I knew, still involved a lot of running around, so that was out.

At the time, the girl I was dating announced that she was looking to buy a house. It was an idea that seemed absurd to me, considering the closest I had ever come to qualifying for a mortgage was getting approved to finance a DVD player from Best Buy. Her confidence in tackling the task made me question how unbelievably out of my league she was.

I'd never seen the house-buying process before. It was astounding. It reeked of responsibility with all its forms and appointments and phone calls and emails and bank . . . stuff. It dawned on me that a real estate purchase might be an ideal solution to my problem. For two solid weeks, I reveled in telling folks that I was "looking into buying a house" when they asked how things were going. It was marvelous, but the dream was short-lived. As it turned out, while I could afford a house, I could not afford any house within a zip code I was familiar with. It was 2012, and Seattle-area home prices were the lowest they had been in more than a decade. There could not have been a more affordable time to buy a house, but I was nowhere near being able to do so.

Outside of Seattle, there were options. I'd sit at my computer, zooming out farther and farther until I saw listings that matched my "financial profile." They were far from the city. Far from traffic and streetlights. They were in farmlands and river valleys, and still farther yet, they were nestled in the foothills of Washington State's Cascade Mountains. And often, they were not homes at all. They were cabins.

I'd grown up in the woods, on a few acres about an hour and a half south of Seattle. My childhood was spent tromping through dense forests of hemlock and Douglas fir, pushing through ferns and blackberry bushes with the family dog, a chocolate Lab named Mud, who had a taste for sticks and deer shit. When the long days of summer allowed, friends and I joined one another in the woods building tree forts with my dad's rust-covered hand tools. When they were complete, we'd pack ourselves inside and spend hours practicing swear words, farting, spoiling our appetites with Cheez-Its and warm cans of Mountain Dew. Scrolling through pictures of cabins on real estate sites let loose a torrent of nostalgia from those tree fort days. Though adult life included summers with frequent camping trips, I still missed the woods. Certainly a vacation home was the sort of surefire totem of responsibility that I was hoping to find, but when I saw those cabins, my real estate pursuits became fueled by a desire to return to that magical feeling of being in the woods, cramped into a cozy space with good friends, maybe swinging a hammer around from time to time.

There was a problem, though. While I could afford a cabin, I could not simultaneously afford a place to live in the city. Escaping to a woodland retreat was what I wanted. Becoming a full-time hermit was not. Nonetheless, I kept looking, gawking at log structures in snowy mountains, drooling over humble cottages alongside lakes and rivers. It became the mindless thing I did on my laptop or phone in the morning when I woke up, on the toilet during work, and late at night when I couldn't sleep. This went on for months.

Until late one night, in the early fall of 2013. I was on Craigslist looking for ads featuring any one of a number of items that had been stolen from our house during a recent burgling. Having no luck, I returned to the search bar and, on a whim, typed in "cabin" and hit Enter. The inquiry had the sophistication of an eleven-year-old typing "boobs" into Google. It was just as effective.

My eyes locked onto the top result: "Tiny Cabin in Index."

I knew Index. The little outpost hemmed in by brutally beautiful mountains consisted of a shabby mini-mart, whose shelves of dust-covered beans and out-of-date camping equipment never seemed to change, a small coffee shop, whose OPEN sign was always illuminated even though the door was always locked, and an adventure rafting company that offered guided trips down the Skykomish River. Apart from that, Index maintained a volunteer-run fire station, a small collection of cabins, a school, and a decrepit inn that had been neglected for decades despite a constant stream of new owners with grand plans to renovate. My visits to the town were always quick stops on my way to hikes or camping spots. Index was a last chance to stock up on ice or a few cases of cheap beer before diving deeper into the mountains.

But it wasn't the town's name that drew my attention to the ad. It was the picture and the price. The simple, tiny cabin was set against a backdrop of moss-laden trees. Only ten by twelve feet, it looked more like a big chicken coop than anything else. I knew people that had larger places to store their lawn mowers. Architecturally, it took inspiration from drawings of houses made by preschoolers. Box on bottom. Triangle on top. All around it, the forest floor was covered in a sea of bright ferns. Here and there, the first leaves of fall added a pop of gold or crimson, donated by a few mature maples that towered overhead. Nestled into the forest, the cabin begged for someone to cozy up inside, light a fire, take a slug of whiskey, and let the world drift away, all for the price of a used Hyundai. They were asking $7,500.

I sent an email immediately, requesting more info and a visit as nonchalantly as possible, so as not to appear overeager. When I heard from the owner the next afternoon, the reply was quick and equally casual:

Yeah, that's no problem. The key is above the door. It's the fourth place on the left up on Wit's End Pl.

The owner's name was Tony. He seemed about as concerned about the place as a dog is about climate change. I told him I might go check it out, *if* I had time. I didn't want him to think I was desperate, didn't want him to know that within twenty minutes of receiving his message, I was speeding northeast, feverishly trying to cut out of the urban sprawl of Seattle before armies of tech workers swarmed the highways on their commutes home. By three o'clock, I had made it to U.S. 2, a two-lane, east-west corridor that roughly followed the Skykomish River as it wound down from the Cascades to Puget Sound.

In the winter, the highway was clogged with powder-hungry skiers headed to the resort at Stevens Pass. In the summer, it was equally clogged with a combination of hikers and campers looking to escape the bustle of Seattle for a weekend. And in all seasons, city folk streamed over the pass to reach Leavenworth, a stunning mountain town that had been transformed into a strange, pseudo-Bavarian theme park promising big pretzels and overpriced beer. It was, and continues to be, bafflingly popular.

It didn't take long for the landscape to begin shifting as I made my way east. The chain restaurants and clogged intersections gave way to one-light towns and rolling farmland. An hour after I left, the road aligned with the wide banks of the Skykomish River, flecked by the occasional retiree in full waders casting a line. I passed through Sultan, Startup, and Gold Bar, a trio of tiny places that were all too easy to mistake for one another. Experiences on previous road trips had taught me to remember that Sultan was home to the bakery that made cinnamon rolls the size of spare tires and giant cups of coffee that never cost more than a dollar. Startup, of course, was home to the drive-in with the best milkshakes and saltiest fries, and Gold Bar had the Prospector, where a kids' karaoke night turned the establishment into a makeshift day care on odd evenings.

I found myself daydreaming about a life where I would lean into the nooks and crannies of the town's homespun businesses. I imagined stopping in the little lumber store to buy bags of nails by the pound like my dad and I had when I was a kid. I pictured ducking into the studio apartment–size post office in Startup to send out letters to friends and family over longer cabin stays. And when I passed by one of the many white water raft companies that shuttled tourists down the Class IV rapids farther upriver, I took special notice of the road sign calling for "New Seasonal Guides! Now Hiring! Training Provided!" picturing myself as a summer raft guide. I hadn't even seen the cabin yet, and I already had a whole new life picked out to complement it.

After Gold Bar came Index, but not immediately. Index had something akin to intro music. In the few miles that separated the two towns, the road got tight. Gone were the farms and rural housing developments. There was no room here, no more flat.

Groves of massive Douglas fir and cedar guarded the shoulder. At the edge of Gold Bar, a long bridge revealed the Skykomish River below. No longer wide and calm, it had transformed into a mesmerizing display of shifting blues, swirling from deep cobalt to turquoise to snow white as it churned and tumbled over granite boulders the size of minivans. Taking inspiration from the river, the road began to snake through the valley. Around each bend were teasing glimpses of Mount Index, whose nearly six-thousand-foot peak loomed over the forest below.

U.S. 2 was known for being dangerous. It was the only highway in Washington I knew of that had a permanent sign erected to keep track of how many days it had been since a fatal collision. In over a decade of visits to the area, it felt rare to see the number top twenty-five. The sign itself was just outside of Index, and I often wondered if the dangers came not from the icy conditions in winter or the high speed limit (sixty miles per hour on what were very windy mountain roads) but from the sheer beauty of the place. When you approached the town, it was instinctual to shift forward in your seat, pulling yourself over the steering wheel to see even just 5 percent more of the surrounding granite spires. It was as if the mountains themselves had the power to draw you straight through the fucking windshield.

It seemed too good to be true that I wasn't driving through but diving deeper into those woods. I could only imagine what sort of picture-perfect cabins and cottages would be tucked along the river here, built by those who wanted to complement the surrounding environment rather than impose themselves on it. I figured I'd see folks chopping up firewood in preparation for the cold weather ahead. Maybe there'd be a father and son casting their lines into calm river pools for salmon, or someone out with their dog just enjoying an early-autumn walk.

The directions seemed fairly clear. When I took a right off the highway, I started getting excited. Crunching over a well-maintained gravel road, I slowly cruised along a winding drive that paralleled the river. Up and over a small hill, a homemade arch welcomed me to the Mount Index Riversites.

As the car found its way around a high bend, the road quickly dropped, and I hit the brakes. There was a monster below: a massive waterfall shooting out of a long, bottleneck canyon. It looked like something out of an Old Testament story. Later I would learn that Sunset Falls only drops 104 feet, but it does so over a span of rock about as long as a football field. With most waterfalls, there is an element of grace, a moment when the water is free to slip over the edge and drop without influence. Sunset Falls was not graceful. It was an aquatic mosh pit, a cocaine-fueled waterslide designed by Poseidon himself. I rolled down the window and slowly followed the road as it wound around the pool at the base of the cascade. Mist from the falls drifted through my open window and settled on the dash. It smelled like cedar.

Past the falls, the road turned sharply to cross an old wooden bridge above a straight section of railroad. I was supposedly getting close. According to Tony, Wit's End was not far beyond the bridge, but nothing by that name showed up. Before long, I started second-guessing my directions and my desire to stick around.

Until that point, I had seen an odd structure here and there, a few cabins, nothing out of the ordinary. Here, though, deeper in the community, a different type of neighborhood began to emerge. There were piles of rusted car components being overtaken by thick clumps of blackberry vines and muddy driveways packed with vehicles that clearly hadn't run in decades. Around one corner, I came across a large cleared lot with the charred remains of several RVs. Police tape still clung to some of the tree branches. It was hard to imagine any explanation other than a thriving meth business that had met an explosive end.

The only things that seemed bright and new were the ample orange-and-red NO TRESPASSING signs affixed to random trees, fence posts, and scattered bits of junk. I wasn't sure what was more frightening: the dangers that lurked behind the signs or the type of people who would desire to find out.

I would later learn that the Mount Index Riversites consisted of a few hundred lots, most under half an acre. It may have once been a pristine settlement of vacation properties in a gorgeous mountain environment, but at some point, Uncle Methadone moved in and really kicked some shit around. Whatever it might have been in the past, there now seemed to be two kinds of places in the Riversites: junk-strewn drug dens and everybody else. From the looks of the quirky lawn ornaments, everybody else was mostly grandparents, retirees, and the odd ski bum. I drove to the end of the road, where it finished with a big loop that had me soon heading back out. I'd passed by several road signs, but none that were close to sounding like Wit's End. I checked my phone, which hadn't had service since pulling off the highway, and checked the directions again. There were no additional hints to help me out. Without reception and with no desire to knock on the door of one of the many nightmares that surrounded me, I decided to turn back and head home, asking Tony for better directions or simply abandoning the prospect altogether.

As I made my way out, the glint of a green road sign caught my eye where I hadn't noticed one before. It wasn't on a post but rather rammed into a large maple. It read 's END PL. The rest of it was buried deep in the tree's bark, grown over after being placed there, likely decades before. It wouldn't be long before the apostrophe would be consumed and the tree would continue its gradual process of renaming the road. Hoping it was indeed Wit's End Place and not Lunatic's End Place, I unnecessarily flicked on my turn signal and hung a left, creeping up the gravel drive and looking for the fourth cabin on the left, not knowing whether to count the spray-painted school bus, overgrown with weeds, that sat at the corner.

Wit's End rose up a steep hill. Although the streak of abandoned structures continued here, there was a subtle difference. These were tiny cabins. Most were simple, the sorts of things more likely cobbled together by weekend warriors rather than full-blown construction companies. They resembled the kind of sheds that you'd see falling apart in the parking lots of Home Depot or Costco. Granted, there was far more character to these simple getaways. Little chimneys poked up from cedar shake roofs, ornamental stained glass windows provided pockets of vibrant color, and well-worn decks offered views toward the river and mountains. Though the overgrown driveways and weed-filled gutters indicated they weren't regularly occupied, they still felt tidy. They did not feel like the hideouts of a ne'er-do-well. They felt like forest refuges, clearly well loved at one time or another even if now they seemed forgotten.

My station wagon came over the top of a hill, and I counted the third cabin. Just beyond, over a steep drop to the left, the corrugated metal roof of a tiny structure sat cloaked in dried bits of moss and a red-brown blanket of fallen maple leaves. I parked in the middle of the road near the closest thing the cabin had to a driveway, a slightly cleared mud pit with a few patches of salmonberry bushes. Turning the car off, I hopped out and took in the scene.

Anticipation is an underrated feeling. It is that moment when all the possibilities of what could be pile up, and you can't help but wonder if there's a chance that what's to come might just be the best thing that's ever happened. Often, I felt like the anticipation before a grand adventure or a first date could feel as big or bigger than the experience itself. I stood there for a moment, savoring the anticipation of weekends spent with friends, crisp fall days burning leaves, long summer nights by the river, cozy winters huddled up inside, big snow, deer, bears, drinks, smoke, fire, wood, axes, sweat, tears, laughter. The structure was already a lifetime of memories and I hadn't even taken a step toward it. I checked my phone and saw that it had put itself into emergency mode on account of the lack of reception. While the lower road felt like the sort of place one might have the need to call 911, I felt safe up here, so I tucked it into my jeans and crossed the few broken planks of wood strategically arranged for safe passage across the swampy ground that led from the road to the cabin.

In person, it felt bigger. The steeply pitched roof was rusty, but seemed solid. Neatly arranged cedar shakes covered some of the exterior. The rest was some kind of cheap exterior paneling, with little grooves cut out to mimic the aesthetic normally provided by actual boards. Though the windows looked almost brand-new, the remainder of the cabin appeared to be cobbled together from miscellaneous spare parts. In front, the skeleton of a deck waited to have its top filled in. A few pieces of rotten plywood served as a substitute in the meantime. On the small ledge above the cabin's only door, my fingers pushed through a curtain of cobwebs to find a key. Curiously, there was no knob; two dead bolts held the heavy door in place. The key turned easily in each lock, and the door swung open, though not all the way.

About a third of the way into its swing path, the bottom of the door caught against the floor, indicating that either the door, or the floor, or both, were not level. The inside smelled like a good scotch, wet earth, and punky wood, which didn't bode well for the hopefully dry interior of a house or cabin. Even with three windows, there was not much light inside. The floor was mostly dirty plywood. In the corner were scraps of even dirtier linoleum. Some of the walls were covered haphazardly with cedar boards that had at one point been painted a shade of pink whose name, if you were to come across the swatch at a hardware store, would likely be Pepto Bismol but Gray Somehow. Where the walls weren't covered, exposed hunks of pink fiberglass insulation hung loosely from within the cabin's framing.

Beneath two of the windows was a small cabinet that I didn't dare open for fear of getting ambushed by a startled woodland creature. Opposite the cabinet, a crude ladder led me to a dark, cramped loft. The loft floor appeared to be made of more plywood, held on by a parade of rusty, half-driven nails. There was a window opposite the ladder, but I was too unsure of the date of my last tetanus shot to consider making the hands-and-knees journey to see if it was operable.

Back on the main level, I tried to picture where things might go, what work might have to get done. New flooring, new wall coverings, and fixing the door or the floor or both for starters. I'd need to cover the deck, figure out a place to poop, and fill in the swamp of a driveway. That was just off the top of my head. In reality, it was a dark, musty, disgusting hole. There were spiders everywhere, skittering around the floor like extras in a Godzilla movie. It was the sort of place where you wish your shoes had shoes. There was no electricity, no water, no plumbing, no wires, no bathroom, no lights, no Wi-Fi, no cell service. If you counted gravity and rain, the total number of utilities would have been two. It was a wooden box with a roof and a door. It was perfect.

Like a new parent with a hideous baby, my eyes glazed over the flaws. At that moment, I only saw what I wanted. Weeks later, I would see the holes in the floor. I would see that not a single support beam was level or straight. I would see the gaps in the siding. The rotting rim joist failing to support an entire corner of the cabin would eventually catch my eye, and a militia of mosquitoes would soon welcome me to the neighborhood. But I noticed none of it then. I didn't see that there were signs of a leaking roof or of a rampant mouse infestation. I overlooked the swamp of a driveway and the tetanus-riddled loft and the old wood and the bent nails. Instead, I saw the flushed faces of friends after a day of snowshoeing. I saw boots drying by a woodstove and a pot of soup warming on the fire. I saw summer days, the car filled with new wood, a trunkful of tools. I saw only potential, and I saw a version of myself that was capable of making it better. Not great, necessarily, but better. Most importantly, for the first time in a while, I felt the pull of something a bit bigger, a grand pursuit, a thing to dive into that was different and new and exciting. I could buy a cabin and fix it up. Why not?

As I locked up the door and replaced the key, a new wave of anticipation began to grow inside me, one that obscured the meth houses and scrap-filled yards from my vision on the way out. Instead, my eyes belonged only to the waterfall, the trees, and the mountain, and I took them all in while wondering how much a circular saw might cost.

2

DOING THE DEED

The drive home sobered me up a bit. Reflecting on the sexy-cool cabin-fix-it-guy dream as I waded through traffic on my way home, I admitted to myself a few potential problems. Small problems. For example, I didn't know how to fix up a cabin. I could hang a picture and put IKEA furniture together with the best of them, but I hadn't held a saw since my adolescent days building tree forts when I considered sap to be a fundamental component of a structure's integrity. As such, I was also a poor judge of the cabin's current condition. It was either a few swift kicks from crumbling to the ground, or it was merely the victim of many aesthetic shortcomings. My total lack of experience made it impossible to tell.

Beyond the cabin, there were other issues. The neighborhood and its gallery of horrors were certainly not inviting. The cabins on Wit's End were charming in a dystopian sort of way, but the abandonment was troubling. It was clear others had the same idea as I did, to create a cozy escape in the woods. But the evidence indicated their dreams were unanimously abandoned. I worried there was a reason.

I also had to admit how far I'd come from the initial idea of a cabin, an idea partially born out of a desire to plant a flag of responsibility, to show others or maybe just prove to myself that I was doing more with my life than just sitting at a desk churning out marketing emails. It felt absurd to think that a leaky, moss-covered box in the woods was just the thing to propel me into the alum of adulthood. Even so, there was something about it that felt right. When I got back into town, I decided to play it slow with Tony. I'd take a few days to decide if I even wanted it, then I'd offer him $5,000 and definitely not pay more than $6K. I dialed the number. He picked up after the second ring.

We exchanged pleasantries, and I asked him to tell me all he could about the place. The story wasn't complicated. He worked in Seattle as a tugboat captain, had always wanted a little place in the mountains. He'd bought the cabin at the county auction for tax-foreclosed properties. The idea was to have it as a weekend retreat, a place to fix up when he had the time. But that time hadn't come. The tug business was a bit too good to afford him the free weekends he'd hoped for, so he'd decided to pass the cabin on to someone who might pick up the project where he couldn't. Besides, he told me, a buddy of his had just bought a place down the road that was bigger and finished and—shockingly—apparently much, much nicer. He'd just abuse that relationship and skip the whole working-on-it part.

"Well," I said, getting down to business. "It looks like it definitely needs some work, so I think I'm gonna need to give it a few days of thought, then maybe make you an offer."

"Well, I've had a few other offers, so I think I'll probably let them know it's still avail—"

"I'll take it," I cut him off.

"Okay, I'll grab the papers. Can you meet tomorrow night to sign it over?"

"Yes."

"All right, I'll let you know a good place. We'll need a notary."

"Sounds good," I replied while simultaneously heading to my computer to Google what a notary did. It was happening. I was terrified.

Committing to the sale brought up the final problem with buying the cabin—namely, that I did not have $7,500. But I was confident that obtaining a loan from a local bank would be easy enough given the low price.

Credit where credit is due, none of the loan officers I met with outright laughed at me when I showed them pictures of the cabin. Their reaction, however, was about what I would have expected if I'd asked to borrow money for a pizza-powered time machine. The meetings were short. There was no creative work-around as far as they could see. When I ran out of banks to call, I dialed my last option: my mom. Parents must dread conversations with their children that immediately sound like business proposals. To her credit, she let me make my argument, which was basically, "Please?" and a promise to pay her back at an interest rate better than her savings account. Ultimately, she agreed to loan me the money, although I could tell she would have preferred if it were going to something more like grad school and less like a dank tree house for aimless millennials.

With the funds secured, I turned to the transaction itself.

From my brief foray into looking for real estate, I knew that in standard deals there were a litany of safety measures. There were appraisals and inspections and insurance companies involved to protect folks who didn't know any better from making terrible financial decisions. But this was not a half-million-dollar house in the city. This was a $7,500 shack in the woods without so much as a light switch. Employing the normal professionals for this transaction would have been like putting a helmet on to empty the dishwasher. Instead, there was just Tony and me and the hope for trust between strangers. Tony suggested we take care of the deed ourselves, and I happily agreed to the version of a deal that cost both of us less money. I imagined our exchange would be like the scenes in old westerns, where a grizzled cowpoke would throw a few coins to a bartender, make their mark on a slip of paper, slam a shot of whiskey, and walk out of the saloon a landowner. The reality wasn't far off, although there wasn't any whiskey, the saloon was a UPS, and the rough-hewn bartender was an acne-riddled teen in a brown visor.

When Tony arrived, he looked every bit the part of a modern-day tugboat captain. About five foot ten, dressed in a ratty baseball cap, paint-splattered sweatshirt, and heavy canvas pants, he looked strong enough to pull cargo ships around the bay without much more than a rowboat. He met me with a smile and a crushing handshake. Greetings were exchanged, and he produced the necessary papers. Inside, the UPS boy efficiently stamped and notarized our forms, I handed Tony $7,500 in cashier's checks, and somehow, that was it. In less than five minutes, it was over. Tony had all my money, and I had a piece of paper.

As we said our goodbyes, I asked Tony, "Oh, anything I should know about the neighborhood?"

Backing up slowly, he casually responded, "Uh, no, not really.

There can be drama up there, but I'd just stay out of it. There is one guy next to you who thinks he owns part of the cabin, but it's fine," he said with a final wave to let me know there'd be no more discussion about it. And with that, he disappeared down the crowded sidewalk. Assuming I'd been scammed, I started thinking about which power tools to buy first.

3

TOOL CHATTER

For someone who imagined they'd like to build a thing or two, I had an embarrassment of tools. Most of what I had was acquired by occupation or accident. In college, I'd worked as a delivery "driver" for Jimmy John's. I say "driver" because I, along with every other delivery person there, distributed late-night sandwiches to drunk kids on sorority row by bicycle. The remnants of that job were a few wonderful friends and a collection of wrenches and tire-changing implements that were largely useless for anything other than repairing a bike. Nevertheless, I added them to a corner of my room I'd set aside for cabin supplies. I also scrounged up an old hammer, a measuring tape, a dull handsaw that I was pretty sure was for cutting metal only, and a collection of screwdrivers, all flathead in nature. The one power tool I did possess was an electric drill on loan from my brother. Considering the drill had to be plugged in and the closest outlet to the cabin was probably a quarter of a mile away, its presence in my cabin tool corner was mostly symbolic.

I had used the drill once before. The goal had been a small hole in some drywall for a modest hook, but I underestimated the drill's power by a factor of six or seven million. The drill bit and then the drill itself went through the wall much like that Kool-Aid fellow tends to enter a room. Subsequent attempts produced smaller and smaller holes until I finally got what I needed. Thankfully, it was a big picture. As the proud yet incapable owner of a cabin vacation home in need of a few updates, it was clear that I'd need some new tools. Chief among them would be a battery-powered drill that I could take into the woods and operate, as they say, off the grid. But the search for drills had been far more stressful than I had imagined it could be, the sheer number of options and combinations of power tools available seemed designed to break down people's sanity.

One evening at home, while my roommate, Indy, stood over the stove slamming thick burgers into a cast-iron pan with a spatula, I recounted my troubles.

"It's the sort of thing where it's going to cost between two hundred fifty and probably four hundred dollars, no matter what I do. I want a cordless drill and circular saw, which seems simple enough, but it makes sense to get both the same brand; that way, you can share batteries. I learned this," I said to Indy while I paced the kitchen.

"Yes." Indy was really on board so far. Smoke from the burgers was rapidly filling the kitchen, so I opened the side door and continued explaining while batting the door back and forth to encourage the smoke into the yard.

"Now, for whatever the hell reason, manufacturers don't offer, 'Here's a box, inside is a drill and a battery. Here's a box, inside is a drill and a saw. Here's a box, inside is just a drill.' No, it's, 'Here's a box that contains two drills and two batteries.' Now, one of those drills, you don't even know what to use it for. That box is twenty dollars more than the box that only contains the drill you want, but do you want to spend twenty dollars extra for a drill you don't even understand?"

Presumably someone understood what the extra drill was for, but it wasn't about to be me.

"And! Then you need a saw, and saws typically like larger batteries, larger than the ones that come with your drill. But Home Depot doesn't carry 'saw with battery' kits. They have the saw only, so should you buy a larger battery for the saw? Well, that's ludicrously expensive, so now I'm thinking maybe I'll get the kit that contains *all of them*! But that has a light too and a holder bag that I don't need, and it doesn't matter, because it's not in stock anyway. Now, add to that, there are three different brands, and I was stuck in there, talking to a fifty-four-year-old father of three, grandfather of seven Home Depot guy who's been selling tools for thirty years, and he's telling me to trust him because he 'sees a lot of that Milwaukee stuff gettin' returned.'

"And according to this guy, Paul, there's 'a friggin' killer sale on Bosch drills right now.' So I say, 'Yes, Paul, but do you have Bosch saws?' And Paul says to me, 'Nah, they're online only.' And so now I'm back to square one, because if you don't get all the same brand, then the batteries won't work between them, ya know?"

Indy was smiling, either because he enjoyed watching me unravel or because he didn't want to provoke someone who was already so clearly unhinged. "All right, these are ready," he said, clicking off the stove's burner and moving the burgers onto a plate.

Most of the smoke had dissipated—though, in hindsight, I realized that fear of a smoke alarm would have required our smoke alarms to have fresh batteries in them or at least, and possibly more importantly, to exist in the first place. I shut the door, grabbed another beer out of the refrigerator, and sat down at our kitchen table. Pushing a week's worth of mail aside, Indy slid the plate of burgers toward me. This is how we ate then. No sides, just a pile of burgers.

Grabbing one and squirting a healthy dose of mustard underneath the bun, I ranted on.

"I spent an hour and a half in Home Depot last night. I only left because they closed and kicked me out. Just so they didn't think I was insane, I impulse bought a drill set at random. Now I've got a roomful of tools I'm too scared to open for fear of not being able to return them, and if I do return them," I said, bits of burger likely spilling from my mouth, "I'm gonna have to drive to the Home Depot in North Seattle, because if Paul sees me returning drills that aren't Bosch, I won't be able to stand the humiliation. So I'm back to square one with this stuff I don't know anything about, and there are eighteen different tabs open on my computer, and I've got Excel documents opened up with specs on torque ratios for drills I don't even understand how to turn on, and charts and manuals like you wouldn't believe."

Calmly, Indy asked, "Why don't you just return all of it and go to McLendon's?"

"Dude, McLendon's doesn't even carry Bosch," I replied, sighing with the undeserved confidence of someone who had learned less than twelve hours ago that A) Bosch was a company, B) they made power tools, C) they were considered good, D) McLendon's didn't carry them, and E) McLendon's was a hardware store.

"Does the entire world agree Bosch is the way to go?" he asked.

"Paul seemed to think that was my best bet. He had a real Little League coach vibe. I felt uncomfortably in his control. I have heard amazing stuff about Bosch, though. If I can get a Bosch drill, four batteries, and the saw for eighteen dollars more than what I've spent to get the Makita saw and drills with only two batteries, then I think I'll be in business."

Tossing the dishes in the sink, Indy said, "Makita?! What ever happened to DeWalt?" Now he was invested.

"Bud," I said with a chuckle that made it clear how far behind Indy was, "DeWalt is for plumbers. Know what I'm sayin'? That's what Paul says anyway. He also says I should quit my job. And he said I'm dropping my hands on the curveball."

We wrapped up the dishes, and I grabbed another beer to take into my room and revisit my drill research project. There was no clear answer. But a decision had to be made, so I went with what seemed most convenient: a drill set combo that I hoped would have plenty of battery power for weekend trips, a circular saw that seemed ideal for a wide variety of tasks, and a Sawzall, which—according to YouTube footage I'd seen—was about as destructive as it was dangerous and the perfect tool for any kind of demolition work.

When I got the tools home, I brought them into my room and shut the door. Carefully, I opened each one and turned them over in my hands, marveling at the sheer number of settings, dials, and gauges. The heft of them felt good. I pored over the manuals and fiddled with the settings. From outside the room, you would have heard the crinkle of plastic wrap followed by the intermittent whir of an electric motor. For the rest of the night, I practiced. I swapped different bits in and out of the drills, I adjusted the cutting depth of my circular saw back and forth until it felt natural. And at some point, the fever got the better of me, and I drilled a few holes in a corner of my closet where the landlord was unlikely to ever notice.

Climbing into bed that night, I felt a glow that reminded me of Christmas nights growing up, falling asleep to the reality of new toys and the knowledge that the future held many, many days of good times. In months prior, it was all too easy for me to feel restless at night, wondering what to do with my time, wondering if I should quit my job and try something else, start a new workout routine, investigate some new hobby. Nights were all too easily turned into sessions of self-doubt about how I was spending my time and whether it was something I'd reflect on fondly or look back at with regret. The fear that I had about not having an answer to the question "What are you up to these days?" was ever present, especially when that question was asked while I looked in the mirror. But for now, even if the cabin was just a distraction, I felt like I had an answer.

Merely looking for tools had occupied my mind for weeks. The work had not even begun, and I felt cured of a listlessness that had gone on for what felt like years. It was a welcome change, and I felt myself drawn to go even deeper into whatever it was that was offering up the reprieve.

There was one other tool I acquired early on, in addition to the drills and saws. Foreseeing the need to charge batteries if and when they did go dead, I purchased a small, gas-powered Honda generator from a kind woman on Craigslist. She had mostly used it as a power source when camping at Burning Man. I wondered what kind of hellish treatment the little engine had gone through, but the price was right, and when she invited me to pull the cord and start it up, it purred to life immediately. The generator was the last big tool purchase, but I couldn't help myself from going into the hardware store whenever I'd pass by on my way to work. And so it was, within the first few weeks after I bought the cabin, that I ended up with a new level, a good pair of leather gloves, a fancy new extra-long measuring tape that snapped back into its case with spectacular vigor, and some earplugs and safety glasses that would almost certainly go unused because they were so easy to misplace. Luckily, I was good at squinting.

4

WORK PARTY

It was still dark when the alarm on my phone rang at 6:00 a.m. on a mild mid-October morning. The faint glow of lights at the milk processor across the street illuminated my bedroom in a pale shade of green. I could just make out the clumsy paths of maple leaves falling outside the window.

The alarm was unnecessary. I had been wide awake for hours going over lists in my head. Eighteen sheets of quarter-inch plywood to use as paneling for the walls. Sixteen one-by-four-inch cedar boards for trimming around the door and windows. Three hundred square feet of cedar boards for the deck. Would it be enough? May as well bump it up to 350.

I had been up to the cabin twice since buying it nearly a month before. Once to show my brother, who eyed it with the sort of suspicion only a loving family member can, a complex mix of feigned enthusiasm, general concern, and sincere fear as he stood balancing on the skeletal frame of what I promised him would one day be a charming little deck.

The other time I went up, I took measurements, dutifully jotting down dimensions of the windows, walls, and floors. I bought graph paper and made meticulous drawings to help me plan what was needed for the deck and soon-to-be driveway, now just a boot-sucking puddle of forest goo, sprinkled with bent nails and rotten wood.

It wouldn't be long before winter set in. I had little time to get major cabin projects done that would allow me to enjoy the space with some low level of comfort during the colder months when snow, or at least lots of rain, was basically guaranteed. For a standard two-day weekend, completing all the critical projects was a tall order. As I got out of bed to throw on a pair of old jeans, I went over the list for the hundredth time in my head.

The deck was merely framed in, requiring an acrobatic effort from anyone trying to reach the front door. The plan was to cover it with cedar boards, purchased from a lumber outlet about twenty minutes west of the cabin. Due to some unknown cause, the door only opened halfway before it collided with the floor. Without knowing whether it was due to the sloping floor, whose angle could have allowed it to function as the base of a pinball table, or an unevenness in the door itself, I merely had "fix door" on the agenda. The driveway swamp, an area big enough to park two cars end to end, needed to be filled in with gravel. I'd already called a local materials supplier who had cheerfully offered to deliver the necessary goods later that morning.

On the inside, wide cedar boards covered portions of the wall with the alignment normally reserved for glued letters on a ransom note. The plan was to take it all down and replace it with the cheapest plywood I could find. The floor would get discount laminate planks featuring a not-so-believable faux–wood grain pattern. A not-so-surprisingly large portion of materials in my budget range featured a not-so-believable faux–wood grain pattern.

Finally, over a large pit that had already been dug next to the cabin, we'd build an outhouse. I say "we" because, in keeping with my memories of childhood days putting together forts in the woods, one thing had been clear from the start. The cabin would not be a solitary place. It would exist and improve at the hands of friends too kindhearted to question weekends sacrificed to providing free labor. Besides, beyond the good times, warm beer, and free sandwiches I offered, there was another prize to be had, rooted in the reality that none of us had the slightest clue what the hell we were doing.

Growing up, most of us didn't have the benefit of a father who taught us the sorts of things you see fathers teach their kids in movies. And if we did, we didn't have the sense to listen to them. We didn't know how to build houses or fix cars. We didn't know the difference between a jigsaw and a scroll saw or why you might want an orbital sander versus a palm sander. We faked our way through engine trouble when girls were around, and we tried our best to offer firm handshakes whenever we could, even if the strongest thing we normally gripped was a Nintendo controller or a guitar neck. As adults, our fears of lost security deposits kept us from the sorts of trial-and-error projects that might have offered a few lessons in home renovation, but that certainly didn't mean we didn't want to.

The cabin was practice. Most importantly, it was practice in a place far from the prying eyes of people who might see what we were doing and offer some criticism. It was a safe space. They say dance like no one's looking. We wanted to build like no one was around to sarcastically offer, "Huh, that's certainly one way to do it." At the cabin, we knew it didn't matter if a cut wasn't straight or a nail was bent. No one cared if the floor sloped a little or if the driveway wasn't really firm enough. We just wanted to play with power tools and cut wood. We wanted to squeeze the triggers on drills and rip boards with saws. And when we needed to plug something in, someone would say, "Fire up the gennie!" and we'd all know what they meant if we didn't actually know how to start the generator. With no one but the trees to judge us and a fistful of Band-Aids to keep everything in order, we'd pick up where we left off as kids, making forts, learning how to build things again.

I flipped on the lights of the kitchen, added some beans to the grinder, and gave it a whir, hoping the clattering sound and smell would function as an alarm for the sleeping figure in the adjacent living room. When Bryan sat up, still half stuffed into a bright red sleeping bag, we locked eyes and nodded, knowing what had to be done. It only took a few minutes to gather our bags and pour a few big travel mugs of coffee before we were outside. I started my mother's red 1994 Ford Ranger to get the heat going while we loaded things up. I'd borrowed the truck for the weekend. It felt good to have a vehicle that matched the task at hand. We added all the new tools and a few buckets to the truck's bed, already loaded with plywood and flooring, then topped the whole thing with an aluminum extension ladder, unwittingly on loan from my landlord. Once everything was in, we crisscross applesauced the whole deal with about a hundred feet of rope and at least as many square knots to keep it from bouncing out onto the highway.

The sky grew lighter as we headed northeast. Thirty minutes in, we could see the jagged silhouettes of the Cascade Mountains in the distance. A quick stop to fill the generator with gas and we were back on our way, pulling off the highway and into the Riversites just as we finished the last dregs of our coffees. The truck bounced along the gravel road, following the river past Sunset Falls and then over the train tracks until we came to Wit's End. I parked in the middle of the road, just a few feet from the driveway's wormhole of mud. Soon after, a second car arrived, and finally, a third. Three cars, six idiots, a couple of hundred bucks of lumber, and a truckful of tools no one knew how to use stood between us and that cabin. It was 9:00 a.m., and it was time to get to work. But first, we'd shotgun a beer. I passed them out.

There was Indy, the youngest among us. He was constantly ridiculed for his dad-like character and was prone to fit the image with common accessories, including a belt-attached cell phone holder and a baseball cap bearing the name of the bowling supply warehouse where he worked.

There was Matt, a talented musician, my closest friend, and the person I was most likely to engage with in an argument or a fit of hysterical laughter. Usually the latter. He was stubborn, though. If something was worth talking about, it was worth him having a strong opinion.

There was Bryan, a fellow writer I'd met years before. He was as jaded about the job as I was. A native Californian, he had come from Colorado simply to help out.

There was Kellen, Matt's brother-in-law and our former manager at the sandwich shop where we delivered hoagies on fixed-gear bicycles to drunk college kids. Kellen probably had the least experience, which wasn't saying much, but he more than made up for it with pure enthusiasm and by far the best beard among us.

And there was Lucas, whose annoyingly constant reminders about having the most experience led us to task him with building the outhouse, force him to wear an embarrassingly bright yellow construction hat, and address him by "sir" at all times.

Tossing my empty Rainier can into the bed of the truck, I went over the plan with everyone, letting people claim tasks along the way. There was a lot to do and no time to spare. Naturally, people had their own ideas. Matt was focused on the driveway.

"There's too much water in here, man. You've gotta drain this somehow," Matt told me.

"The gravel guy's gonna be here in two hours. We don't have time. Besides, you're working on the deck, right?"

"Sure, sure, I'll do the deck. It's just this swamp, ya know?"

He was probably right. There was a lot of water, but I didn't know what draining it would entail. I hadn't thought of that, hadn't researched it, but I knew we didn't have time given everything else that needed to happen. Plus, if we started digging into the swamp to make room for some kind of drainage trench, like he was now suggesting to the other guys, I worried the gravel would simply fill the new hole as opposed to spreading over the whole area. As I finished unloading the truck, I looked at him square and said, "I get it, but there's no time. The gravel guy is gonna be here in two hours. Okay?"

"Yeah, okay," Matt said, eyeing the shovel just a few feet away.

"I'm gonna go get the cedar. Don't you start digging around now."

"Okay, I won't."

"Don't dig that trench, bud. Work on the deck. You'll love it."

"Sure, sure."

I slammed the tailgate shut and hopped in the cab of the truck. After turning around at the end of the road, I rolled past slowly. I could see Matt talking to the others.

"Don't do it!" I yelled as I drove past. They waved and smiled the way serial killers might if you let them babysit your kids.

Nearly two hours later, returning with a full load of decking and a gravel guy set to arrive any minute, I came over the hill that crested just above the cabin and saw Matt and several others covered in mud with shovels and buckets. There were more empty beer cans than when I'd left. The cabin looked exactly the same, but now a crude trench stretched across the driveway along with a big, beefy pipe I didn't recognize.

"I knew it!" I said as I jumped out of the truck. "The gravel guy is coming. We don't have time for this! We have to cover up the trench so the gravel spreads out!"

Hearing the urgent call, everyone flocked to the scene to begin filling the trench. We appeared as ants in a time lapse, Matt digging the trench out farther and farther, seeking lower ground, others sourcing some more sections of pipe they'd apparently found under a pile of leaves behind the cabin. We covered the whole thing with whatever we could get our hands on—old boards, branches, scraps of metal roofing, unearthed glass bottles.

I could hear the grumble of a big truck coming up Wit's End as we tossed more of the forest's detritus into the gaping hole, which had taken on the appearance of a giant booby trap, hastily camouflaged with nearby foliage. As the truck's engine grew louder, we jumped into the cars to move them out of the way. At the top of the hill, the faded yellow cab of a big diesel truck came into view before coasting down the hill. Popping into park, the truck shook to a halt just beyond the driveway. Out of the door came a pair of exhausted leather boots, followed by bare legs, cargo shorts, a Hawaiian shirt, and a safari hat that framed a wiry smile and a wizard-like beard.

"Howdy, I'm Cal. Where we doin' this?"

Cal climbed down from his rig, an enormous truck with dual rear wheels, a dump truck back end, and what looked to be a few different truck faces welded together to make a Franken-cab that shook violently during its gentlest idle. His beard was long, wispy, and white. Each strand bent and hooked out of his face like a tiny lightning bolt, clearly contrasting the red hue of his face, saturated from a bit too much sun, an excess of physical effort, or sheer beaming enthusiasm aimed at the prospect of dumping a load of rocks on something. In the years of rock deliveries that followed, I'd come to realize it was the latter without question. I shook his hand and we walked into the mud pit together, past the sound of Matt still diligently digging a trench to some distant location in the forest, now well clear of even the most generous of imagined property lines.

"I was thinking about here, Cal," I told him, indicating a spot near the end of what would be the driveway. "And do you think you can sort of spread it as you dump it?"

"Oh, sure," Cal replied confidently and hopped back into the truck with the agility of a gymnast. His face made him seventy. His leap made him closer to eighteen.

A few of us assembled near the unload point, equipped with rakes and shovels and the expectation of doing a minimal amount of heavy lifting and rock moving. Cal would lay out the gravel in a dark gray ribbon, and we'd merely iron out the edges. In twenty minutes, we expected to have a driveway. A shrill beep rang out to indicate the truck intended to start coming backward, and with a violent shake, the promise was made good. But with about twenty feet to go, it lurched to a stop. The bed lifted swiftly upward, and without the slightest hint of a spreading-forward motion, Cal dumped the gravel just off the road, a solid thirty feet from the proposed drop zone. Jumping out of the truck with the utmost of pride, he scrambled onto the pile and admired the view from the top before saying, "Yeah, it's too muddy over there. This is a good spot. That'll be two hundred dollars."

Without having the gumption to spoil his infectious good mood, I handed over the cash and watched him climb into the truck, tossing a wave out the window before disappearing back down the road in a cloud of smoke and noise.

Expecting grief from the road crew, I turned around to find them aggressively attacking the mountain of rock, stabbing and slashing at it with dull shovels and flimsy rakes. They poured it into a rust-eaten wheelbarrow nursing a flat tire (also found in the woods nearby) and dragged the overladen contraption through mud and our own pile of nonsense until they reached the end of the driveway.

Matt finished and we all inspected the pool of water where the drain began, following the pipe, now covered in an increasingly deep layer of freshly shoveled gravel, in our minds' eyes all the way to the end of the line, where a dribble of water had started coming out. It was working. It was draining. We dubbed the whole project Badger Creek in honor of Matt's efforts (his last name is Badger) and each shotgunned another beer to celebrate.

Working in shifts when our arms got too sore to shovel, we fell to other construction projects with similar fervor. The cabin came alive with activity and sound. A tiny speaker blasted music from an iPod, the generator roared with the effort of charging batteries, saws whirred through fresh cedar, and hammers beat out a rhythm against bent nails in the cabin's framing.

Bryan and Matt took to the deck, cutting up the cedar boards and fastening them down with screws. Indy had the door off its hinges faster than most people could peel an egg, which impressed me, and was slicing off the bottom at a steep angle with a circular saw, which worried me. Assuming he had found the solution for the door jamming on the floor, I left him to it. Meanwhile, Kellen began ripping out the old wall paneling inside in a series of high-pitched, screaming hammer pulls, and Lucas started on the outhouse foundation. The old wall paneling was removed and clean plywood installed in its place. Rarely did the ends meet cleanly, but we made up for the gaps with laughter and a surplus of nails. If it wasn't pretty, we could at least make it strong. I found myself bouncing between projects as needed, setting people up with tools, materials, and high fives.

As we worked, it became obvious that whoever had gotten the cabin to this stage was almost as clueless as we were. Nothing was level or square or consistent. None of the wood matched. The walls and floor were not squares or rectangles but rather slightly askew trapezoids that would have required advanced degrees in geometry to effectively measure and fill. We got around these problems with a belief in good enough, ensuring that with every driven screw our mistakes and those of our

predecessors were merely compounded. We did not untangle
the knot, we simply found more string to add.

It went like this for hours, us feeding the cabin with our
efforts, pausing only to pee, slam beers, and eat peanut butter
sandwiches covered in sawdust off the tailgate of the truck.
With each task, we gathered to test a new tool together, to take
turns using it. The inaugural pull of the trigger on a circular saw
or an impact driver or a Sawzall always met with smiles and
laughter and rounds of "Hell yeah."

By the time the sun began sinking over the hill above the
cabin, the deck was nearly finished. Indy reattached the door. A
twist of the knob and a gentle push sent it swinging gracefully
all the way into the cabin. It did not come near the floor, and we
rejoiced. Unfortunately, in its closed position, it now featured
a rather sizable gap between the bottom of the door and the
jamb. Convincing myself it wouldn't be a problem, I put it out
of my mind. (When a bird literally walked through the gap the
following morning, I found the problem significantly harder to
ignore. Even the bird seemed surprised.)

Night fell. We gathered our sleeping bags on piles of plywood in the cabin, passing a bottle of whiskey around, followed
by salty bags of chips that served as our dinner. With the outhouse only halfway to completion, we took turns with the headlamp and a shovel, heading into the woods, where the fear of
bears proved to be an effective laxative.

In the dim light of a hurricane lamp, the cabin looked even
better. At times, you didn't even have to squint to appreciate
our unique brand of craftsmanship. We sang, we drank, and
we warmed ourselves by a hissing propane heater I'd picked up

on a whim. Slowly, I realized the scene I had imagined on that first visit to the cabin was materializing. Warm and happy, we were stripped of phones and TVs, of noise and distraction, enveloped by our own creation and fueled by an oddly powerful sense of camaraderie. What had started the day as the sort of place people dared one another to enter was now suitable for a group of friends—albeit quite inebriated—to cozy up and fall asleep. We had made this place. It was ours.

In the morning, we awoke stiff and cold, gathering around the heater while Indy made a run into town for hot coffee and greasy sausage sandwiches. By the time he returned, the frenzy of activity had continued. The outhouse rose and got a roof, the plywood floor disappeared under wood-like laminate, and the deck was finished with cuts that looked a little straighter than the day before. In the late afternoon, while everyone else started packing up, Bryan and I hopped in the truck to head back to town so I could drop him at the airport. As we drove away, I wondered if we might learn how to do a few things after all.

Five friends joined me that weekend. Their visit was clarifying. Clearly, the cabin struck a chord with them the way it had with me. They saw its potential, saw the weekends spent chopping firewood and learning the power of power tools. They saw early mornings eating pan-size ham steaks and afternoons letting sawdust fly on some new project. Whatever reservations I had about buying a ramshackle shed in the middle of nowhere began to fade away. The cabin was clearly something we all needed. It wasn't just the opportunity to learn a few things. At a time in our lives when each year brought a move to a new apartment, or a new relationship, or a new job, the idea of having a place that was permanent was an immense comfort. It soothed a type of homesickness that we felt but maybe couldn't describe. And when we talked with excitement about the projects we could eventually work on, we were really talking about the relief that we now had a place where we could always meet, laugh, and stockpile memories.

For me, there was more to learn that weekend. I felt more engaged with the work we'd done in those two days than I felt about anything I'd accomplished at a desk or behind a computer back home. For years, I'd poured myself into a keyboard for re-sults that were rarely tangible. Certainly, I had coworkers and friends who did the same thing and found gratification in it. But all too often, it seemed like I was simply casting my efforts into an empty void. The cabin, on the other hand, could not have been realer. In a matter of hours, I went from teetering on bits of pressure-treated wood to standing confidently on a freshly sawn cedar deck. What had been a swamp was transformed into a clean patch of gravel big enough for a few cars. I found myself happily lost in the thousands of little puzzles that came naturally out of building something. And I loved being outside, feeling the morning chill get cut by the first bright shots of sun-light, smelling the wet earth when you hopped on the shoulder of a shovel and it sank deep, and looking up from your work to see, in the distance, the unimaginably grand peak of some giant mountain, ever keeping watch.

5

CABIN SCHMABIN

Even before I owned one, I'd always taken issue with the casual way people throw around the word *cabin*. It seemed that somewhere along the line, the definition of a cabin went from a primitive, basic-needs shelter to any structure that had more than six or seven trees around it. I'd once been invited to a friend's supposed cabin only to arrive and find that it had a basketball court. Cabins do not have basketball courts. Cabins have tetanus.

True cabins are hardly better than tents. They have limited amenities, basic comforts, and inefficient systems that make you thankful for the plush life you live 95 percent of the time. They are not anyplace with a sign above the toilet that says, "Life Is Better in the Woods."

Cabins are small, musty places. They are poorly finished, outfitted with the hand-me-downs of people's real homes. They are repositories for knives that are a bit too dull, furniture that no longer matches, and artwork showcasing anything but good taste. When you enter a cabin, there should be a sense of encountering how things used to be, not just a variation on how they already are.

My irritation with overuse or misuse of the term *cabin* didn't come from some inherent need for accuracy. Rather, it upset me because I wholeheartedly believed that true cabins had something unique to offer, but that value was lost when people strayed from the real thing. People who visited eight-bedroom "cabins" with heated driveways and Wi-Fi fridges were missing out on something they likely really needed.

All too often, an average evening at home would consist of little more than sitting on the couch, phone in hand, letting my attention lazily ping-pong between Facebook and Instagram and YouTube and whatever happened to be on TV. Hours were spent like this. Days were spent like this. Weekends were lost to this behavior. Sure, there would be evenings spent cooking dinner with friends, Sunday afternoons doing laundry or other house chores that demanded some energy and time. But so many tasks felt like they required a Herculean effort to break free from the malaise of modern life. Maybe I was just incredibly lazy or mildly depressed or who knows. Whatever it was, it was just too damn easy to live like that. Worse was seeing so many others living the exact same way, making it almost impossible to justify the feeling that something about it was wrong.

In the weeks that followed the work party, I hustled up to the cabin as often as I could. There were critical little projects to finish here and there, a few last pieces of faux-wood flooring to put in, attaching the toilet seat to the bench in the outhouse, and general cleaning. Simply washing the windows had seemingly doubled the amount of light that made it into the cabin. Between tasks, there were other potentially less critical projects to get involved with, things like hatchet throwing and unloading hell on empty beer cans with a pump-action BB gun. With each trip, I took up a few more amenities, stocking the outhouse and the cabinet that came with the cabin with essentials like extra paper towels, tea light candles, hurricane lamps, spare lantern fuel, boxes of dehydrated hash browns, and the largest bottle of Tabasco I'd ever seen.

Even after only a few visits, I found myself falling into a rhythm there. Achieving the comforts of day-to-day life at the cabin demanded a consistent hum of activity that felt like an antidote to the doldrums of modern amenities and big-city living. It was through a parade of chores that the real value of the cabin came out. Sure, you could try to sit on the floor and try to use your phone, but the closest Wi-Fi was fifteen miles away at the McDonald's back in Sultan. Not that you had time to be on your phone anyway. There were things to do. The lanterns needed to be carefully filled with oil. Water for tea or coffee had to be heated on a Coleman stove that required manually priming the fuel canister by pumping it with a little rod. If I wanted entertainment, I'd read or play guitar or walk into the woods and explore a bit, almost always finding a new vantage point of one of the surrounding mountains, or a little creek, or a particularly gnarly old tree. Everything took time. There were days when simply staying warm and fed felt like activities that took hours to complete. At home, people would talk about the importance of taking time out of your day to be "present" or to be "mindful," a mental state that came as a natural side effect of cabin tasks. When boredom might have crept in, I found myself simply sitting in the quiet, listening to the woods or the river, enjoying, if not becoming, the calm.

Indy knew what I meant when I talked about the value of real cabins.

We grew up in the same area, separated by the county's power lines and a few hundred acres of private forestland, though we hadn't met until college when we both signed up for a study-abroad trip in Colombia. His real name was Tyler, but on the first day of that trip, I came down through the lobby of our hotel in Cartagena to find him staring down a cobblestone street at sunset. He was sporting a gratuitously unbuttoned linen shirt, leather satchel, canvas pants, and well-worn hiking boots. To top it off, a canvas fedora. I began mocking him immediately. Having the gumption to dress like the world's most famous archaeologist in a city so perfectly antiquated it felt like a Hollywood back lot was plenty of fodder to start calling him Indy that day. The name stuck.

After the trip, we'd kept in touch, hung out here and there. When he decided to move to Seattle, we got a house together with another friend. About a year later, he began dating my girlfriend's roommate, and we settled into a sort of sitcom lifestyle where we all hung out in a pair of crappy houses that were always way too hot in the summer and freezing in the winter. During the limited time of year when Seattle was warm and dry, we'd spend our evenings playing cards with all the doors of the house open. Sometimes, Indy and I would sit out on the back porch and pass a bottle of red wine back and forth, a few frozen burger patties on the grill nearby, and talk about the places we grew up, out-of-the-way towns where we spent most days outside, lost in a sea of trees and ferns. When I bought the cabin, Indy was one of the first people to jump on board with the idea. He knew as well as I did that the place offered a way to access our joint nostalgia.

About a month after the big work party, we planned a visit up to the cabin. It would be the first overnighter where the only agenda item was to simply enjoy the space, now equipped with a driveway that you could park in, a deck you could actually walk across, and interior flooring that you were at least less likely to fall through or contract hepatitis from.

On a Friday afternoon, we packed up the car with the basics of survival—two cases of Rainier beer, one bottle of cheap whiskey, two rib eye steaks with bones in, two cheap folding chairs, one plastic card table, three hatchets, another BB gun, several thousand BBs, two sleeping bags, one large bottle of ibuprofen, one gallon of water, six rolls of toilet paper—and headed into the mountains. We had intentionally brought a surplus of items so that we could add to the cabin's stockpile of essential supplies. The gallon of water, for example, would be left there for emergencies along with at least two of the hatchets.

The drive up was glorious. Fall was in full swing, and we took the long way, weaving through farmland along the Skykomish River as it traced its source back into the Cascades. In all directions, huge maples were cloaked in fiery hues of red and orange that popped against a backdrop of evergreen conifers—pine, cedar, hemlock, and fir. When the trees broke away, we were greeted with views of Mount Baring, Mount Index, and Gunn Peak, each dolloped with the season's first snows. It was the perfect day to relish in everything we knew a cabin visit should be: a smoky campfire, impromptu forays into the forest, amateur whittling, and the unnecessary sharpening of hatchets followed by the necessary arguing of the best ways to sharpen a hatchet, a skill neither of us possessed. When we arrived, though, our moods shifted.

On the front porch, we found a handful of cigarette butts. Someone had clearly been to the cabin and hung out awhile. No windows were broken and the door remained locked, but it looked as if someone might have tried to pry it open. There were scratch marks near the locks. We took a few minutes to investigate nearby structures, but saw no similar butts or signs of break-in attempts. They seemed entirely abandoned and thus unlikely to draw the attention of some opportunistic criminal. I wondered if the cabin's ribbon of fresh gravel and bright, clean deck boards had made it a target for the Riversites' more nefarious residents or guests.

It had only taken a single positive work weekend for me to forget about the lots filled with burned-out RVs and tatters of police tape. Now those scenes came flooding back to the forefront of my mind. I wondered if it was only a matter of time before my retreat was a place to escape from rather than to. Just a few days before, I'd gotten an email from someone associated with the community's volunteer board, responding to a message I'd sent to make sure I was up to date on the community dues that paid to keep the roads plowed in the winter. The previous owner, Tony, had assured me they were up to date. They were not. Among the back-and-forth to settle the issue, the board member offered the following as a sort of welcome message:

I would be happy to chat on the phone if you have questions about MIRCC [the Riversites] and road assessments
but please don't be too hopeful about a warm and fuzzy
community when you come up. We have more than our
share of hermits, social misfits, and general low life in our
neighborhood . . . but hey, welcome aboard!

I had written off the message hoping it was just a bit of snark,
but now wondered if they'd meant more by it than I imagined.

Nonetheless, the cigarette butts and door scratches led to
an uneasy beginning of what I had hoped would be a phe-
nomenally relaxing night. Listening intently for the sound of
someone sneaking around in the ferns, we unloaded the car and
began setting up.

The card table was placed where I imagined a small kitchen
area would eventually be. Beside it, two camp chairs were unfolded
and squared to the propane heater strictly meant for outdoor use.
We laid out the old Coleman stove on the card table and set to
work priming the fuel tank to test the burners. The stove was as
laden with nostalgia as it was with rust. It had been the heart of
family camping trips growing up. As soon as I smelled the gas,
I pictured my mom behind the stove fixing up a huge batch of
spaghetti while I read *Goosebumps* in the fading light of a summer
evening beside a lake on Washington's Olympic Peninsula.

With the stove fired up, Indy got to work on the rib eyes,
and I lit the propane heater in an effort to maximize carbon
monoxide dangers. We had intentions of a campfire, but rain
had kicked up and beckoned us to stay indoors. While the
steaks cooked, I stocked the small cabinet with our reserves of
toilet paper, whiskey, and BBs.

If I had been nervous upon arrival, I was relieved to find how powerfully calming the cabin was once we settled down. We cooked and drank and set the standard for what a traditional cabin night would look like for years to come, all to the soundtrack of rain crashing against the rusted metal roof. We played cards by the dim light of hurricane lamps and eventually pulled out a tiny battery-powered speaker for music fed from an old iPod. Often, we found ourselves sitting in silence, looking around, admiring the work that had already been done, and imagining what future projects would come next. Already, it felt like there was some magical quality to the space, some atmospheric power that held us in contemplative moments we were lacking back home. Or maybe it was just carbon monoxide poisoning from the outdoor-use-only propane heater.

Gleefully ignorant of the actual time, we decided to roll out our sleeping bags when another pull from the whiskey bottle felt unnecessary. Just as we had during the work party weekend, we slept on the floor that night. It stopped raining at some point, but errant drops were still pachinko-ing their way through the canopy, intent on being heard slamming into the cabin's roof before sliding to the forest floor.

The following morning, I awoke and stood up to be startled by the presence of a car that appeared overnight just down the road. It seemed as if a neighbor had arrived at one of Wit's End's less shabby cabins. I was immediately anxious wondering of the board member's cast of characters if this would be one of the hermits, social misfits, or general low-lifes. Too scared to find out and not knowing what the protocol was for introductions, I decided the best course of action was to stare out the window and continue feeling nervous. Halfway through the morning's first cup of coffee, a figure appeared on the road heading for the cabin.

Murphy was about five foot six, maybe midfifties, balding, and excitable. He was all handshakes and smiles when Indy and I greeted him outside, but it didn't take long before he started to criticize our work. According to Murphy, there was a lot wrong. For starters, the deck boards were too close together.

"Those are gonna get full of pine needles and cause the boards to rot out way faster," he told us.

"Oh, okay," we replied, unsure if we should set to work immediately ripping them up or set to work immediately asking him to leave.

"Looks like you put new gutters on?" Murphy asked.

Expecting something less than a compliment, I hesitantly confirmed that, yes, we had put those gutters on.

"Yeah, snow's gonna rip those things off," he said with absolute certainty.

Murphy knew these things because he'd been around awhile. He had one of those seen-it-all, done-it-all type attitudes. A decade had passed since he first bought his little escape on Wit's End, and he'd had his fair share of rotten boards and mangled gutters. His criticisms weren't meant to be dickish, but for how proud we were of the little work we'd done, it was hard not to take them personally.

Once he'd done a once-over of the place, Murphy seamlessly switched topics from the complexities of cabin-building to tales of his exploits in the mountains. Murphy—apparently—was a bit of a badass. Before we had a chance to stop him, he guided the conversation away from my failings as a carpenter to his successes, mostly at kayaking white water and riding dirt bikes.

With his arms extended to grip a set of imaginary handlebars, Murphy brought his past adventures to life. Flicking his wrist and letting out a "BRAAAAAAAAAP!," he gave us a little taste of the kind of stuff he got up to.

"I'm out on that forest service road that goes toward Lake Serene, and I'm, just, ya know . . . BRAAAAAAAAP! Ya know."

And we dutifully nodded to let him know we knew, so he could continue.

"There's just so much mud, so I gotta just . . . BRAAAA AAAAP! . . . with my legs down and just covered in muck, and I get totally stuck so I'm just . . . BRAAAAAAAABAAABA AAABAAAABRAAAAAAAAAAAAAP! YA KNOW?"

We continued to nod, afraid of what might happen if we didn't know, and he continued on, transitioning from tales of dirt biking to his white water thrills on the Skykomish. As it turned out, holding imaginary motorcycle handlebars and holding an imaginary kayak paddle were not so different, so I was glad for the update of sound effects that clarified what sort of gnarly ride I was meant to be imagining. BRAPs were exchanged for WOOSHes, and the stories continued.

After about fifteen minutes of his play-by-play, where the only contributions Indy and I had made were exclamations of "Whoa!" and "Oh man!," Murphy finally wrapped up.

"So anyway, wanna shoot my BB gun?" he asked.

"Absolutely, I do."

Murphy and I left Indy, who decided to skip the BB gun session and the near certainty of more motorcycle tales so that he could throw on another pot of coffee. I got a tour of Murphy's place, an amalgamation of many impressive DIY projects that he was quite proud of, including a small outdoor shower fed by a rainwater catch system and a cozy breakfast nook surrounded by massive antique windows that offered an intimate view of the surrounding cedars. He was quick to admit all the mistakes that he had made, and I realized that his criticisms of the cabin were merely meant to help me avoid the same pitfalls. All in all, he was just being neighborly.

True to his word, our punctuated tour ended on Murphy's BB gun range, a muddy patch of ground between an old out-house and a board with rusted cans nailed to it. We crouched together in the outhouse and took turns firing off shots. I'd brought my plastic, pump-action rifle with me. Unsurprisingly, Murphy informed me that my gun was no good and that I'd better shoot his instead.

We plinked away for ten or fifteen minutes, Murphy filling me in about his life back in Seattle as a middle school teacher and giving me the rundown about Wit's End. It seemed that there wasn't much activity anymore. The golden days of adventures seemed mostly in the rearview. There were a few neighbors he thought I might run into from time to time, but most of the properties were, as I expected, abandoned. Murphy himself didn't get up nearly as often as he hoped. A new kid back home meant that most of his weekends were spent in dad mode. But, he hoped, it wouldn't be long before the kids would be old enough to appreciate a cabin trip here and there. He knew that time spent up in the woods would be as good for them as it was for anyone. As for me, he seemed glad to have some young blood on the block, enthusiastically bringing life back to one of Wit's End's potentially lost properties. At the very least, he was glad I wasn't a meth-addicted squatter.

When we parted ways, he told me to come and pull from his firewood pile anytime I wanted, and he promised to check in on the cabin whenever he came up. We exchanged numbers, and I headed back, glad to get out of the rain and enjoy a fresh cup of coffee. I could see the propane heater's freakish neon glow from the road. It looked damn cozy inside.

6

HEART AND HEARTH

Winter came on early. During the week, I'd wake up extra early in the hopes of beating traffic (which never really worked) and make the thirty-minute commute east of the house I shared with Indy. The commute ended at a park and ride because I couldn't afford to park at the actual office building where I worked—or anywhere near it, for that matter. The lot was a two-mile walk to the office and almost always miserable, especially in winter, when it was usually completed in the pre-dawn darkness. Often, it was raining. If there's anything to make an unlikable job more unlikable, it's trudging through the rain in the dark for nearly an hour to get there.

Being in the office had only gotten worse over time. I'd come to dread the small talk, the obligatory elevator chitchat, the social templates that seemed impossible to avoid. On Mondays, you'd ask everyone about their weekend. Tuesdays were harder since weekend adventures had already been discussed, so we'd discuss the weather. If you were lucky, someone had been fired or hired, or some other office gossip had emerged. The boldest and most bored among us would begin discussing upcoming weekend plans on Wednesday. The rest of us would try to wait until at least Thursday. On Friday, all talk was of recognizing how glad we all were that it was Friday. These conversations were repeated ad nauseam every week. They were as reliably bummer-inducing as the constant, drizzly rain. They were the sacrosanct threads of a social fabric that held together people's sanity just enough to keep them from leaping out of sixth-story windows just to feel the fresh air. Perhaps I was being overly dramatic about it all, but that's how it felt sometimes.

If it weren't for the immediate team of folks I worked with, I would have lost it. Many of them were also aspiring writers, documentary filmmakers, musicians, and artists. It was a group full of people who didn't intend to be there but had just sort of wound up in the job for one reason or another. Or maybe it wasn't a coincidence they were like that at all. Maybe that was how everyone was. Maybe no one wanted to be there. But we all played the part. Maybe the worst aspect was how easy it was to do so.

The money was good. The benefits were too. I had a fairly flexible schedule. There were opportunities to get better positions and make more money. There was the potential for a life with retirement options and nice big houses and new cars every other year. There was a decent way to rack up paid time off and travel discounts. Like looking into a crystal ball, I could imagine a future where I convinced myself that the job simply didn't matter, that it was something to merely put up with in order to have a comfortable life during the other 128 hours that were in a week. Maybe, I thought, I'd learn to put up with the discomfort of sitting stagnant under those fluorescent lights and talking about the weather and weekend plans. Plus, I had a decent shot at getting a parking spot in a year or two.

So much of that time was spent feeling like I had come too far to turn back, to choose another direction. Each year older, each year deeper into a field meant more experience but less flexibility. It was like digging a hole and then stopping to wonder if it was too deep to get out of, then going right back to digging. The problem with that kind of reasoning and being the sort of person who buys into it is that the trap it creates only becomes stronger with each passing year.

I tried hard to rationalize the feeling that I wasn't getting all that I could out of life. Often, I managed to believe that I was just being lazy or whiny about a career that by all objective metrics was ideal. But the feeling never lasted long, because when I zoomed out, imagining doing that same thing in five, ten, or twenty years, when I pictured myself at a retirement party in those offices, I cringed at the thought of all the regret I'd feel for staying put and playing it safe. It seemed obvious that I should leave, but I'd done most versions of the writing gig and found the same results. And if not the writing, what else was there? I had no appreciable skills in any other field, unless you counted sandwich delivery boy. Whatever change I made, I'd be starting from scratch, and what were the chances that I'd get five or ten years into that new thing and feel exactly the same: burned out, bored, trapped? The fear of that possibility was real enough to keep me frozen where I was.

The peak of these thoughts started happening around the time that social media platforms like Instagram and Snapchat were spreading like wildfire. It felt like overnight, at least to me. In hindsight, it was a hard time for anyone to start feeling insecure about their purpose or how they filled their days. I was pulled in by pictures and videos of woodworkers, cabin builders, chefs, and comics, things I was interested in. But it was not possible to wade into that world and avoid exposure to the rest of it, the highlight reels of the most extreme, attractive, creative, wealthy, adventurous, intelligent, powerful people on the planet: all ranked and sorted to shake dopamine out of your brain like a disobedient vending machine. Logically, I knew that it was absurd to compare an entire life to the best 2 percent of someone else's, but it was damn hard sometimes. I would stare into a screen where people were leaping out of helicopters with snowboards or diving into the Mediterranean for fresh lobsters or surrounding some acclaimed musician in a candlelit room or taking the time to sort their dried goods into appropriately sized and labeled mason jars, and then I'd look up to my own reality, sitting on a beat-up couch, covered in dog hair, adjacent to a pile of laundry that'd gone unfolded for who knew how many days, and, faced with the choice of folding wrinkled shirts or living vicariously a world away, I'd tip my head down, swipe, and disappear again.

At times, I wished for some sort of test for contentment. I wanted to walk into a clinic and give my blood or swab my cheek and run my numbers to determine if my happiness levels were average or not. If they were low, I'd feel justified in making some big change. If things were fairly typical, I'd find ways to cope. My biggest fear would have been finding out that I was above average, that I was better off than most, that the aimlessness I felt all the time was actually as good as it could get. There's a hopelessness that comes with reaching the peak of anything because once you're at the top, there's nowhere else to go. All you're left with is the realization that the promise of reaching someplace higher was always the best part of climbing in the first place. In the end, I just wanted to know that there was a lot more to gain before I threw away a life raft of comfort and routine, and that was assuming I had something to throw it all away for, an idea of where to go next, which I didn't. And so, I stayed stuck in that place, wondering.

On weekends, the cabin brought me back to life, even if the increasingly frigid winter made it harder and harder to force myself out of the sleeping bag in the morning. I would lie there, watching my breath rise into the mishmash of salvaged boards that made up the ceiling, waiting for the urge to pee to overwhelm the desire to stay warm. I hadn't seen snow yet, but it certainly wasn't due to high temperatures. Every morning, the ground was hard with frost despite the clear and sunny conditions. The start of those days usually looked the same: me, sleeping bag around my shoulders, endlessly futzing with the propane heater.

I had a love-hate relationship with the heater. Love, because without it the inside of the cabin would be inhospitable unless you were doing constant jumping jacks. Hate, because operating it terrified me.

Having lost the manual for the heater almost immediately, I'd come up with my own set of instructions, which were as follows:

Step 1: Mentally prepare to light the heater.

Step 2: Get into position so that your body is not directly in front of the heating element, which resembled a large metallic sunflower.

Step 3: Open the valve on the propane tank and depress the ignition switch to allow gas to violently hiss out.

Step 4: Frantically jab at the element with a match or lighter, terrified in the knowledge that every second it goes unlit means more propane around your face and the assurance of an exponentially more aggressive and larger fireball once it does ignite.

There were times when I'd shadowbox at the thing for a few rounds without success, the smell of propane becoming stronger and stronger until I'd have to give up, turn off the valve, open all the windows, and let the cabin breathe for a bit before trying again. When I did manage to get it lit, it glowed like the sun and provided ample heat, but the danger was only half-over.

As a device exclusively recommended for outdoor use, the propane heater constantly belched a deadly supply of carbon monoxide, the type that lulls you to sleep before it slowly and gently puts your brain into a full nelson. Luckily, the cabin was not exactly airtight. Drafty windows and larger holes, like the one under the door from Indy's fix, created an almost constant supply of fresh air inside. In the end, running the heater in the cabin was probably not dangerous enough to kill a person, but it might cause you to forget how to tie your shoes every now and again.

Knowing these things, I had dutifully purchased a carbon monoxide monitor to make sure I wasn't being overly stupid. I assumed the packaging, which depicted a calm little boy asleep on his bed, was meant to be reassuring. It seemed like more of an ironic oversight, advertising as a benefit the primary symptom of carbon monoxide poisoning—namely, drifting off into an eternal sleep.

Having also lost the instruction manual for the detector, I filled it with fresh batteries and pushed its only button. It emitted a single shrill beep and then nothing. Not knowing whether this meant it was working, was broken, or was immediately overwhelmed with high levels of CO, I promptly set it on the windowsill and decided not to trust it. When guests came to the cabin, I assured them it would save their lives. Needless to say, I never kept the heater running overnight.

During the moments the heater did work and we managed to maintain consciousness, it still wasn't quite right for the cabin. For starters, there was an odor. The subtle, almost chemical scent seemed to seep into blankets, food, and clothing. It also offered what I thought of as a wet heat, producing the type of warmth that would burn your hands but never warm your bones. On freezing mornings, I would sit in front of the heater's blazing orange face and wait to hit that magical moment where your body kicks over into warmth, where bubbles of pleasure rise up from the base of your spine and percolate through your neck before cascading down your arms and fingertips in a wave of goose bumps. But that moment never came. You could get hot with the propane heater, but you couldn't get cozy, and that was a problem.

I needed a dry heat, something that would seep into the body's core. I needed something that wouldn't kill you if you got too close or left it going while you slept, something that would give the cabin some heart, some spirit, some personality. I needed some real fire, some crackles, some sparks, some smoke. I needed a woodstove.

Growing up, I always associated woodstoves with wind-storms. A few times a year, usually in the fall, the wind would kick up around our house enough to topple some branches and kill the power. When it happened, we'd all gather in the lowest room of the house with flashlights and candles. My dad would light up the woodstove, a big black thing with silver squirrels on the front, and my mom would open a can of Campbell's bean-with-bacon soup to set on top. While it heated, we'd play cards or read and listen to the sound of fir branches slamming into the roof. Every now and again, I'd follow my dad out to the woodpile, bracing against the chaos of wind and rain to bring in another load. I loved the contrast. Everything outside all dark, loud, wet, and angry. Inside, everything was still, soup, and blankets.

I'm sure my parents were anxious during those storms, worried about damage and insurance claims, but those firelit moments were pure gold to me. Surrounded by a crackling fire and my folks, I never felt safer. When the power did come back on, everyone would go back to their usual, watching the news, doing laundry, pretending to do homework, probably playing video games. But on rare occasions, the power would stay off all night, and we'd sleep down there, curled up on the floor while the weather raged outside. Because we only used it during storms, I think I came to view the woodstove itself as a sort of spirit guide for those perfect nights. Putting a woodstove in the cabin seemed obvious. Anytime I imagined the finished space, there was always a woodstove in the background. I pictured foggy mornings, me armed with a steaming cup of black coffee, a heavy woolen vest, and a sharp axe, going out into the woods and felling dead trees between sips of Folgers. The fantasy was frequent and strong. Unfortunately, there were also challenges.

It didn't take long to become almost violently apparent that the majority of woodstoves were far too large for the cabin. Most were meant to heat entire houses, places with rooms, corridors, hallways, and high ceilings. Installing the same type of woodstove you would add to a normal house would instantly turn my tiny space into something less like a cozy cabin and more like a place to bake calzones or glaze pottery. Thanks to modern high-efficiency standards, even petite new stoves were seemingly capable of heating Wrigley Field, and the smallest stoves available, micro versions made for sailboats and tiny homes, were obscenely expensive. Ornamented with brass rails and specialized wall-mounting hardware, these gems of the woodstove world were a bit too high class for the cabin's tastes. I needed something small, but well used, something old, something that wasn't designed on a computer to maximize every possible BTU. Weeks of searching antique stores, flea markets, and Craigslist finally led me to a candidate.

It was a little potbellied fellow made by Sears and Roebuck in the 1920s. At just over three feet tall with a midsection about the diameter of a basketball, it was made in an era when stoves leaked enough smoke to put some character in your lungs. From the pictures in the ad, it looked like a previous owner had painted it green and added a little sunflower on the side, but the passage of time and elements had replaced most of the paint with a dull coating of rust. There were two small vents on the front. Each was in the shape of the logo for nuclear radiation, which seemed like a good sign for some reason. At the bottom was a little door for clearing out ashes. Just above, a slightly larger one for feeding chunks of wood. The top was the perfect size to accept a mug and keep it warm. Knowing its age and seeing the significant rust, I hoped the little stove would be delightfully inefficient. More importantly, at only $200, I could afford to be wrong. Plus, it was located in Gold Bar, only twenty minutes from the cabin. It was meant to be.

I made a trip to check it out on a dreary Saturday morning in early December. It was just a few minutes off the highway, so there was no trouble finding the place. When I pulled up to the pale yellow trailer home, surrounded by a graveyard of forgotten cars, I saw the stove sitting glumly in the back of an old box truck. Without its chimney, it looked a bit helpless.

The seller's name was Aaron, who mumbled something to the effect of, "Came across it . . . cousin," when I asked him about the stove's history. It was one of the few questions I could ask without betraying my complete lack of woodstove know-how. Instead, I let my suspicious eyes do the talking and began circling the stove with an analytic expression. The chimney hole on top was in the shape of an oval, not a circle. Every chimney I'd ever seen had a cylindrical shape to it. I silently wondered if there must be some adapter to make such a thing work. I briefly considered asking about it, but kept quiet out of fear that it was perhaps a classic chimney hole design. Asking might have revealed that I had no clue what I was doing. I certainly didn't want to look like a fool. Then again, calling it out might show that I was a scrupulous buyer, not some soft-handed cosmopolite who didn't know their chimney hole from their butthole. But again still, what if he didn't know about it, and my bringing it up to him caused him to get shifty and evasive as he tried to protect his own sense of woodstove pride? By now, it had been too long, I was nearly loitering, and a whole new wave of anxiety began to form.

"How about a hundred and sixty?"

"Sorry, I have to get two for her."

"I'll take it," I surrendered, making a mental note to read a book or something about negotiating.

Money and stove were exchanged, and Aaron did me the honor of letting me load the thing into the back of my car unaided. Tempting a hernia, I wrestled the stove into my station wagon and wrapped it in blankets as a protective measure, albeit one that was probably mostly symbolic. If there was an accident, the ninety-pound hunk of cast iron would probably be the only thing that made it through unscathed.

I finished the drive and promptly dragged the stove out onto the deck, where I packed it with an assortment of junk mail that had been accruing in my back seat, and started a fire. Smoke poured out of the top. I quickly gathered a handful of twigs and dropped them inside, smiling when I heard the first crackle emanate from within. After a few minutes of dumbstruck amusement, watching the flames glow through the sizable gaps between the stove's various components, it started raining. I let the fire burn out, cleared the smoking debris, and stomped it out on the driveway. As I carried the stove inside the cabin and set it in the corner where it would eventually live, I couldn't help but notice the warmth radiating off the thick metal. It was a good heat.

7

CHIM CHIM CHER-EE

A cquiring the stove and actually having a fire in the cabin were two very different acts, separated by an event that intimidated me to no end: installation. Certainly, there were plenty of DIY articles and how-to videos showing me all the ways in which to install a woodstove. Most of them were the same. There would be an expert of some kind, usually dressed in khakis and a polo shirt, standing in a controlled environment next to an aesthetically pleasing arrangement of chimney and stovepipe components. They'd go on for ages about different types of pipe, adapters, flues, dampers, flashings, all items you, the viewer, might potentially need for your chimney installation. But at no point would they be so kind as to highlight what determines what you need, or go to the trouble of showing you how in the hell even two of dozens of potentially necessary pieces joined together. After the chimney stove component roll call was completed, the video would cut, and suddenly, the presenter would be by a roaring fire—chimney installed, golden retriever napping nearby—with a big smile on their face. No part of the actual installation process was shown. They wouldn't even show the person making the fire or acquiring the dog. Over and over again, I watched lengthy videos that were like a highlight reel of chimney installation, filled with advertising and a few of the best shots without the tedium of a full game. It was easy to dismiss the videos at first, but once the stove was sitting in the cabin anxiously awaiting its lifeline to the outside world, it was hard to ignore the challenges ahead. Feeling overwhelmed by a project whose spectrum of success ranged from cozy cabin to inescapable inferno, I decided it wouldn't kill me to go out into the world and talk to a professional directly. Of all the jobs at the cabin, I thought maybe this one was worth a bit of expert help.

I cut out of work early and fought traffic through town to chat with someone at a home-and-hearth store. Waiting in the showroom for a responsible professional, I feigned sincere interest in a wall of roaring gas fireplaces, each with price tags that were in the thousands of dollars. The prices brewed in me a fear that if they knew my budget or somehow saw a picture of the cabin, they'd kick me out for wasting their time. When it was my turn, I nervously approached the counter and described the project. I had a woodstove and just needed it installed. They asked what the cabin looked like, so I carefully drew the box with a triangle on top. "This is the roof," I said, pointing to the triangle.

Probably assuming I was a terrible artist and not the owner of what amounted to an oversize doghouse, the responsible professional started sketching out what I'd need and they'd provide.

I followed along at first, but soon was lost in a stream of chimney component lingo. When he finished, I asked—with the utmost of casual tones to denote how appropriate it was that I was there considering the cabin's record-setting score on the rinky-dink scale and my own near-terminal economic status—how much a project like this might cost.

The responsible professional began tapping away at a calculator, sketching a chimney design out over the top of my ridiculous drawing, and mumbling the names of parts and hypothetical sizes. At some point, even if he'd been pressing one plus one the whole time, I knew he'd blown past my budget. Fortifying myself to act naturally when the total was announced, I waited for him to finish. When he did, with a confident stroke of the equals sign, he belched it out.

"Six thousand, six hundred, and forty bucks. Now that's just an estimate. Once we get up there, we can give you a more reliable number," he offered, handing me the drawing back with the number written at the top.

Taking it, I managed to wheeze something that sounded like, "Suuuuuuuuure."

The price of the chimney would be roughly equivalent to what I had paid for the cabin. I had budgeted $900 to put in the woodstove, and by *budgeted*, I meant it was all the money I had. Breathing hard and backing away slowly, I reassured him.

"Well, that's great. I'll give you guys a call when I'm ready for you to come out."

I rushed out of the store and back to my car, where I pulled out the estimate and the drawing: a piece-by-piece breakdown of exactly what pieces I needed to install the woodstove. To hell with it, I would do it myself.

Back at home, I started making a list. Standard black stove-pipe from the woodstove to the loft floor, a support box to hold the chimney securely at the level of the loft, a transition to eight-inch, double-insulated stovepipe from the loft and through the roof, two support arms to hold the thing steady above the roof, a silicone boot to seal the chimney against the roof, and a snug little cap to keep the rain out and the sparks in. It was all there, neatly assembled on paper. But one thing was still eluding me. How did the pieces literally, physically, attach to one another? Was it glue? Was it tape? I hadn't ever seen a chimney with tape. Was it some secret internal mechanism I was unaware of? Baffled, but determined, I decided the best way to find out was to go somewhere where I could get my hands on the various components and just fiddle around.

I started at the closest hardware store to my house, a busy Home Depot in downtown Seattle. It was pure chaos during the day, when armies of drywallers, carpenters, framers, and landscapers descended on the place for their day's supplies. At night, it was usually quiet, save for the occasional apartment dweller buying paint or Drano.

When I arrived, a prompt and courteous greeter asked if I needed any help finding anything. I replied that I would love to see their selection of stovepipe. He informed me that he would be delighted to do so, and together, we strode through rows of bright orange aisles until we arrived at a selection of pipes and metal bits of all shapes and sizes. Both satisfied we had received what we wanted, we thanked each other for the pleasure of the other's company and parted ways, happy as clams to have been helped and to have been helpful.

Something about the pipe seemed off, but I persevered, taking out various sections and wrestling them together. When I couldn't find parts I needed, I attempted to improvise with other things that looked close. It was only after assembling about eight feet of some kind of chimney that I realized I was in the dryer vent section.

Notably irritated, I returned to the front of the store and found a different Home Depot associate, one with far more badges than my previous buddy had. This associate had an arsenal of Sharpies, box cutters, and duct tape hanging around a casual-but-firm-fitting tool belt. They had weathered work boots and unfashionable blue jeans. They had a walkie-talkie that crackled with the muffled requests of other associates who were lost, dead, or being beaten by unhappy customers in some far-flung corner of the store. This new, clearly more knowledge-able associate led me through the aisles again, turning around a final corner before announcing, "There you go!" and walking off into the halogen sunset.

Something still didn't seem right. Going now immediately to the small-print descriptions of this assortment of pipe, I found that these were indeed chimney pipes, but specifically for propane stoves. Though they looked similar, they were far smaller and didn't feature the necessary capacity for a wood-burning stove. Again, I returned to the front of the store, where I put all my trust in a bright young man named Alex. I explained very carefully.

"Alex, I need to find the chimney pipe section. Here's a picture on my phone. Chimney pipe. Stovepipe. The black stuff. For wood-burning stoves."

With a knowing look, as if he had just come from there, as if this happened all the time, as if he were constantly taking confused customers to the chimney pipe section, Alex led me directly to the dryer vents. We went over the game plan again, but he was even more confused than I was. And so, I struck out on my own, determined to walk every inch of the store until I found the mythical pipe. When I finally found it, it was easy to see how it would be overlooked. The section was tiny and mostly picked over. What pieces they did have did not match in size or were severely bent out of whack. Almost nothing from the blueprint I had from the home-and-hearth store was present. I returned home no more informed than when I had left, but feeling slightly superior in that I had made queries that were beyond the capabilities of Home Depot's part-time staff to answer. Perhaps I wasn't the least knowledgeable cabin fixer-upper guy.

That week, I made several phone calls, leery anytime someone on the other line sounded confident that they had chimney pipe in stock.

"It's not dryer vents, is it? Are you sure?"

Finally, I found a place that seemed to have promise: McLendon's. Luring him with the promise of a visit to his favorite hardware store, I half begged Indy to come with me and provide support, or at least to keep an eye out while I built an entire chimney system on the floor between aisles. When we arrived, a helpful worker pointed us exactly where we needed to go. What we found when we arrived was the promised land of woodstove chimneys. An entire aisle was filled with all the stars of countless installation videos. The flashing, the adapters, the support arms, the insulated, the double-insulated, the triple-insulated pipe! It was all there.

We spent two hours gathering the necessary, assembling them in the aisle as quietly as possible so as not to attract the attention of a store employee. Many of the parts were unreasonably packed away in boxes or tightly bound in plastic wrap so they couldn't be added to our Franken-chimney, but they were indicated on the diagram from the home-and-hearth store, so we made a little pile and checked them off the list. When we assembled all we could, we gave it a satisfied look and then tore them apart to cart up to the register. The total came to just over $1,000, over budget, but far more reasonable than the colossal sum it would have taken to have it done right, which was certainly never going to happen.

8

RAY

She came in the middle of the night. I was out, and she just showed up with a big trailer and stole all of them. Twenty horses. Just gone."

Ray was about ten minutes into a real yarn about his ex-wife. He thought they had ended things on good terms, she apparently thought he owed her some horses, and I was wondering why I was listening to any of it at 7:15 in the morning, especially considering that A) I had only known Ray for about four minutes and B) I was paying him twenty dollars an hour to help me put in the woodstove.

I found Ray on the Mount Index Riversites community website, the digital version of the cabin's underdog neighborhood. Just like the community, the website was severely outdated, forgotten, seemingly lost in time. Abandoned community forums mirrored the area's crumbling, overgrown cabins, grainy photos of grandchildren by the river testified to the area's retired full-time residents, and the vast majority of recent posts spoke to the only real bit of consistent Riversites news: burglaries, suspected drug havens, squatters, domestic violence, wildlife sightings, noise complaints, and the weather. In most places, the top posts were months, often years old. At the top of the page was a stunning shot of Mount Index, whose six-thousand-foot peak erupted from a rain-soaked river valley full of towering Douglas fir, hemlock, and cedar. The website was a perfect digital representation of the Riversites, a hodgepodge of criminals, cabin dreamers, and solitude seekers all drawn, for better or worse, to the beauty, solitude, and privacy that the mountains offered.

I'd returned to the site after buying the woodstove components because I recalled seeing a classified section and wondered if there were any carpenters listed. Ray was the sole entry. The title of his post was simple: "Carpenter for hire." The ad's description merely repeated the title and provided an email. When Ray actually responded to my message, I was astonished. In his reply, he'd assured me that he had "done a few stoves for friends," which set me at ease, but then ended the message asking, "Do you have tools?" Granted, this was my first carpenter hire, but due to some amount of basic common sense, I figured he'd be supplying the tools and, hopefully, some actual carpenter skills. But at a price a third or less of what an actual carpenter would charge, I thought the risk was well worth it. I immediately hired him.

When Ray arrived fifteen minutes late—no small feat considering he lived at a now horseless ranch about five minutes from the cabin—his truck full of tools made me feel better, but it was his attitude that made me feel great. With a confident stride, wearing paint-splotched pants, a tie-dyed headband, heavy leather boots, and a faded blue sweatshirt, all six foot one and 230-ish pounds of Ray walked right up to the place and gave it his seal of approval by exclaiming, "FUCK YEAH!" and then shaking my hand heartily. Without invitation, he walked past and strode inside, getting the lay of the land and muttering to himself in short bursts of approval. Even though I knew he'd be working with me on the cabin, I hadn't quite prepared myself or the interior for him or any stranger to see it.

His tour didn't take long. Ten feet across and twelve feet long, the entire cabin was about the size of a cramped bedroom. The sum total of a few previous weekends of work with friends had resulted in thin wooden paneling that mostly covered the walls. Large gaps and jagged cuts evidenced inaccurate measurements, bad cuts, and dull blades. Where you could see directly into the wall itself, bits of electric-pink insulation spilled out like unsightly pubic hair. Spiders filled every corner and nook, and on top of the faux-wood flooring I had installed was an arrangement of amenities normally reserved for the clammy hideouts of desperate fugitives: a flimsy plastic card table held a grease-spattered Coleman camp stove, two folding camp chairs provided the only seating, and the floor pulled double duty as both mattress and storage area. My crumpled-up sleeping bag lay in one corner. In the other, an unorganized pile of paper towels, half-empty whiskey bottles, and baby wipes. The cabinet, filled mostly with backups of what was already on the floor, was the only true piece of furniture around. But Ray, God love him, he saw a kitchen, late-night conversations with a good friend, and deep sleeps with nothing but the sound of creaking trees and the distant river.

As we talked and I learned about his divorce and his two

girls that he got to see only on the weekends, I began to wonder if the cabin might have been a glimpse into a parallel life, one just down the road, but light-years away from his own. I think he may have imagined himself in the cabin, with no house to look after, no responsibilities to worry about. Just a man with the potential to sit by a warm fire, look out at the trees, and build a few things on his own terms. I envied his ability with a hammer. He envied my freezing box of a cabin and childlike responsibilities. After he took it all in, I met him at the doorway. "Yeah, man, I get it," he said. And I really believed that he did.

We went over the basic plan, something I had fretted about for months. It went something like this: place the stove in the southwest corner of the cabin, run the pipe up through the loft using a so-called chimney box to serve as the conduit, transition to triple-walled insulated pipe through the floor and an expertly cut hole in the roof, and then extend it outside to a height just above the roof's peak, supporting the outside pipe with two stabilizer arms. In hindsight, it was pretty straightforward, but figuring out that plan had been one of my life's greatest puzzles and, ultimately, the reason I had hired Ray.

From day one, it was always clear that the cabin was not up to code. Whoever had come before me had approached carpentry more like a bird building a nest than a carpenter set upon a job. Bits of timber had clearly been gathered from odd places for years, brought to the cabin, and nailed together whenever a weekend opened up to allow for a few hours spent in the woods.

No two pieces of wood matched in color, stain, or age. Some were bright, blond, and new. Others were grayed, twisted, and split. Boards that were too short to cover their intended span were simply nailed to other bits of wood to make them longer.

Half of the loft flooring was made of a real estate sign advertising "Great deals!" on acreage in who knows where.

Whoever had laid the first support beam in the middle of this dripping rainforest must have had a similar idea as I had. This was not the project of someone that needed a place to live or wanted to make money on real estate. It was a diversion, an excuse to get out into the woods, make some noise, and create something that didn't need to be perfect. Of course, I loved it that way, recognizing it as the origin story for things that end up a version of perfect that can never be replicated. I knew for certain that I was the owner of something completely unique, filled with histories of people who maybe didn't know what they were doing, but adored the cabin all the more for its crooked boards, bent nails, and other scars, because each mistake offered a memory of a moment spent doing something they loved.

The cabin's humble profile carried another benefit as well. At only 120 square feet including the loft, it was too small to come under the radar of any county-required inspection, leaving it in a Wild West when it came to building things correctly. It was a nice loophole for systems like decks, doors, windows, floors, and walls. If those systems failed, the results were fairly drama-free. Small leaks, drafty interiors, splinters, and so on. Without electricity or plumbing, the number of poorly installed features that could go wrong in some dramatic way was basically zero. Until, of course, the stove.

There were volumes of information on the necessary precautions for installing stoves. The distance from the pipe to the wall, the type of pipe for the living space, the type of pipe for passing through floors, the type of pipe for outside chimneys, the pipe cap and support system, the dimensions and slope of the roof, the type of stove being used, and on and on and on. Consideration of all these details made my head swim, made it easy to imagine an errant measurement or a crooked pipe that would end up causing the cabin to engulf itself in flames.

Of course, one of the primary goals of the cabin was to learn how to do things myself, but installing the woodstove bore a risk-to-reward ratio with a much higher delta than, say, screwing on a deck board. Do it right, have a cozy woodstove. Do it wrong, burn the cabin down or, at the very least, blast a giant hole in the roof of a place that contends with an average six feet of rainfall every year. I'd looked to the Riversites page because I hoped I could find someone who wouldn't just put the woodstove in but would let me help. What I wanted was something more akin to neighbors helping neighbors, rather than carpenter and client. Ray seemed like the perfect fit.

I showed him the various chimney pipe pieces and their corresponding attachments, all displayed proudly out of the back of my car. From a distance, it probably looked like I was selling him bombs or rocket parts. Ray randomly picked up pieces of the chimney, examined them, and then put them down. It was apparent almost immediately that he didn't recognize several items, a reaction I gathered from him based on subtle clues, like the repeated utterance, "Huh, what the fuck is this thing?," which meant either my attempt to purchase all the pieces was a failure or Ray didn't know what the hell he was doing. Confident it was probably a mixture of both, we set to work.

Before we could cut through the roof, we'd have to bring about ten feet of pipe up through the loft. After twenty or thirty seconds of hard deliberation about where the stove would go, Ray climbed into the loft and prepared to cut out a hole in the floor with the power tool equivalent of a loose fire hose, a Sawzall. The Sawzall's only purpose in life is to utterly destroy things while giving the operator the illusion of control. Its single blade attaches to an arm that moves in an oscillating pattern, imitating the motion and far exceeding the speed of a runaway train wheel. It's what you'd come up with if you were tasked with creating a new product that would ultimately be named the STABS-A-BUNCH 9000. Sawzall, as intense as it sounded, was the mildest thing they could have used.

Understandably, I had always been more than a little intimidated by my Sawzall. With Ray at the helm, it seemed like a great time to learn how to harness its power and chaos from a true master of the craft. Or at least that's what I had in mind when I decided to stand more or less directly beneath the area of the ceiling that was about to be cut out. I crossed my arms, looked up, heard Ray yell, "Here we goooo!," and then . . . there was nothing, unless you count the ringing in my ears and a very deep, but general sense that the world was coming to an end.

Everything was everywhere. Insulation rained down from loose corners in the ceiling. Mouse shit, broken nails, and bits of drywall added to the downpour, an element of the chaos that was nearly miraculous when you considered there wasn't any drywall in the cabin. It was possible then that the Sawzall had opened a hole into another dimension and started ripping things apart there too. Time seemed to slow as I sought refuge behind the cabinet. I imagined Ray as a maniac Civil War surgeon, amputating soldiers who'd come into the infirmary with sore throats or lightly twisted ankles, only to have him dismantle their bodies with a steam-powered Sawzall. Seconds, minutes, days, who knows, later, the circle of ceiling came loose and clattered to the floor, replaced by Ray's smiling face. He looked full of joy, confident, excited. I hoped that my twisted expression didn't betray my anxiety that the hole's position was a bit off. Oh well. It was too late to go back.

With a hole in the loft complete, it was time to install the metal bracket that would provide support to all the pipe upward of the loft. The bracket was meant to screw into a simple wooden frame. A simple wooden frame that we needed to build. The job was exceedingly simple. Ray only needed to cut four pieces of a two-by-four and nail them into a square. Approximately thirteen bent-over nails later, he forced what looked like—incredible, considering it was made out of only four pieces—a hexagonal wood frame between the floor joists. He tested it the same way I would have, by whacking it with a hammer. Instantly, it fell and broke apart on the floor. A second attempt was equally unsuccessful.

I wanted to help, felt confident that I could help, but Ray seemed determined, so I made work of "organizing" the rest of the parts outside while he continued making new-and-improved wood frames. Finally, he got one that worked, and we attached the black stovepipe from the woodstove to the loft ceiling. We were halfway there. It was time to saw through the roof.

After the first Sawzall episode, I had the sense to watch the next event from outside the cabin with my hands clamped over my ears. From that safe distance, I heard Ray's indiscernibly muffled yet clearly excited yell from inside. The generator's RPMs ramped up as the Sawzall called for more power inside, and then the whole place came alive. Like wind-burdened flags, the cheap, rusty panels of corrugated metal began to wave violently, rhythmically from the power of the Sawzall. Underneath, Ray was wrestling the blade through a lasagna of old plywood, nails, and metal. It seemed as if the cabin might explode or lift off, and I couldn't help but think of those old black-and-white Mickey Mouse cartoons when animators would try to show that a building was really rocking to some serious jazz by making the walls swell and collapse, or having the roof blow off on the high notes. Things were definitely rocking in the cabin.

After what seemed like an eternity, the mayhem stopped. Ray gingerly pushed out a hunk of roof and stuck his head through.

"Wooooooooohooooo! She got to shakin', huh?!"

Struggling to imagine that any of what had just happened could be described as "accurate" or "intentional," I carried the first two sections of chimney pipe up to Ray with resignation, bracing for the moment when he realized something was irrevocably ruined. Maybe we'd try again some other time and use a well-aimed cannon instead of the Sawzall. Little of what Ray was doing seemed to echo the decisive, smooth movements of carpenters I had spent hours watching on PBS as a kid. His hands did not flutter over a carefully organized belt, selecting the perfect tool at any given moment. I did not see in him the same professionalism that I saw in lifelong DIYers on YouTube. Instead, he seemed to be crashing about, trusting his eye a little too much, firing from the hip, so to speak.

Ready to bear the almost certain consequences of his brash work, I quietly ferried the remainder of parts up to him in the loft. As I went back for the final piece, I realized I had been very wrong. Extending up through the hole, like a gleaming steel totem, was a real, honest-to-God chimney. When Ray came back down from the loft to take a look at it himself, we stood back together, arms crossed, and just stared for a moment.

"Is it crooked, Ray?" I asked tentatively.

He had obviously identified the chimney's rakish, almost Seussian relationship to the cabin's roof. I say *obviously* because his response was locked and loaded, ready to deflect any fault directed at the quality of his work.

Without hesitation, he replied, "Nah, your cabin is!" and gave my back a hearty slap before grabbing the ladder and heading onto the roof.

He fit the bright red silicone collar around the base of the chimney to keep rain from creeping in at the edges, and soon, even the pieces he hadn't recognized found their home. Support arms were drilled into the cabin's framing members, sealant was laced around the seams, and a special, grated rain cap finished off the top. Before I knew it, Ray was crumpling up bits of paper and going on about the cabin again. "Yeah, man, I get it. This is the spot, man. You got a good spot."

Still in awe that it was done, I watched as he arranged the paper, lit a match, and tossed it in. Soon, a fire was born. Had I been alone, I imagined there would have been a bit of ceremony to go along with the lighting of the first fire. Perhaps a moment of silence or a special piece of kindling would have been added, or at least a moment for safety, fear, and superstitions. It would have been nice to have a chance to make the sign of the cross, or shield my eyes, or cross my fingers. I wouldn't have minded an opportunity to check the fire extinguisher one more time or make sure my shoes were tied in case I had to run. But Ray allowed for none of this. Instead, like a skydiving instructor with a nervous first-timer, he just jumped, confident that I was strapped tight right behind. As the first bits of kindling caught, Ray began nodding, a big smile on his face, and extended two thumbs way up. I could only stare, slack-jawed, and listen to the noise.

With a growl that started low and grew like an approaching train, the stove began to draft, sucking great gulps of air through the open door, up through the loft, and past the roof, belching the first column of smoke out of the bright steel chimney. With a bit of dry wood, I heard the first crackle, and the smell of pine began to fill the room. Ray was ecstatic. "Whoa, listen to how she draws, man! She's sucking it right up!"

And she did draw. The little stove roared when the flue was opened all the way and relaxed to a gentle purr when it was closed. I found that the tiniest of adjustments to the various doors and vents on the stove itself could have a profound impact on its performance. It would take time to learn. Even years later, I would find myself discovering new things about the stove's personality, like how the flue needed to be warmed up with a fistful of newspaper on particularly cold days or how it was better to listen to the fire rather than look at it in order to tell if it was running at maximum efficiency. When things were just right, it would just barely murmur. Too much air and it would roar exponentially; too little air and its crackle sounded more like a series of burps. Learning these things would take a while, would be lessons that had to be earned. But for now, the cabin was heating up.

As Ray began cleaning up, we chatted more about the community and his two little girls. It was for them that he had always wanted the horses and why he suspected his ex-wife had taken them. And, hell, maybe the horses were actually hers after all, but he sure had looked forward to giving his girls a child-hood where he could have put it all together. The conversation was kindled here and there with future plans for the cabin. Expand the deck, maybe add a rain catch system, address the foundation to fix the cabin's crookedness, whatever was causing it. We traded ideas back and forth until there were moments when it wasn't really clear whose plans were whose or whose cabin it was. Before he left, I happened to point out the massive gap under the front door. Without a word, he grabbed a scrap piece of pressure-treated lumber, eyed the gap a second time, and then ripped off a thin, angled slice with a saw gathered from the back of his truck. With a few nails, he smashed it into place, and I looked on in wonder. It fit perfectly.

"Yeah, that'll work for the meantime, but we'll get that floor straightened out real soon," he said.

He packed up his tools, slammed the tailgate of his truck, and I gave him the cash, a hundred bucks for five hours, includ-ing the extra hour he stayed to chat about future plans for the cabin. As I expected, he turned down the extra cash, and with a final wave, he drove away, leaving me to split some wood.

9

SETTLING

The installation of the woodstove marked a major phase shift in the cabin's interior. Things were starting to come together. Over the next few weeks, I spent every free evening and weekend making runs to Wit's End, outfitting the space and preparing for winter. A futon with a thick brown mattress slid in perfectly between the woodstove and the ladder to the loft, still unfinished and primarily occupied by spiders. For warmth, a mishmash of blankets, including a bright-green-and-gold Seattle Supersonics fleece I'd had since second grade. A plastic folding TV tray became the official dining and coffee table. A gnarled jute rug, too ugly for any space that received a decent amount of natural light, provided some relief from the cold, uninsulated floor. It pulled double duty as a welcome mat, keeping wet boots in check. In one corner, the plastic table that held the Coleman camp stove was outfitted with some real plates, a few pots, pans, and an assortment of cutlery. In the opposite corner, the whitewashed cabinet that came with the cabin was now full of all kinds of necessities (batteries, whiskey, and toilet paper). Above the cabinet, I hung up an old hammock to use as a make-shift shelf for blankets, pillows, spare gloves, and stocking caps. This setting up of the cabin pleased me to no end, bringing back the best of memories.

I had always been a camper. From as early on as I could re-member, our family spent summer weekends up at Lake Cres-cent on Washington's Olympic Peninsula. My mom and I would pack up the car, filling her tiny Subaru sedan with tents and sleeping bags and sandwich supplies and inflatable boats. We'd fill out the tiny gaps between supplies at the end with firewood, feeding the last pieces in through the front seat or the window so they could fall in and fill the void next to the door. The two of us would leave on a Thursday morning and make the three-hour drive to get there at the ideal time, that transitional period when the weekday people were packing up, yet before the week-end families arrived in full strength. Getting there on a Thurs-day afternoon usually meant we'd get our pick of spots, and we certainly had our favorites. Choicest among them was number ninety, the last of the waterfront sites, the one with the most pri-vacy. Unfortunately, also the farthest from the parking lot, which was several hundred yards away up a steep hill.

After claiming the site with a few towels and a bag or two, we'd hoof it back and forth up the hill for what felt like hours, struggling with heavy plastic tubs of camping goods, bags of groceries, and overladen coolers. Each round trip was a danger-ous traverse of steep gravel trails and root-laden paths fraught with tripping opportunities. Often, we'd stumble and lose our grip and some Rubbermaid tote would go careening down a hill, tossing out paper plates and bacon pans as if it were in a yard sale parade. Despite exhaustion, carrying things around was only half the battle. Then there was the setup itself, wrestling broken tent poles into graceful shapes, looking for tools that had long been lost, and listening for the firewood guy who roamed the road above with a megaphone. When we heard "Firewood!" in the distance, I'd go sprinting back up the hill with a five-dollar bill to buy an extra bundle. A little before dark, we'd finally be settled and collapse into green folding camp chairs beside a little fire. As if on cue, it was at that point my father would arrive, trucking one or two pieces of wood and his toothbrush, just in time for dinner. His excuse for arriving separately and conveniently late was always rooted in some supposed work conflict, but looking back, I wonder if he was just trying to avoid the sweaty initial struggle of setting up.

As annoying as it was to lug everything from the car and down the hill to the lake, I always found comfort in having everything we needed for our home away from home, neatly packed away in tubs and totes, whittled down to just the essentials of sleep, food, and entertainment. After all, what more could you need than a dry place to sleep, some spaghetti and a way to make it, a chair to sit in while the noodles boiled, and maybe a deck of cards for after dinner? Later in life, I would trade the heavy trunks and long weekends at the lake for ultralight backpacking supplies and extended hikes on backcountry trails. Even though the gear and the scenery was different, the reassuring feeling of being out in some wild place totally self-reliant was always the same. In so many ways, staying at the cabin was like those camping trips. There were no flush toilets. The only shower option was to dive into the freezing-cold river.

Staying warm meant making a fire, and staying entertained meant good conversation, cards, or a book. The golden difference was the opportunity to revisit those experiences without having to schlep the gear around every time.

I fantasized about a well-stocked cabin, where the oil lamps had plenty of fuel for a few days, the propane tank was always full enough to cook several meals, and there were piles of replacement batteries for headlamps and flashlights. I imagined the corner cabinet ever loaded with a full bottle of some dark spirit, a few boxes of dehydrated hash browns, a bit of olive oil, an assortment of hot sauces, a repository of canned chili and soups, and a few jugs of water. Upstairs, there'd be some dry socks, maybe a few good wool sweaters, and enough extra blankets that if you ran out of firewood, it wouldn't be the end of the world. I wanted the cabin to be a place that I could run to at any moment, secure in the knowledge that everything I needed was already there.

It's easy to make comparisons to folks who seek security in preparing for natural disasters or economic collapse by having go bags and hidden bunkers full of everything they'd need to survive a nuclear apocalypse or bad election or Black Friday event gone wrong, or whatever it was. But the prepper mindset never felt like it matched what I was trying to do with the cabin, and regardless of how well stocked it was, I always ended up swinging by the grocery store or the hardware store to pick up a few items before going out anyway. Bringing extra stuff on each trip was inevitable. But when I was back in Seattle, stuck at a job I didn't like, feeling the malaise that's unavoidable when you spend most of your time under a field of fluorescent lights, I would close my eyes and imagine the cabin. I'd picture it there, in the quiet calm of a rainy forest, ready to provide a cozy escape even if I arrived with nothing but the clothes on my back. During meetings, I'd imagine getting up, walking out of the room, and driving straight to the cabin without stopping. At any given time, I knew I could be sitting next to a fire with a cup of coffee in under two hours. That possibility was like an antidote to the invisible claustrophobia that I felt when confined to an office, a desk, and a computer. Knowing I had the perfect escape made the desire to escape more manageable, as if seeing light at the end of the tunnel made being in the tunnel a bit more tolerable.

10

FIREWOOD

Bryan was up. It had been a couple months since his initial visit during the work party weekend. I was excited to show him what'd become of the place, what with the woodstove and the furniture and blankets and extra cans of soup and all.

I'd met Bryan years before at an outdoor gear convention, where we had both been conscripted to write reviews on the latest camping equipment for magazines that talked about that kind of thing. When we met, we were just beginning careers as hopeful writers. What we really wanted was to one day be real journalists, flying around the world to uncover all sorts of strange and exciting stories. Yet in the years that followed, as we worked toward that dream, we found that writing for a living did far more to force us behind a desk than it did to free us into the world. We'd commiserate over sending in story pitches that would never get answered, dealing with bad editors, and always, always we talked about the boredom we felt when confined to an office. There was a kinship to our misery that made it a bit better, especially because we'd also developed a shared source of relief in building things.

At the same time I was working on the cabin, Bryan was turning a derelict sailboat into a tiny home. He'd bought the vessel for a dollar from the marina owner, who saw the boat as far more of a liability than an asset. Bryan was told it was a true racing sailboat, that it had even been to Hawaii, but its past exploits did little to distract him from the reality that it was little more than a floating biological hazard. Inside, he'd discovered piles of porno mags and jugs of piss, the only supplies left over from the previous owner, who had apparently drunk himself to death. Sheer economics had forced Bryan to buy the boat and make it a home. He lived in Oakland, worked in San Francisco, and knew that a one-dollar boat was likely the only chance he had of sustaining himself on the comically small stipend of a journalism internship. But he also saw the boat the same way I had seen the cabin, an opportunity to make something out of absolutely nothing.

We'd chat often online while we were supposed to be working on some project at work, finding time between meetings and emails to discuss the best features for a little cabin kitchen or sending each other photos of cabin designs we found particularly intriguing. Whenever one of us needed help with a project, we'd save up and split the cost of a flight between Oakland and Seattle to forget about writing for a bit and make something together. He'd been there for the initial work weekend at the cabin, had helped put in the flooring, and had followed along from afar as I'd struggled through the woodstove installation.

On a frigid early morning in December, I picked him up

from the airport, and we headed toward the cabin, intent on picking up a few supplies he would need during his stay. The forecast called for cold, dry weather. Despite a string of sunny days predicted, it likely wouldn't get above freezing for the entirety of his visit. Bryan seemed excited by the weather and the opportunity it presented to put the woodstove through its paces. What he didn't know was how much of a pain in the ass it was to actually use the thing.

It hadn't taken long to discover that standard-size firewood wouldn't fit in the woodstove's little belly. Since Ray had helped me install it, many panting, arm-destroying hours were spent huddled over pieces of wood with a rusty handsaw, vigorously gnawing them down into bite-size bits for the stove to nibble on. I felt like a mother bird, half digesting the baby stove's wood to be, at most, the size of a decent grapefruit. Without anything adequate to secure the wood, I usually ended up holding it in place with my boot, slamming the once-dry fibers into wet earth, where they would absorb so much moisture while I sawed away that the resulting chunk of adequately sized fuel would be difficult to light and slow to burn. They say that chopping firewood warms you twice, once when you chop it and again when it takes flame in the stove. At the cabin, preparing the firewood indeed warmed you, but to the point of complete exhaustion, into a sweat-filled delirium where you no longer cared about heat, or the cabin, or much of anything in the world, as long as you didn't have to tear firewood apart with the world's dullest saw anymore. When I was feeling especially motivated, I would rip up an extra batch of firewood and leave it inside for the next visit so at least my future self would have something to start with. The nature of the task ensured that I never felt especially motivated.

At a hardware store where we'd stopped for extra lantern fuel and other odds and ends, I couldn't help but think of Bryan feverishly trying to keep up with the dropping temperatures while he manually prepared a full day of firewood with a saw as sharp as a fresh baguette. Looking past the traditional impulse buys of gum, candy, and magazines, my eyes focused on a wall display on the far side of the store. I'd walked past it many times before. It featured a row of chain saws, all dramatically backlit and surrounded by pictures of lumberjacks clad in canvas overalls and leather gloves, covered in sawdust, ripping through trees with ease. In my darkest hours of firewood deconstruction fatigue, I'd fantasized about having a lightsaber, slicing through dozens of pieces with just a flick of my wrist. Though I'd never owned a chain saw, I figured it was about as close as you could get.

As the cashier began to ring up our purchases, I looked to Bryan and said, "Is it crazy to buy a chain saw?"

With absolute understanding, he responded, "No, absolutely it is not."

Turning to the checker, I proudly informed them that I'd be buying a chain saw as well, half expecting balloons to fall from the ceiling in celebration of such a rad purchase. While someone went to the back to fetch the box, Bryan and I strolled over to the chain saw section and loaded up with everything we'd need: a gas can, some engine oil, lubricant for the chain, a pair of sturdy leather gloves, and some eye protection to please our mothers should they ever find out we were chainsawing stuff. We also bought more firewood than usual, confident that breaking it down would no longer be a chore but a high-octane montage of horsepower and steel and wood chips and high fives.

When we got to the cabin, we tossed a cellophane-wrapped

bundle of firewood onto the soggy earth and read enough of the manual to find out what oil went where and how to start the thing. Within minutes, the little orange saw sprang to life with a chipper puff of oil-tinted blue smoke.

We fell to the bundles of wood with reckless abandon, stepping back with wide-eyed caution whenever the chain would catch wrong and scramble the logs like they'd been caught in a blender. Often we'd miscalculate the force of push required to cut and plunge the saw straight through the wood and into the earth, sometimes catching the edge of a rock and flinging it into a nearby tree or the cabin with a spark. Danger aside, the efficiency was something that couldn't be ignored. We felt like King Midas, were his fingers made of chain saws, and his wish, a simple desire for smaller wood.

After the initial thrill, we did have to recognize a few chain saw shortcomings. For starters, the same problem of stability existed with the chain saw as it did with the handsaw, only with far more dramatic consequences. Working the blade through a prepackaged bundle of firewood, it was inevitable to hit a knot or a pocket of sap or something that would cause the blade to kick and rear, usually sending pieces of firewood exploding into the air like kettle corn. In an effort to tame the chaos, we held the wood down with our feet, a practice that seemed more and more likely to end up leading to ambulances and wheelchairs and prosthetics and lifelong haunting regrets with every violent cut.

There was also the noise. It goes without saying that chain saws are loud, annoying devices, unless you're the one using them, in which case they sound pretty rad. Nevertheless, the thought of having to start it up late at night to process a few extra pieces of wood didn't sit well with me. No one wants to hear chain saws roaring to life in the middle of the night, and I certainly didn't want folks coming around to find out where the noise was originating, especially after dark.

Our introductory session ended without dismemberment and with a sizable pile of bite-size firewood bits. They'd be enough to get him started, but he'd certainly need more. He was going to be up for a while, a ten-day sojourn alone in the woods. I planned to return the following weekend and join him for the end of his trip before giving him a ride back to the airport. I was jealous of his time at the cabin. A stay of ten days obliterated the longest period of time I had spent there. And I was jealous of his tasks. Beyond staying alive in single-digit temperatures and trying not to cut his foot off with a chain saw, he'd be working to add bits of trim around the windows, build a small table to go beside the futon, and dive into whatever other improvements struck his fancy with a limited supply of wood and nails and screws.

Intent on dedicating my week to the cabin mentally even if I was physically in the office, I focused on solving the issue of firewood. The chain saw was fine for a pinch, but I wanted something a bit more predictably safe and reliable. The week started with me making several calls to firewood dealers. If anything, I thought, I could buy my way out of a problem.

Browsing the websites of firewood suppliers, the options available seemed endless. Cherry and oak, maple and madrone, pine and fir, custom sizes, different ages of seasoning, bark on, bark off, delivery and pickup, half cords and full cords, small piles and big shipments. They had it all and my request was simple. I just wanted small pieces. I felt better as the phone rang for the first dealer.

"Hello?"

"Hi. I was interested in picking up some firewood and need it in a custom size."

"No problem, how big did you want it?"

"Chunks about six inches across."

There was silence on the line, as if I had been cut off.

"Hello?"

"Ummm, we don't have anything that small, sir."

"I thought you did custom sizes?"

"Well, yes, sure, you can have twelve inches, or fourteen inches, or sixteen inches."

"Okay, but you can't make it smaller?"

"I just don't know how we'd do that."

"You don't know how to make the wood smaller?"

"No, we don't do that."

"Can't you cut it?"

"I don't think it would work. Can't *you* cut it?"

We were at an impasse. Of all people, I knew exactly how hard it was to cut it, but surely it wasn't my job to make firewood. Thinking I had just gotten an unsympathetic company, I tried again.

"Hello, Richardson's Fuel."

"Hi, I was wondering if you sold small firewood chunks, like six inches long or smaller."

"No, why would you need anything that small?"

"That's how big my stove is."

"Huh. Well, we only sell twelve inches or sixteen inches."

"Can't you cut it smaller?"

"Nope."

Seven companies, seven stumped firewood salespeople. It was the ultimate riddle. How to make firewood smaller. How could it be done? Surely the wood came from a tree, and at some point, that tree was cut into pieces, and at that point, it had to be decided how small the pieces would be, but at no point after that could it be conceived to cut the wood again. Once it was cut from the original tree, it could not be severed again, except into thinner, longer pieces for kindling. It was as if some biblical decree had been passed down, as if Moses had come down from the mountain, read off the Ten Commandments, and then added in at the last minute, "And thy wood shall be twelve or fourteen inches long, and once cleaved from the tree, it shall not be cleaved again, or your children shall be covered in boils!"

It became obvious that I'd have to cut down my own tree and slice off rounds that were six inches long, then split those into the chunks I wanted, but it was the beginning of winter, and I didn't have time to season a tree's worth of wood. Not to mention I wasn't nearly skilled enough to know how to cut a massive tree down. What I was skilled enough to do was imagine the nightmarish scene of dropping a gigantic evergreen directly on the cabin, the irony ultimately being that the splintered remains of the cabin would likely fit perfectly into the woodstove. And so, it was back to the drawing board. For now, the chain saw would have to do the trick.

11

A RECIPE FOR COMFORT

I returned to Wit's End to join Bryan for a few days before his return flight. When I got there, he took me through his week's projects. There were now little shelves in the windows, perfect for spices and silverware and miscellaneous kitchen items. In an empty corner beside the futon, he'd built a tiny table perfect for a tea light candle, a few coffee mugs, and a book. Much of his time, though, as expected, had been dedicated to staying warm. Nearly all of the firewood was gone, and the chain saw was completely out of gas. A well-worn fire-poker stick was more evidence that he'd spent hours quietly tending the woodstove. It had been a good week.

We spent a few days indulging in late mornings, too much coffee, big ham steaks, and leisurely afternoon hikes. In the evening, we talked about his new gig working at a well-respected magazine back home. It was a big job, one that he'd desperately wanted for a long time, but the day-to-day reality was not how he'd imagined. Like me, he felt like work was something to endure rather than engage with. We joked about the cliché office dramas, about people not washing their dishes, about the one guy that didn't think twice about microwaving fish for lunch and subjecting an entire floor of a thirty-story office building to the smell of day-old cod, about the pointless meetings where you spend an hour hearing people using mountains of acronyms you don't understand to explain the solution to problems you don't care about.

For me, one of the most frustrating parts about the work was how much I wanted to like it. I wanted to feel challenged and interested. I wanted to care enough to get frustrated and overcome things and feel real pride at the year-end holiday parties. I wished that the metrics and the ROIs and whatever the hell else there was, that any of it mattered to me. I tried working harder, taking on extra projects, hoping the extra effort would unlock some feeling of ownership or sense of shared accountability, but it never did. Inevitably, I'd slip back into just sort of plodding through the day, doing about the minimum required, because working harder didn't seem to help me and didn't seem to matter to anyone else.

Even the environment began to bother me. It was custom-designed to feel like nothing. The temperature was always perfect. The lights, always bright, but never casting a shadow. The colors of walls and floors and cubicles, all designed to blend into one another so the space felt larger and more open, attempting to hide the fact that you were technically in a maze with a hundred other people. Everything was tan and gray and white and light and straight and smooth. It was an absurdly comfortable work environment, its ergonomics customized to be easy on all the senses, but I began to feel like the comfort was more of a curse than a blessing. When the work felt meaningless and the environment matched, it was easy to go through the days in a sort of fog.

The cabin offered a reprieve, although it too was getting dangerously comfortable.

When I first saw it, it was the sort of place that inspired shallow breathing to minimize exposure risk. Now, it was hard to leave. Despite the futon and roaring woodstove and thick blankets, on paper, the cabin was still a terribly uncomfortable place to be. Splitting wood for the stove demanded loud, downright dangerous chain saw sessions. Cleaning up meant taking dishes outside with a headlamp and a freezing-cold jug of water and worrying that a bear was sneaking up behind you while you rinsed out greasy bowls. Even going to the bathroom was an adventure, the experience ever sprinkled with the chance you'd suddenly encounter a raccoon or a wood rat, thanks to an early decision to make sure the outhouse had lots of holes in it for ventilation.

The thing was, there was a benefit to each of those little adventures.

The best steak of my life was burned to a crisp. It was my brother's idea to carry the sirloins up a few thousand feet and into the Goat Rocks Wilderness on my first backpacking trip. It seemed like a strange addition, considering the amount of money and time he'd spent trying to shave weight from his pack. He had a camp stove smaller than a soda can and a sleeping bag that weighed less than a pack of gum but decided that a few fat steaks were worth the extra effort and back pain. It was my inaugural backpacking trip, so I didn't question the logic. "It'll be worth it," he reassured me.

We ate them on the first night, after a brutal day of elevation gains in the hot August sun. When it got dark, he made a fire while I sharpened a couple of roasting sticks. We sat there, considering the stars a bit more than we considered how long the meat had been in the fire. At some point between well done and Kingsford, we took them off and let them cool while we scraped the burnt bits off with dull rocks. Objectively, they were destroyed. On a purely carcinogenic level, they were probably dangerous to eat. But damn it if that wasn't the best thing I had ever tasted.

There is a magic sweetness that comes from unlikely comforts. As any camper will tell you, food tastes better around a fire. Sleeping bags are somehow improvements on thick memory-foam beds. Brisk dips in a lake create memories that no shower could ever contend with. For the non-outdoors types, imagine the tingle you get when the seat next to you on an airplane is unoccupied. No one would choose a pair of economy plane seats for their living room, but if that's what you end up with on a flight, you'll feel as though you've been transported to a golden cloud. When people ask about your flight, the extra seat will become the highlight of your entire trip. People will ooh and aah at the thought, even when they are actively sitting on a reclining leather sofa in their own living room.

When I was outside, soaked to the bone, risking my life awkwardly hacking at firewood with the chain saw, I'd be happily lost in anticipation of the well-deserved tingle of warmth that would trickle up my spine once I was inside and feeding the woodstove. I liked the rush of doing dishes knowing that my list of potential foes started at burnt eggs and ended at mountain lions. And when the chores were done, even though I was sitting on a crappy futon in a dark cabin without most of the amenities of modern living, the sum of the efforts that it took to get there made me into a slumpy pile of human goo. The work involved in achieving *warm* and *dry* and *clean* and *fed* made the comfort that derived from it all the sweeter. It also made me appreciate what was at home, where after a long stay at the cabin I'd return and find a mild sense of glee the first few times I flipped a light switch, turned on the water, or twisted the dial on the thermostat.

Switching back and forth between the cabin's comforts à la adventure and home's comforts à la laziness gave life a contrast. It was hard to define, but the net result was that I spent more days of my life simply feeling appreciative for what was around me. Maintaining that contrast demanded the cabin couldn't get too good, too fancy, or too easy, and yet I couldn't help but get lost in grandiose plans. I pictured complex plumbing systems with copper coils that wrapped around the woodstove to heat water for showers and loads of dishes. I imagined kitchen areas on the inside and outside, so that when I inevitably became a seasoned angler, I wouldn't have to get scales and fish guts all over the countertops. In my mind, there would be outdoor showers too, maybe even a wood-fired sauna or hot tub. Perhaps I'd knock down one of the walls and put in a set of French doors that led onto a second deck. Or, hell, at least I could add a few windows to let more light in.

I worried, though, what these additions might do to the spirit of the place. Adding everything might mean creating a space that was not different enough from day-to-day life. Without contrast, I worried that the cabin would lose a bit of its magic. The outhouse was a joy to use because as miserable as it seemed to crouch down in a dark plywood closet with fears of spiders crawling up your backside, you knew the alternative would be heading off into the forest with a shovel to straddle a hole. If you could step out of the cabin into a well-lit bathroom with a flushing toilet and hot water, you may as well be at home.

One comfort the cabin was devoid of was electricity. That's not to say there weren't electrical "things" at the cabin. When I bought the place, I took note of some kind of breaker box or panel, loosely mounted to the front of the cabin. A bouquet of wires emanated from its mysterious core and, as far as I could tell, ultimately led to nothing. Looking around, it was easy to see that none of the other cabins on Wit's End had power either. The closest power pole was on the main road, down a steep hill, easily three hundred yards away. When I called the Snohomish County PUD and asked about approximate costs to bring power up the road, it turned out that I could probably only afford to bring power about five and a half inches closer to the cabin. When the kind woman on the phone heard my electrical budget, we both had a much-needed chuckle and bid each other a quick farewell. Connecting to the grid was not an option, which was fine by me because I could not begin to comprehend what that process would have entailed. Plus, it seemed appropriate that the cabin would have some kind of off-grid power source. I was already without septic, water, Wi-Fi, mailbox, and cell reception. Not having an electrical bill every month didn't seem like a big deal. There were plenty of options. Or so it seemed.

Since the first work party weekend, I had had a generator. At first, it was a critical helper for longer days of work. It charged speakers that we used for music, it replenished tool batteries, and ran a crucial Mr. Coffee machine that kept us rattling on. For most visits, though, the generator felt a bit industrial. It was hard to sit on the deck, admire the mountain, and lose yourself in the ambient calm of nature when there was a two-cylinder Honda motor chugging away right next to you. It was loud and obnoxious, and no matter how carefully I attempted to fill it with gas, no matter what kind of gas can I bought, I could not for the life of me get gasoline into the thing without spilling most of it on the outside of the generator and onto the surrounding earth. Side note to all those who have struggled with the so-called safety pour mechanisms of modern gas cans. You are not alone. They are impossible to use.

Actually, let's pause on the gas can problem for a moment.

I still recall when I was a kid and the "honor" of mowing the lawn was passed down to me by my father. The gas can we had was simple, red, plastic. It had a nozzle that tucked itself backward into the opening. To pour gas out of the can, you'd simply remove the cap, attach the nozzle, position the nozzle in the general area you wanted gas (like inside the lawn mower), and then tilt the can so that gas poured forth. When you wanted to terminate the flow of gas, you stopped tilting the can and let the wonders of gravity take care of the rest. As an eleven-year-old with no primer on gas management, I don't remember ever spilling more than a drop or two.

But now, as an adult with a college education, albeit a liberal arts one, pouring gas out of a can feels like a never-ending prank. The problem is the modern gas can. As far as I can tell, at some point, some safety nerd realized that if you have a gas can set up in nozzle mode, flammable gasoline fumes are escaping and, therefore, causing a fire hazard. A simple solution would have been to remind people to simply put the gas can cap back on. But what I assume happened is that some gas can manufacturer got together with the nerd and some crooked politicians and decided it would be a hilarious way to make money if there was a new law that basically required every gas can on earth to be remade with a safety mechanism that prohibited not just fumes but literally anything to come out of a gas can unless you had an advanced degree in mechanical engineering.

The safety mechanisms seemed simple enough. There was a small plastic tab that supposedly slid from Store to Pour (rhyming makes things easy!) when you wanted to use it. Presumably, I'd slide the tab to Pour and then go about my business putting gas wherever I wanted to put it. But the tab always seemed a little stuck. I'd slide it as far as I could and then figure that was maybe enough and try to pour some gas, but nothing would come out. So I'd try again and again, always putting more pressure on the little tab, encouraging it toward Pour. Simultaneously, I'd start to get a little bit angry. *Boy, this is kind of tricky!* I'd think, smiling through gritted teeth to no one in particular.

Out of desperation, I'd slide the tab back to Store and try again, feeling foolish the moment I tilted it to no avail. "Ha ha, what a puzzle!" I'd chortle, the tips of my teeth grinding into bread flour. Then would come a bit of shaking, hoping the momentum might smack some critical part loose and into proper action. At this point, gas would start to come out, but not out of the nozzle, oh no. Instead, it would begin to leak from around the base of the cap and onto my hands, my clothes, basically everything except the vessel I was trying to put gas into.

Perhaps it was those fumes, those dangerous fumes, that would then propel me into a sort of existential crisis: *Why have they done this? What was wrong with the old cans? Or maybe I'm the problem? Maybe I'm not strong enough? Maybe I'm not smart* enough? Am I so feeble of mind and body that I can't effectively disperse the contents of a simple gas canister? Is this just a microcosm of my life as a whole? Am I literally always fumbling this hard at everything I do?

Eventually, in a blind rage, I'd rip the whole nozzle and cap assembly free, destroying its plastic components in the process, and then feverishly dump gas wherever I damn well pleased. Free of all constraints, it would gurgle with intoxicating fervor and tremendous inaccuracy, ensuring that everything within a two-foot radius was baptized in petrol and the can was empty; me, chest heaving, eyes wide with lunacy. That is the kind of safety we have now. Luckily, I've always sorta liked the smell of gas.

That being said, I didn't always want to smell like gas and deal with buying new cans to tear apart, so I knew I had to get beyond needing the gas can, which brings us full circle into the issue at hand: getting beyond needing the generator.

Electricity is a problem many small cabin and small-home folks run across when living off the grid, meaning that you are not connected to any municipal power, water, or waste lines. Many people leave said grid as an act of defiance. As if to say when you fired up the generator, "Hey, Snohomish County Public Utilities Department! Try to stop me from making coffee now, you sons of bitches!" But I was not grid-less because of any anarchist bent. I was grid-less because by circumstance and poorness, I couldn't get the grid anywhere near me.

The problem with most off-grid energy solutions was their reliance on natural resources that I simply did not have access to. The trees eliminated any chance that solar could work. Wind only came in big storms and was not consistent enough for me to rely on turbines. And unless I could harness energy from the rain directly, I had little chance of constructing some kind of water-powered solution. That none of these options worked for me was probably for the best anyway. Researching electrical systems was an aggressively humbling experience. No matter how basic the video or article or blog post or infographic about power was, it wasn't long before I'd find myself reading Wikipedia about electrons and protons and orbital shells and feeling the powerfully nostalgic anxiety of high school science.

The night before Bryan left, we sat on the futon with a fire raging, a few hurricane lamps placed around the cabin, a tea light or two, and a couple of battery-powered puck lights I'd picked up at the hardware store and slapped on the ceiling. As usual, the firelight played out across the wall in ways that, at times, seemed to match the music coming out of my tiny battery-powered speaker. The hurricane lamps added perfect pops of illumination to necessary work surfaces, the countertop, and the tables. The camp stove was bubbling away making hot water for tea. In the morning, it'd do just fine for coffee, and I realized there was truly no need for unlimited power. Bringing a light bulb into that environment would have felt like a sin. The lighting was perfect, the stove was effective, phones were useless and therefore required no charging. I realized that electricity would do more harm than good to the cabin's analog personality. This was not the office; it was not home. It was the cabin. Its charm and beauty and magic existed because it was different, because it was hard, and I loved it for that.

When the fire died down and the tea lights began flickering through their last bits of wax, we flicked on our headlamps and arranged the sleeping bags. Our backpacks were already loaded in anticipation of an early departure and waiting by the door.

In the morning, we struggled out of our sleeping bags and loaded up the car without time for coffee or a fire. We'd stop by the bakery in Sultan for doughnuts on our way to the airport.

As we drove, we talked about when Bryan might come up next, what projects there were still to do. Maybe he'd be able to make it in the spring. The loft still needed to get finished. I wanted to build stairs to replace the ladder. Maybe he could help create a little area for a firepit outside. There was plenty to do. Wouldn't it be nice, we thought, if he wasn't heading home today and instead we were just headed to the hardware store for materials. Wouldn't it be nice, we joked, if working on the cabin was somehow our job.

I dropped him outside the terminal and waved him inside as it started to rain heavily. The dry, cold weather had broken. On the way home, I found myself continually upping the speed of my wipers to keep up with the onslaught of water. In the morning, I'd return to work. I was already dreading the dark, cold, wet walk into the office from the park and ride. Thankfully, it was the end of the year, and long stretches of holidays meant less time at work and more time at Wit's End. And soon, I expected, all this rain would be turning into snow up at the cabin, cloaking the place in a delightful blanket of white. I couldn't wait to hole up and let the woodstove run.

12

RAIN'S COMING

Not long after Bryan's trip, I made a solo run up to Wit's End. There was no real project in mind, just an opportunity to disconnect and play cabin for a bit by myself. Weeks before, I had received a heavy package in the mail. It was my late uncle's typewriter, a gorgeous green-and-chrome machine from the '50s. He had been a professor and used it to punch out his dissertation decades earlier. It was he who had encouraged an early interest in writing and, later, a curiosity about woodworking. The basement of his home in Michigan's Upper Peninsula was filled with an army of tools dedicated to shaping bits of cherry, oak, walnut, and maple into cutting boards and intricate boxes. When he passed, his brother asked if I would be interested in the old typewriter. I said I would be honored to take it and immediately began fantasizing about evenings in the cabin with nothing but the mechanical thwack of metal on paper, the pop of a good fire, and rain thundering down overhead.

With the typewriter belted into the passenger seat, I made the dark drive along U.S. 2 toward the cabin, wipers on full blast to combat the downpour. At this time of year, the light was usually gone by 4:30 p.m. I don't mean sunset was at 4:30 p.m. There was no sun. But half past four was about the time the dim gray sky gave up its weak attempt to illuminate and gave in to black and night. It was a miserable ride at first, crawling along the cramped, clogged, waterlogged lanes of I-5 and I-405. But it slowly got better. I whipped past Woodinville, up over the hill, and down into Monroe before sweeping through Sultan, Startup, and Gold Bar. I loved the small towns, loved seeing the sign for one-dollar coffee at the Sultan Bakery, loved looking at the holiday light displays around the town welcome signs, loved that the Prospector bar was advertising Spaghetti Night on Thursdays. Despite a healthy appetite for spaghetti, I never usually ordered it at restaurants. It's never made much sense to me to pay going-out-to-dinner prices for a plate of something I could make at home for four dollars. Yet there was something unbelievably enticing about the offer. A whole night dedicated to spaghetti and a guarantee that you'd be surrounded by folks who thought such a thing was a reason to get out of the house and head into town. I made a mental note to visit on a Thursday soon.

As I neared Index, the streetlights disappeared, the oncoming cars lessened, and the heavy rain turned to snow. I slipped the car off the highway and onto the gravel road that led through the Riversites. The swirling snow caught the headlights and made it feel like I was warping through space, trading planets for tiny cabins and suspicious RVs. As usual, I slowed down when I rounded the corner that revealed Sunset Falls and rolled the window down. Even in the heavy dark of a stormy evening, I could make out the white glow of cascading water that made up the falls. The power of the place never failed to captivate me. It was unlike any waterfall I'd seen before. Eschewing the cliché waterfall design of a straight vertical drop, Sunset Falls went on for a while.

You could fit two football fields between the start and bottom of the falls. At the top of the falls on a clear day, the shape and color of smooth river rocks ten feet underwater were easy to make out, the clear green water like glass. But as the water converged into the tight granite canyon and began to drop, it picked up speed, and all hell broke loose. Undulations in the rock sent the rolling river into a frenzy. Halfway down, water was slamming into itself from all directions. There were moments when it seemed like the river had changed its mind and might start to head back up. At night, from the road, it looked and sounded like a white train was derailing, exploding through a canyon hemmed by hemlock, fir, and cedar. When the chaos finally clattered into the wide-open pool below, the water swirled in all directions as if bewildered from the journey, unsure of where to head next.

I left the window down and listened to the falls as I followed the road around the river. The car snaked up the switchback next to the falls and deeper into the woods where Wit's End and the cabin waited. When I arrived, I eased the car back into the driveway and left it on so I could unload in the taillights' red glow. I unbuckled the typewriter and carefully transferred it into the dark cabin, where I set it on the futon and returned to the car for a few bags of groceries and a fresh tank of propane. When I finally shut the car off, the darkness rushed in. It was unbelievably quiet. Occasional drips from wet branches echoed off the roof while the new snow fell. The rain was always quieter outside of the cabin. Inside, when it was really coming down, it sometimes felt like you were inside a snare drum. I stood there awhile, absorbing the quiet and the smell of wet moss and of smoke from some neighbor's fire.

I flicked on a headlamp and headed in to crumple up some of the blank paper I had brought up to supply the typewriter. The loose balls were tossed into the belly of the woodstove and topped with a handful of kindling, mercifully stocked by myself a few weeks earlier. I grabbed a lighter, tried it, realized it was empty, and then tossed it back into the pile for another. This went on, as it always did, for five or six dead lighters until I found one that worked. As usual, I neglected to dispose of any of the empty ones. Sometimes, they seemed to regenerate. Far be it from me to deprive them of the chance for resurrection.

The fire caught, and I headed out the door to grab more wood from the outhouse. It was the only place outside the cabin that had a slim chance of keeping things dry. Once I had ripped pieces down with the chain saw, I stacked them against the wall around the toilet seat. For the most part, they stayed dry—the outhouse roof had suffered many extraneous nail holes during its construction—but there were unfortunate side effects. The number of logs seemed to have a close relationship with the number of spiders found on, in, and generally around the toilet seat. Of all the real estate for a web, it seemed the choicest spot was the one that spanned the space directly below the seat. It made sense, when you considered the next floor down was likely the most attractive place on earth for bugs and other flying insects that spiders might be interested in. Matt and I joked about the spiders who lived in the space below the toilet seat, imagining it as the arachnid version of Tornado Alley.

"It's a nice place to live," the spiders would say. "Yup, not bad. Lotta bugs come through here. But ... every once in a while, this thing happens."

Defecating directly onto a spiderweb always felt like asking for bad karma, so I'd usually reach for the broom and clear a path before doing my business. If I was visiting with friends, it was a service I provided, the cabin equivalent of leaving a mint on the pillow. That night, the seat hole was clear when I grabbed an armful of stubby logs and retreated inside.

In my brief absence, the stove had made short work of the kindling. I added a few more pieces and encouraged the bright embers with a few lungfuls before putting away the groceries, lighting a handful of tea candles, and unfolding the TV tray that pulled triple duty as kitchen countertop, desk, and coffee table. It was warming up now. I took my jacket off and set the typewriter case on the TV tray. The clasp on the front of the clamshell case opened easily. Lifting the lid, I pulled it out carefully, slowly. It was a gorgeous machine, as beautiful as it was heavy. The firelight landed a reflection on the chrome trim and carriage return, and I couldn't help but smile.

It only took ten minutes and a few trees' worth of paper for me to successfully slip a blank page into the maze of rollers without crumpling it into oblivion. I had no idea how typewriters actually worked. Like the nervous, curious primate I was, I slowly pressed down on the k and watched its corresponding metal arm move toward the page, colliding in slow motion with the ink ribbon before kissing the paper. I let go and the arm dropped back into place. Evidenced barely in the dim light was a shadowy *k*. It seemed too light, so I initiated another trial. This time, I hit the key a bit harder. A new, darker *k* had formed. More impressive was the sound. The hearty *thwack!* seemed right at home in the cabin. Soon, a series of progressively darker *k*'s filled the page and the cabin. When I got to the end of the line, the final *thwack* was punctuated with a cheerful *ding!* This was the part I did know how to do. With utter satisfaction, I pressed my palm against the carriage return and slid the whole mechanism to the beginning of a new line.

Not wanting to ruin the moment by trying to think of something clever to type and then disappointing myself, I slid the TV tray back and crawled off the futon to work on dinner, which meant opening a can of chili and standing between it and the woodstove with a bag of Fritos. Above the sound of my crunching, I could hear the shift from snow back to rain as the drumming upped its pace on the roof.

It certainly felt cold enough to snow when I returned to the outhouse for a few final pieces of wood before bed, but the rain had clearly taken over. Back inside, I stripped down and crawled onto the futon, still in couch mode. I lay there listening to the fire die and the storm gain strength. The windows were black, but a few heroic tea lights still struggling on offered enough light that I could see drops of water collecting on the glass outside.

When I woke up, the cabin was frigid. It was still raining, but harder now. Peeking over the edge of the futon, I assessed the wood situation. There were two chunks left and no kindling. At most, after a bit of work, I was likely to get half an hour of good heat out of them. Instead, I grabbed another blanket and slept a bit more before finally getting up and packing quickly while the car warmed outside. I secured the typewriter back in its case along with its page of *k*'s and tucked it all neatly beside the futon. I swept the floor, emptied the ash compartment beneath the woodstove, and washed the chili pot outside with a jug of cold water. It was pouring. The jug was almost unnecessary. I was soaked through in minutes. Unhappy about driving home with a wet butt, I slid into the car and cranked the heat.

If you live for any length of time in the Pacific Northwest, specifically on the western side of the Cascades, you get used to the rain. Seattle, of course, has the reputation of being a gray, overcast, wet, miserable place. The stats back that reputation up. Eighty-four percent of our days are cloudy, and it averages out that half of all days you can count on measurable precipitation. But in most cases, it's a drizzle here or there. It's an annoying, sporadic mist. Miami, for all its sun-soaked stereotypes, gets more annual rainfall than Seattle does. Of course, the hurricanes help.

Index was a different story. On the welcome mat of the Central Cascades, it was in a prime position to get absolutely dumped on. Here's why, as far as I can tell, thanks to about two minutes of Google research and a lifetime of barroom conversations focused on complaining about the weather.

As any classically trained meteorologist would probably tell you, weather is basically just different types of air. There's hot air and wet air and dry air and fast air and slow air. Some air even has electricity in it. For the most part, the PNW gets its air from the Pacific Ocean, which, as you might expect, tends to be very wet. As our air bumbles around the Pacific, it gets drunk on salt water and shows up to our coastline, wet and irritable. Moving east, those moisture-laden clouds eventually find their way to the foothills of the Cascades, where, faced with the prospect of having to drag their sodden masses over ten-thousand-foot peaks, they choose instead to dump all their extra weight in the form of rain, directly on the cabin.

It rained a lot at the cabin. On average, Seattle, the poster child of rainy places, managed to soak up thirty-seven inches of rain per year. Less than forty miles away to the east, Index nearly doubled that. Even when it wasn't raining, it was. The outstretched bows of cedar, hemlock, alder, and Douglas fir trees were like a holding tank for every day of drizzle. Their delicate needles and cones filled with water that would drip, usually straight down the back of your shirt while you were scampering to the outhouse, for hours after clouds had passed by. To be at the cabin between October and July and have it not be wet was virtually a miracle.

There were—of course—some benefits to the rain.

At any time of year, the cabin was surrounded by a thousand shades of green. Evergreen trees were a mainstay of intense, dark emerald hues throughout the year. Ferns were everywhere. Behind the cabin, a steep hillside covered in waist-high bracken ferns gave the area a prehistoric vibe. In spring, delicate ostrich ferns beyond the deck delivered tightly coiled fiddleheads that were delicious sautéed with a bit of olive oil and salt. Like a glue holding it all together were thick carpets of moss that gave the forest floor the appearance of shag carpeting. It made the bare winter branches of maples and alders look like they had donned fur coats to stay warm. Up close, the colors were incredible, ranging from a pale blue to a green so neon bright you'd swear it would glow in the dark. The world of a temperate rainforest was a verdant, spongy, drippy place that was a welcome change from the city's hard and grit and gray. Healthy doses of rain ensured the cabin's backdrop of green stayed that way.

I loved the rain for the days and nights it kept us inside. I loved listening to the dull drumming of drops on the cabin's rusted roof. I loved stepping outside to the cold and wet, sometimes just so I could look forward to diving back inside and soaking up *warm* and *dry* from the woodstove. When we finally did go outside, we did so with a sense of adventure, with an intent to embrace the sopping, dripping world and play in it. We'd gear up in an abundance of grubby layers and, like low-rent astronauts, we'd set off into the empty, rainy forest as wet-weather explorers, knowing that, when we were a bit too sodden and cold, a crackling fire was not far away.

Just a few hundred yards from the cabin was the boundary of the Mount Baker–Snoqualmie National Forest, a 1.7-million-acre swath of land that cut down the middle of the state. It was a hell of a backyard. Without any dedicated trail, we'd head for the woods and tromp overland, enjoying the sense of exploration as much as the acrobatics required to traverse a landscape of huge, fallen logs, creeks, and moss-covered boulders, though we'd never make it too far before we were soaked to the core. In some ways, just getting to that point seemed to be the point.

After all, the best part was returning to the cabin, throwing a can of something on the stove, and stoking the fire. The wet layers would get stripped off and hung from anything that would hold them—errant nails in the ceiling, the front doorknob, and every last rung of the crude ladder leading to the loft. The windows would fog up with steam from the drying clothes, and we'd sit there, flush-faced, happy, glad to be warm and dry again. As usual, the cabin provided exactly what we needed—a base camp, a refuge, a launching place, a landing pad, a place to reliably return for whatever it was we needed, even if we weren't sure ourselves.

13

BIG MUD

The first slide happened just before Christmas. That it had been raining for weeks without stopping was not unusual, nor were the warnings about area rivers reaching critical flood stages. Floods, in fact, were common. Many of the waterfront cabins in the Riversites were built on raised foundations for this very reason. Mudslides—at least minor ones—weren't uncommon either, but there was less to be done about preventing them. In most cases, there wasn't much prevention beyond hope and luck.

I saw the first post about the slide on the Riversites' Facebook page, which I'd come to idly visit when at home or bored at work and thoughts of the cabin made it hard to focus on other things. Checking in on the community's digital version of itself was a way to stay connected to the cabin. The page was, for the most part, a calm, collected, quaint little gathering place to post the sort of news you would expect from a mountain community of cabin owners and senior citizens sometimes plagued by misfits and ne'er-do-wells. People would post about missing dogs, only to have them found hours later at some neighbor's house. Happy-reunion pictures would follow and everyone would breathe a sigh of relief, expressed through emojis. You could also find out what kind of stew was on at the local distillery during the Seahawks game, enjoy amateur photos of the nearby mountains and river, or watch aerial videos from one Riversiter who had received a drone on his birthday. Sometimes, the character of the message would allude to the community's shadier side and give the page a bit of illicit excitement. One woman complained that "a few" of her "outside refrigerators" had been stolen. Instead of commonsense follow-ups inquiring about the necessity of exterior refrigerators—or several of them, for that matter—most comments merely offered their condolences and expressed concern about their own out-of-doors appliances.

When I logged in on a dreary morning in late December, I was met with a photo of a gravel road covered in trees and thick clay. I recognized the place immediately. It was part of the switchback that wound its way up the side of Sunset Falls. The hill beside the falls wasn't massive, maybe six hundred feet tall at most, but it was steep. Now, it seemed intent on reclaiming the road that snaked below. Overnight, a grab bag of forest had sloughed off the hillside, taking with it a few dozen Douglas fir and a couple of power poles. As such, power was out and folks were stuck.

Things would have been fine if there were another way in, which there wasn't. The Riversites were a dead end. The entire neighborhood relied on the main road that brought you in from the highway. It was a heavy weight to bear for a thoroughfare that was built adjacent to a powerful, frequently flooding river in the mountains. There had been another option. On the eastern edge of the community, there was once a bridge. It connected the area to the highway a bit past the turnoff to Index. Years before, the bridge had aged to the point of needing significant, expensive repairs. Rather than fix it, the community decided to save a bit of money and simply take it out, relying on the route that brought you the long way and up the switchback by Sunset Falls. Now, those who had been around long enough to remember that decision started dialing in their hindsight.

Photos on Facebook showed crews of folks working in neon-yellow rainsuits, attempting to secure power poles back into soil the consistency of brownie batter, and tired neighbors standing in the rain beside cars full of groceries, trying to get home. The spectacle was enough to lure news crews and journalists out into the elements to take a look.

I convinced myself that things were okay. Real adults seemed to be in charge of the road, issuing daily updates, working to clear the switchback as fast as possible. Besides, I was busy with holiday commitments and had no plans to visit the cabin at the time. I was sure it would be resolved within a few days, which it was, but the relief didn't last for long.

Once the initial slide had been cleared, the mud continued to creep insidiously toward the road, prompting daily updates on Facebook. Posts let folks know how bad the road was and when our diligent neighborly plowman expected to have things cleared. At first, the delays were minor. Every few days, the road would shut down during nonpeak hours and get cleaned up a bit. Everyone hoped for a bit of dry weather to help firm things up, but the rain didn't stop, and neither did the mud. Before long, delays of a few hours turned into full-road shutdowns that lasted a day or two. Back home, I felt powerless to do much beyond check the Facebook page and stay out of the way. Surely, my need to access the road did not compare to the nearly eighty people who lived there full-time. I was a tourist compared to them. Plus, I imagined things couldn't stay bad for much longer.

I had an image of mudslides. They were chaotic events. They happened in minutes and gave no warning. They were explosions of earthen momentum that would stop at nothing. What happened before Christmas fit the bill. What was happening since seemed more like an aftershock, echoes of the original slide that would surely quiet down. It was then, at most, a gentle melting. It was just the hill getting a bit more comfortable. That's what I wanted to believe anyway.

Plowing the mud became a daily ritual. Sometimes, it was necessary twice a day so that people could coax their spinning tires through the slick clay and rain to get home. Power loss became commonplace. People were advised, if possible, to leave a car on both sides of the slide area, just in case. People were tired of delays, and construction was underway on a small footpath that bypassed the slide closer to Sunset Falls. When the road was closed, folks had the option of hoofing it in. All the while, the Riversites were hemorrhaging money to pay for the cleanup. The windows of open road became smaller. A week of closure would be punctuated by an opening of a few hours at most, often with little or no advance notice, and with every clearing, the road became narrower and narrower, hemmed in by impeding walls of earth and rivers of draining water.

When the plow wasn't enough, it was replaced by a bulldozer, and another week went by. When the road itself started to crack and separate, desperate property owners began to install drainage pipes to get rid of the excess water, and another week went by. When the mud started closing in on the nearest cabin in its path, blocking the door, the owner went in through the living room's exterior wall using a chain saw and took out his most valuable belongings. Photos showed the little red cabin, a gaping hole in its side, leaning precariously as a river of mud crept inside to occupy the old couch that was left behind, and another week went by. One tiny cabin near the slide tilted right off its foundation and rolled neatly to the bottom of the hill, where it came to a stop on its side, square in the middle of the road.

January turned to February, and I still stayed away. From the slide, it was nearly two miles to the cabin. On a typical trip, I'd have the car loaded down with dry firewood, jugs of water, cans of food, and a handful of tools for impromptu projects. While I could have made the most of it, packed a light bag of essentials, treated it like a rainy backpacking trip culminating in a cabin instead of a tent, I worried that visiting would only heighten my anxiety. In trying to make sense of the slide, I'd looked at satellite images dozens of times to see where the slide was in relation to the river, the road, and Sunset Falls. What I'd come to recognize was that the opposite side of the affected hill led directly onto Wit's End. If half of the thing was unstable, it seemed only reasonable that the other side might be just as bad. As much as I wanted to see the cabin, I couldn't imagine lying in my sleeping bag trying to fall asleep with the fear of waking up drowning in mud.

In late February, a new video popped up on Facebook. Overnight, the hill had moved sixty feet. Road crews pronounced the area too unstable to even attempt work. The scene was unrecognizable. Debris from destroyed cabins was tangled beneath downed trees and power lines. Great hunks of earth floated on pools of liquefied blue-gray clay. All evidence of the road had vanished, and when it snowed in early March, covering the chaos in a calming blanket of white, you'd swear it had always been like that. Nothing to see but a white hill beside a river and a dead-end road.

News anchors returned and stood in the rain, wearing concerned expressions and rubber boots. The rain continued. Power outages became nearly constant as utilities crews poked around in the muck for something solid enough for a power pole to sink into. When an elderly resident past the slide had a heart attack, the EMTs came across the railroad bridge on ATVs, and another week went by. When inventive owners decided to expand the footpath into an ATV-only trail below the slide, equal parts brave and stupid people charged down the trail in their cars and trucks, getting stuck on the tight turns and rolling their vehicles into trees to be left abandoned. And another week went by. And when another cataclysmic slide killed forty-three people in Oso, about ninety minutes to the north, the news anchors stopped paying attention to Index, the weeks turned to months, and residents wondered when the hill might give way on top of them while they unloaded eggs from their car and prepared to hike home through the woods.

The Oso slide turned people's inconveniences into fears. It was a reminder that things might not work out. Compared to Oso, our mudslide had barely done anything. Or it meant that the worst was yet to come. It was a reminder that trekking through a wall of mud to get groceries, to get to work, to check on their cabins, to get to medical appointments, to receive emergency treatment, that all of that might not be solved. At some point, there'd be no money to fix the road, people would abandon their cabins, and the utility department would simply give up on its attempt to bring electricity farther into the Riversites. And all that would be left would be the remnant of a hill, gutted into the shape of a cresting wave, towering over a sliding, sparking stew of mud, trees, homes, and renegade electrical wires.

March arrived, and I found myself driving east on U.S. 2 for the first time in months. Friends and I were headed over Stevens Pass to a cabin on the east side of the state. I decided it was time to see the mayhem for myself. While it had been easy to avoid the place at first, I'd started to develop a desire to see things up close and personal. As thankful as I was for the Facebook page, I realized it was mostly news through the lens of a single resident, Don. I imagine he got the job with two qualifications: being willing and knowing the Facebook password. I was sure Don was doing his damnedest. But I also wondered if maybe he was a bit too close to the problem, a bit too weary from the grocery hauling to accurately represent the true nature of things. Maybe things weren't so bad. And while I was no geologist, it seemed like a fella could get a pretty good feeling about a mudslide by striding up to it confidently and looking it square in the eye. It was a Hail Mary thought. After all, I'd seen the pictures. That hill was so ass-backward I often couldn't tell if photos were posted right side up or not. But still, a fella could hope.

Optimism cranked to eleven, my friends Yos-wa and Sarah and I rolled up to the base of the switchback in the fading light of a rainy Friday evening. Sitting in the back seat, I had my head pressed against the glass to get a better view as we approached the falls and the slide. When we arrived, I almost didn't get out of the car. The hill's height had always been shrouded by my perspective from the road. Now that the front half was gone, I was staring up to the top of a six-hundred-foot cliff.

Slowly, I got out and took a few steps into the drizzle to get a better look. At the top of the cliff, I could barely make out the half-exposed root structures of massive hemlock and maple trees, teetering on the edge. Below, it looked like someone had put the neighborhood into a blender and hit Puree. There were mountains of snapped trees and tangled branches stuck in great piles of earth. Here and there, the bright, jagged remnant of a red cabin's siding, a shiny bit of stainless steel from an obliterated barbecue, and the tattered ends of caution tape added spots of color to the otherwise gray-brown heap.

Gearing up with rubber boots, we made our way toward the old switchback now cordoned off with massive concrete barriers. There were a handful of cars parked around the entrance to the nearby ATV trail, but no one was around. As we moved past the barriers, it seemed that a little trail on the slide side already existed. To my surprise, it seemed solid. I felt the last embers of hope flicker just a bit. We ducked around fallen trees and piles of branches along the trail. Bits of the old road revealed itself here and there, including a broad section that was completely smooth, albeit a bit muddy. I stopped and looked and hoped. This part of the road looked fine. I wondered if things weren't too bad. If this part survived, maybe a big ol' cleanup was all that we'd need. Sure, things were inconvenient now, but if we had a few days of dry weather, maybe then we'd get back to normal. Two steps later, I was thigh-deep.

"Ah, yep, that's bad. I get it."

The hill was swallowing me alive. Engaging in a series of

impressive, though unconventional, defensive writhing maneuvers, I reassured Yos-wa and Sarah, standing on solid ground just a few feet away, that I was fine. But there's something about a guy who can't stop saying, "It's okay," in rapid bursts that makes it seem like he may not be okay. It also didn't help that all my efforts seemed to do was impair me further, dragging me lower into the mud.

After what seemed like half an hour but was in reality probably about thirteen seconds, I began sprinkling in a few other sayings like, "It's not okay," and "Help!" With quick thinking and an arsenal of solutions they had learned from watching episodes of *Looney Tunes*, Yos-wa and Sarah helped me leverage out of the suck with a collection of branches expertly tossed around my sinking body.

Slowly, I pulled myself out of the earth like a fresh-faced Uruk-hai. My bottom half and arms were covered in a thick layer of slimy clay. Mud had filled every cranny of my boots. Squelching back toward the parking lot, we rerouted toward the ATV trail, and I mentally tossed any hope for a new road into the surging rapids of Sunset Falls. The path wound through a dense patch of forest, blocking what little daylight there was left. I flicked on my headlamp, and we followed the swirling cone of illuminated mist from the falls up around the slide and back onto the road above the switchback. From the top, things looked just as bad. We took the scene in for a minute or two before turning to complete the two-mile walk into the cabin.

Huffing up Wit's End, I couldn't help but glance toward the hill to the west. The slide was just beyond. Being on this side felt like sneaking around the back of some massive beast. I had the instinct to stay quiet, as if the hill might be so delicate a shouted word would bring it down. On the spectrum of tip-toeing to plodding, I couldn't help but notice a kind of comfort when I aligned my gait to something a smidge closer to the former. If my friends hadn't been there to ridicule me, I might have belly-crawled the last fifty yards just to be safe. Just as dark settled in, we came over the top of Wit's End, and I saw the pale outline of the cabin's weathered gray siding and rusting metal roof. That it still existed seemed like a miracle, considering the world was turning itself upside down just beyond the ridge.

Big branches covered the driveway. I took a moment to examine the roof as best I could from the outside, curious if any larger limbs had caused damage. A pile of maple leaves had built up behind the chimney, but otherwise, I couldn't see anything obviously wrong. There were more cigarette butts scattered around the deck. Like the first time, I couldn't find any evidence of a successful break-in or theft. A part of me almost felt glad for the mysterious visitor. It was a small sign that things behind the mud were still somewhat routine. Despite the apparent dangers, both natural and man-made, the door was locked and the windows were secure, and the whole place seemed in good shape. Which is to say, poorly constructed but more or less continuing to exist. When I opened the door, the scent of cedar and smoke spilled out. Everything was in its right place. The sight and smell of it cultivated a small lump in my throat. A few months away had given me a dose of fresh perspective. It felt like coming home.

Not wanting to track mud in, I stood in the doorway and swept my light around. The spiders had made the most of my vacation. A few fairly ambitious webs hung around the room. One, stretching over the futon, felt borderline arrogant, though

I was glad something was still hard at work on cabin projects. Every little bit helped when it came to the structural stability of the place.

A glance at the woodstove caused me to pause. There was something reflective there. It looked like water. I took off my boots and stepped inside, noting the futility of removing a muddy boot to walk around in mud-covered socks. The top of the woodstove was wet. Upon closer inspection, I could also see that things were rustier than they had been. Above, I saw a drop of water clinging to the edge of the chimney pipe. After what seemed like an eternity, it dropped down, directly onto the stove.

The pale pink tiles beneath the stove were also a bit wet, but the surrounding faux-wood flooring appeared unaffected. I took a few moments, kneeling there in front of the woodstove, trying to come up with some way to solve the problem. But there was nothing I could do. If water was getting in through the roof, it could be from anywhere. Most likely, it was seeping in around the chimney. Logically, I knew the cabin had always been a playground for amateur carpenters, but I was still disappointed and maybe a little ashamed that my work had added another problem to its laundry list of scabs. It would be fine, but I couldn't ignore the overwhelming sense of responsibility for the place.

It has always been easy for me to anthropomorphize things. My first car was a 1986 Honda Accord. Exterior and interior were both dark shades of crimson. I'd bought it with a lifetime of money saved from birthdays and good report cards and a surprisingly lucrative First Communion. It was $1,300. Mechanically speaking, on a scale from excellent to poor, it was haunted. Only one of its flip-up headlights worked consistently. Three out of four windows didn't roll down, and the thermostat malfunctioned in such a way that keeping the heat on full blast was often necessary to prevent the engine from smoking. The combo of the window issue and the thermostat issue virtually guaranteed no one wanted a ride from me in the summertime. Toward the end of its life, the biggest problem was that the car would not reliably turn off. I'd roll into my high school parking lot, find a space, turn the ignition off, *remove the key*, step out of the car, shut the door, and stand there watching as it continued to sputter and shake with life. In some cases, it would take several minutes for it to die. Sometimes, I'd have to get back in and drive it around the block before it would settle down.

It's fair to say that the car's myriad of shortcomings filled me with anxiety. But that discomfort was never about the money or the inconvenience of potential fixes. I was never worried about getting stranded somewhere or having it stolen because it continued running while I went inside the grocery store. Rather, I felt bad for the thing. When it was lurching around in its parking space, I felt closer to giving it a hug than a wrench and not just because I had zero mechanical aptitude.

I only owned the car for a few years and gave it the best life I knew how. I regularly washed it on the weekends, taking care where the paint was peeling off the hood. I took alternate routes that featured fewer steep hills whenever possible. I kept the heat on full blast even in the peak of summer to mitigate the chances of a thermodynamic disaster. I felt like a sort of automotive hospice provider, and when I heard that the new owner (the daughter of a woman my mom worked with) got rid of it after it died on the freeway, my first thought was that maybe it just hadn't been loved enough.

With the cabin, I knew I was far from the capablest of people to be its steward, but I was nearly positive that I cared more than most, and that seemed like plenty for now.

Staring at the woodstove without a real solution in mind, I asked Yos-wa to empty the small trash can that held pine shavings for outhouse duties. He handed it to me from the deck, and I positioned it beneath the drip. Despite the constant rain, the leak was slight. It took a few minutes before I heard the first drip plop into the plastic can. I could only hope that it wouldn't overflow before I could make it back.

With a final check of the place, I grabbed a handful of paper towels and crawled out of the cabin backward, wiping up my muddy footprints as I went. Outside, I shoved the dirty paper towels into my pocket and held the door shut while I turned the key and slid the dead bolt into place. Gentle rain was filtering through the trees as we made the dark walk back down Wit's End and toward the slide, following the roar of Sunset Falls down the ATV trail. When we cleared the trees and looked back, a rising moon lit up the white waters so that they glowed as they tumbled into the pool below. I stripped out of my muddy clothes and threw them into the trunk before changing into clean jeans and shoes. Glancing up at the hillside one last time, I climbed into the car, and we headed back toward the highway. That night, I ducked away from a bonfire with friends to use the Wi-Fi and check the Riversites Facebook page for any slide updates. The next morning, I did the same. That afternoon, I checked it again. There was rain in the forecast. Things weren't looking good.

14

WAITING AND LEAKS

By the time most residents realized the road couldn't be fixed, the community funds were all but depleted. The Sisyphean tasks of scraping mud away from the road, bringing in new gravel, clearing downed trees, and cutting new work-around trails had added up quickly. A couple of hundred dollars charged twice a year to property owners was meant to handle the occasional snowplow and some extra rock for the potholes that inevitably emerged after a hard winter. We never had the kind of funds necessary to stop hills from relocating. Without a clear solution in mind and with the money nearly gone, tensions were high. There were monthly community board meetings that anyone could attend, but it appeared that most people enjoyed the ease and convenience of airing their grievances on the Facebook page. There was lots to complain about, apparently.

Some said the community board, a seemingly benevolent

group of volunteers, was full of crooked property owners who lived below the slide and didn't care about those of us who were trapped. Others believed that the road's ultimate downfall was late payments from the board to the resident plowman, all because one board member was dissatisfied with previous work the plowman had done on her driveway. One old-timer blamed the county, which had drilled holes in the hillside as part of some survey work the previous spring. His theory gained steam quickly, but was ultimately extinguished when it was revealed their work was much farther down the ridge. Most people seemed as eager to find someone to blame as they did to find a solution to the problem. That's not to say there weren't ideas.

A few folks thought we could use old forest service roads that hugged the mountains to drop into the Riversites from the south. The closest connection was the end of Wit's End. I cringed at the peace that would be lost if the entire community's traffic came past the cabin. Another suggestion was to load up the hill with explosives, a good start, and blast away until we could be sure whatever might slide had slid. Then we could simply rebuild the road and get back to normal. A few people were ready to give up on the entire thing and seek federal assistance money from the government to move. Even alumni property owners popped up on the Facebook page, some offering messages of support, but most expressing how glad they were to be gone. Before the slide, I had enjoyed checking the community page for the little peeks into the lives of eclectic neighbors and security camera shots of mischievous bears. This new era of division and argument and pettiness and fear and mudslide footage, I liked less. More than anything, it worried me that no one seemed to really be in charge. And all the while, the hill kept sliding. In late March, it had reached the river, infiltrating the clear water with a tide of brown.

Every now and again, there was a glimmer of hope on the human side of the slide. I saw posts of volunteer residents in rain gear scooping gravel onto the ATV trail, now guarded by massive rocks that would prevent anyone from trying to bring their car in or out. I saw offers to help ferry people and their groceries between their home and the parking lot below the slide. The smile and thumbs-up of someone riding backward on a four-wheeler loaded down with Safeway bags kept up the embers of optimism in everyone.

A few weeks after visiting the slide for the first time, I returned intent to hike in and spend the night. Even though it was almost spring, temperatures hovered near freezing most nights. Knowing that any dry wood for the stove would have to be carried in, I only bought a single bundle when I stopped in Sultan for last-minute groceries. I'd already borrowed a few dehydrated meals from my backpacking supplies for food, though there was not much I could do to get around lugging a gallon of water with me. When I got to the slide and the start of the trail, it was just before dark. No one was around, though the parking lot was mostly full.

I loaded up my backpack with supplies and strapped the bundle of wood to the top. The weight was clearly annoying, but I'd be lying if I said there wasn't part of me that enjoyed the forced adventure in the same way that I enjoyed the cabin's off-grid "inconveniences." Even when required by circumstance, the road less traveled is often the way to go. I followed my headlamp up the ATV trail, past the madness of Sunset Falls, and back onto the road. At the top, I switched the light off and settled into the dark walk, passing under the railway, then over top of it on the wooden bridge that led deeper into the Riversites. Most places seemed empty, dark, and cold. Now and again, a warm square of light came from someone's window or a curl of chimney smoke. It was good to see that some folks were home and power was on for them. Getting to the bottom of Wit's End, I leaned into the steep road and switched the headlamp back on with intention. I had to see the eyes.

I'd first spotted them in early winter, when the newly bare branches of maples and alder allowed deeper looks into the forest. One night, I pulled onto the road with my high beams on. About halfway up the hill, I saw the reflection of a pair of large eyes staring back at me from the dark silhouette of a distant tree. Getting shredded by a mountain lion is sort of a de facto fear if you grow up in the northwest. Hell, it's probably a de facto fear of anyone from anywhere, but here, it's a more realistic possibility. Even in the safety of the car, I felt a tingle of anxiety. When the tigers get close at the zoo, I'm not ashamed to admit puckering up a bit, no matter how impenetrable the glass supposedly is. That night, I stopped the car and stared for quite some time, wondering if there was a way to park close enough to the cabin that I could transfer myself from window to window like I was a shuttle docking at the space station. Flicking my lights on and off didn't seem to adjust their position. The eyes were always there, staring right back.

It took me longer than I'd like to admit to realize that the eyes probably weren't real. Brimming with confidence born from a childhood belief that bad things don't happen in the woods in daylight, I took a walk the following afternoon to investigate. It didn't take me long to find the right tree where, sure enough, about twenty feet off the ground were two bits of reflective tape, cut into the shape of eyes and held to a cedar trunk with two rusty nails. Clever. Fun.

You'd think that discovering the eyes were fake would have alleviated the anxiety they caused. But it didn't. If you're in a dark, dense forest where you know mountain lions make their home, the mere idea of them will get your mind turning toward the possibility of getting mauled, a notion it's hard to steer your thoughts away from. The same thing happens whenever someone mentions what an interesting miracle it is that your body just breathes in and out on its own, to which I usually respond with a five- or ten-minute session of panicky, manual breathing. The next time I'd come to the cabin at night, I made a plan to intentionally look away and avoid seeing the eyes, but looking away with intention made me imagine the eyes, which got me thinking about mountain lions, which brought the fear back just as much as if I'd just looked at them. Basically, I was scared of cougars, I guess.

Ultimately, I decided on a practice of looking for the eyes, accepting them. At the very least, it felt like a confirmation that the only cougars that were around were fake and where they were supposed to be. If I ever saw a second set of eyes, or that the eyes had moved, then it would be time to panic.

Walking up Wit's End on the night I hiked in from the slide created a new type of fear, however. Without the relative protection of my car's aluminum-and-tempered-glass cage, my anxiety felt appropriately exacerbated. The thought of being jumped by a massive cat was a strong motivator for the steep walk, and I started to wonder if my quick steps were the inspiration for the eyes in the first place. I imagined a dad telling his kids, "We gotta hustle up this hill or the cougar will get you!" It would've been a sick prank. It was the sort of idea that made me wonder if being a father might be a pretty good time.

As usual, I made it to the cabin unscathed. The flip side of an irrational fear of cougars was a belief that the cabin was a safe zone, a protected area the cats respected. When I reached the deck, my anxiety vanished. Perhaps one of the reasons the cabin always felt so calming was its simple relationship with the ebb and flow of my lion-focused adrenaline.

I unlocked the door, set my bag inside, and grabbed the key hanging from the nail just inside so that I could unlock the outhouse. For a while, it had seemed silly to lock the outhouse, which only contained spiders and, in the best of times, a few pieces of dry wood. Once it became a home for the chain saw and the majority of my ever-increasing AAA battery surplus, locking the place up seemed like the responsible thing to do.

Inside the outhouse, I found two disappointments. First, there was no broken-down wood left—or any wood, for that matter. Second, the chain saw and its associated can were bone-dry. I considered the dull blue handsaw for a few moments and then reached for the old propane heater. As much as I wanted a real fire, using that rusted, warped, loose-handled excuse for a handsaw to make potbellied stove–size pieces of firewood was no kind of fun. It was like shaping diamonds with a tennis ball. Resigned to the fumes of propane, I plopped the bundle of firewood on the floor of the outhouse and shut the door, making a mental note to bring gas up the next time. Back in the cabin, I set my headlamp on the card table, with the beam aimed up at the ceiling to provide some general light while I got things in order.

Fortunately, there was plenty of oil for the lamps. Some fire was better than no fire.

If I felt like I had mastered one aspect of cabin life, it was the fueling, lighting, and maintenance of Dietz-brand kerosene lamps. The lamps were the type you'd expect to find in a cabin, the ubiquitous old-timey style that come in bright red, deep green, dark blue, silver, and brass. The kerosene oil was stored in a wide base, on top of which was a wire-protected glass shade that housed the wick. On the side, a little dial raised and lowered the wick as necessary for more or less light. And on top, a thin wire handle made them easy to carry or hang on a hook. It was hard not to grin when you carried a lantern out into the night on your way to the outhouse. The aesthetics and the activity made it seem like time travel was maybe just a little real. And while I'd never owned a gun, the feeling I got from disassembling the lanterns, installing and trimming a new wick, cleaning the glass shade, and then reassembling the whole thing made me think of movie scenes where someone expertly cleans and breaks down their firearm with focused, mechanical precision. I'd come to know exactly how high the wick should be to maximize brightness and minimize smoke. I knew how to fix a lamp whose flame flickered or kicked off soot. I knew which lamps in which places in the cabin provided the best blend of lighting, bright near the kitchen and dim near the futon and woodstove. And I had come to learn the hard way that the wire handles got hot enough to burn the bejesus out of your hand if you weren't careful.

I filled and lit the lamps before distributing them to their typical homes. A few tea light candles filled in the gaps, and soon, I was unscrewing the propane tank from the Coleman stove to get the heater set up. Lighting it resulted in the typical loss of knuckle hair, but it felt good to be pumping some heat into the place. Ten minutes later, the wet layers started to come off and steam.

Not ready for dinner, I grabbed a mug and poured a bit of whiskey from one of many half-empty bottles in the cabinet and began investigating the cabin's interior, starting with the chimney leak. The bucket I had left a few weeks prior was about a third full, nearly a gallon of water. I'd hoped the dripping had been an anomaly of sorts, the kind of thing that only came about with a severe storm, a sort of cabin quirk, but it was clearly here to stay. At some spot where the roof had been cut away for the chimney pipe to pass through, water was creeping in.

I climbed up the crude ladder into the loft and crawled on my hands and knees to inspect the chimney. The hole where the chimney passed through the roof was oversize to ensure the hot pipe wasn't leaning dangerously against the very flammable plywood in the roof. In the gap between them, I could see the underside of the rubber collar Ray fastened to the base of the chimney to keep the water out. A drop of water clung to the edge of the plywood on the high side of the hole. I wiped it away with my finger and watched as another drop slowly began to form. For a while, I sat there, watching the drips swell and fall.

It wasn't surprising to have a leak in an environment that was like a stomach for cabins. Dry wood in a temperate rainforest is an unnatural thing. Everything was in a state of decay. Even the impossibly strong trunks of massive evergreens would lay their bark on the ground someday and start to rot, the punky results offering footing for new seedlings to take hold and grow: roots wrapped around the remains of their ancestors. And here I was, in the cross fire of decomposition, trying to protect the cabin from a circle-of-life momentum, armed with nothing more than a bright blue bucket and losing, and I wasn't the least bit shocked. For so many structures, all it took to drag them into the murk of moss and ferns and rot was for someone to stop fighting back, to give up on their behalf. The gallon of water I caught felt like a victory, a dodged punch, a bit of time back on the cabin's clock.

Fixing the leak would have meant getting on the roof, which would have meant having access to an extension ladder. The ladder to the loft didn't even reach the gutters. I thought about the possibility of carrying a massive extension ladder up the trail by the slide and all the way to the cabin. It was a heroic image, but one I knew would never materialize. The leak would have to wait until I could borrow someone else's ladder or bring one in on the road, if it ever existed again. I reverse crawled back to the ladder and down, double-checking the bucket's position under the leak before finishing my whiskey and turning my attention to dinner.

When I opened the green, rust-speckled cover, my appetite vanished. The mice had made their mark inside the Coleman stove. Droppings were everywhere. On the floor, in the windowsill, and packed into the stove where flecks of steak grease had popped out of pans to create a little Tony Roma's for Wit's End vermin. Were it not for the droppings, I would not have minded their presence. I'd once dated a girl with a pet mouse that I became quite fond of, but shitting on the stove is a behavior I do not tolerate among even my closest of friends.

Fortunately for them, like the leaking roof, there wasn't much I could do about the mice. Gaping holes in the cabin needed to be solved by adding trim and wire mesh and other materials to critical spots, but hauling material left me with the same problem as the leak. I couldn't get supplies to the cabin. And though a handful of traps go in a pocket easily, the thought of being away from the cabin for a few weeks while two or three mice decomposed on the floor was not enticing. The mice could hang out with the spiders a little longer.

I spent the next hour cleaning, attacking the stove and the table, the floors and walls and windows with a bottle of 409 and a few rolls of paper towels. When I finished, the cabin's pleasant woodsy musk was gone, replaced by the sterile smell of disinfectant and artificial lemon. I pulled out a few pieces of piñon incense from the cabinet and lit them from the tea candles. It was warm enough now to shut off the propane heater and let the heat from the hurricane lamps maintain the cabin's warmth.

I returned to the task of dinner by boiling some water for one of the dehydrated backpacker meals, adding the hot water to the pouch before slumping into the futon to wait for the dried bits of food to rehydrate. The smell of disinfectant was finally gone, replaced by smoke and wood and reconstituted cheddar. The glow from the hurricane lamps was just right, and an occasional flicker from the tea candles made me feel for a moment like there was a fire in the woodstove. Outside, rain still tapped on the steel roof, and I could make out the silhouette of cedar branches bobbing along to the same rhythm. Figuring enough time had passed, I opened up the dehydrated food package, let the steam billow out, dug my spoon inside, and blew on the contents for good measure. Not nearly enough. The molten mac and cheese nearly cauterized my mouth shut. Half setting, half throwing the bag beside me, I leaned back to let it cool, possibly for a few hours.

For all the stress of the mice and the leak and the slide and my own inability to remedy all of it or any of it, there would come a moment during every cabin visit where those problems drifted away. When the sweat of the walk had dried, the floor was cleaned and wiped up, the fire started and stoked, the drip captured and the bucket emptied, the outhouse webs cleared and the mice scared into silence, the steak sizzled and served, the whiskey poured, the music begun and the TV tray set with tea, I would sit in that moment and feel a warm happiness ooze and sparkle through my bones.

Certainly, there were flaws. The boot prints on the plywood we used to cover the wall weren't noticed until there were three or four thousand nails in it. The gap under the door was a welcome invitation to vermin, but Indy cut it, and I'd not trade anything for the memory of his surprise when we tested it out. Even after Ray fixed it, the door bore the hilarious scar of that initial folly. The chimney was leaky, but who knows what torrents of water would be rushing in if I'd done it without Ray's help. The cabin had become a sort of architectural photo album. The gaps and rough cuts and bent nails and stripped screws were born out of good times with great friends. And things were getting better. There was progress after all. Even among the wall panels, you could see the gaps get a little tighter as we worked our way around the room. And still, there was so much to do.

If there was any silver lining to the slide and the months of waiting, it was the extra time for planning. When my mind gravitated to wondering if the rain had found a new spot to creep in through the roof, I countered by picking out wall paneling for the upstairs loft. When I drifted toward the fear that an errant tree branch had punched through the roof, I drew out careful plans for an L-shaped kitchen area. When images of crazed meth addicts ripping up the door for the chance at a half-empty bottle of whiskey invaded my dreams, I woke and meditated on thoughts of curtains, potholders, convertible beds, outdoor benches, and a big firepit area. There was much to do, but for now, just being at the place was plenty.

I gave the dinner dishes a clean, which meant nothing more than wiping the spoon off with my shirt, and dropped the wicks on the hurricane lamps. The remaining tea lights I let go, knowing they would burn out within the hour. Settling on the futon under the green Seattle Supersonics blanket, I listened to the rain and thought of big carloads of supplies, sunny weather, and new tools. I pictured piles of lumber and clouds of sawdust, nights around the fire, and coolers overflowing with ice and beer. It was easy to fall asleep this way. In the morning, I packed up what little I had and swept the place. Then I remembered something else I had brought up—a small, tight bundle of dried sage.

I'd never been a supremely spiritual person. When I was growing up, Sundays meant Catholic Mass in the church across the street from the private school I attended. That often meant I was serving as an altar boy, partly out of boredom and partly because my parents forced it on me. My dad had been an altar boy. It seemed to him like a cool thing to hand down, though as far as generational legacies go, I'd have preferred it if he'd been a pro baseball player. If there was a good part to the gig, it was incense days. In the middle of Mass, I'd get to sneak off to the sacristy (church slang for *backstage*) to light a coal and add some incense to the thurible, a cagelike incense burner attached to a three-foot gold chain so the priest could swing it around dramatically. Especially when compared to activities such as kneeling with your eyes closed and singing with your parents, watching a priest parade around whipping a smoking ball on a gold chain over his head was easily a highlight of church. Against the instructions of the altar boy leader, I usually doubled or tripled the amount of coal and resin called for in the recipe so I could emerge from the sacristy surrounded by a belching of smoke like some cut-rate Vegas magician. The point was, I'd always had a soft spot for the ceremony of smoke and figured a bit of extra good luck in the cabin certainly wasn't a bad thing. Plus, people usually did quite a bit of farting in the place with all the chili and rib eyes. A tradition of cleansing seemed like a good idea.

I gave the place a good once-over with the lit sage, including a brief trip up to the loft, which needed a hell of a lot more than smoke. When I was finished, I put the little bundle in the woodstove to go out on its own and took one last look around before swinging the door shut. Outside, the warm, dry smell of sage was replaced with damp earth, moss, rain, and rotting leaves.

The hike back to the parking area was uneventful. A few post-slide cars passed, and I was reassured to get warm waves and smiles from drivers and passengers. One person stopped and asked if I needed a ride, which I politely turned down, enjoying the walk. The slide itself looked as awful as ever. In fact, weeks before, the parking lot near the ATV trail had to be moved because of continued slide activity. It'd been moved farther down the hill and back along the road near the pool at the bottom of Sunset Falls. We were no longer simply stuck. We were retreating.

I got to the bottom of the slide and threw my stuff in the car before following the gravel road out of the Riversites onto the highway and west. Back home, when it would rain, I would often catch myself daydreaming about the cabin, imagining it cold and dark in the forest, fighting to keep the water out. I could see the bucket, filling drop by drop in my mind's eye. The thought kept me coming back with regularity, but it was always the quiet evenings that reminded me why I was really out there. The more it rained, the more I felt drawn to return, to empty the bucket, to reassure the cabin that I wouldn't let it rot and fall apart.

15

THE KITCHEN (PART 1)

I ndy and I moved into a new house. It was early May. The house was filled with rats. At night, we would sit out on the front porch, which leaned toward the street, and drink red wine from the bottle while waiting for the rats to come out from the basement. You could hear them scrambling through dry leaves, looking for nuts or berries or trash, whatever rats eat. When they came out, we'd go after them with the shovel or throw cans at them, anything to send a message that this was our turf now.

After a few months of work, it was clear our crusade against the rats had been unsuccessful by every metric imaginable. If anything, we'd convinced them that going outside was at least mildly dangerous and it was probably best just to stay in the house. Inside, they were becoming bolder. On a number of occasions, one of us would open the door to the basement to find a rat going after a package of ramen in the pantry. I'm not sure if it was the size of the tread or the angle or what, but in their haste to run away from us and down the stairs, they'd inevitably start to miss a few steps and get to bouncing, always ending the journey windmilling ass over teakettle through the air before slamming into the floor and scurrying away to some distant corner. We caught them in the ramen often. Down in the basement was worse. While doing laundry, it was common to see the plastic that covered the ceiling insulation dipping with the weight of a scurrying critter.

Along with the yard implements and the tossed cans, we'd tried all manner of traps and sticky strips and whatever else the store had that promised to get rid of rats. Our resolve to remove them was both proportional and inverse to our desire to use the basement, which is how we ended up spending more time in the basement hanging out with the rats than we did on the porch trying to murder them. After all, hanging out in the basement was a big part of why we chose the house. Like with the cabin, some activities were just a bit better in a basement. Stuff like listening to Allman Brothers vinyl and drinking cheap beer and organizing tools and reclining in dusty chairs and pretending to play poker and—of course—building things.

In the months since the slide had made working on the cabin basically impossible, I'd found other ways to satisfy the itch to hammer and drill. I spent lunch breaks at work walking to the nearest bookstore so I could browse through titles on anything and everything related to building, from architectural photography books to code guides on electrical and plumbing work. On weekends, I picked up a coffee and wandered the aisles of reclaimed building material suppliers and hardware stores for inspiration on future projects or just to absorb the atmosphere. At home, indulgences in YouTube and Instagram were almost entirely devoted to videos and pictures of carpenters working on projects of all shapes and sizes. The allure of future cabin projects even shifted the type of clothes I got. Soon my closet was stocked with pants and jackets made of heavy, oiled canvas, double-kneed pants, and wide-brimmed woolen hats suitable for rugged work in the harshest of environments. When friends complained about problems at their apartments—a backed-up sink, a squeaky door, a flickering light fixture—I found myself eager to see the problem in person and speculate on what might be done to solve it. In some instances, I even managed to fix a few things. When I did, the satisfaction would last for days. I liked being useful in that way.

Regardless of what anyone says, it's difficult to separate your work from your identity. I reveled in the chance to change mine. When I pictured myself behind a desk, crafting templates for emails, it felt off. But when I imagined myself in the woods with a cordless drill, it felt right. Certainly, there was an element of romance to it. Who doesn't have a fantasy of going off to some cabin in the woods to spend your days drinking crystal-clear mountain water and hewing logs? But it went further than that. There isn't a romance to wandering around Home Depot looking at plumbing parts just for the fun of it. Thoreau didn't put his pen to paper about an hour-long video of someone tiling a shower on YouTube, but those were the things I found myself doing. There was so much joy to be derived simply following the curiosity that stemmed from cabin projects. My investigation into getting power at the cabin made it clear immediately that I wouldn't have outlets or light switches. But even after I'd made that decision, I went on to read about gang boxes, subpanels, ground rods, and solar arrays.

Before the cabin, when I was desperate for some passion, some calling, something I could point to when people asked about life, I think I felt that pressure because the reality was, I wasn't doing much besides going to work, coming home, and going to sleep. Sure, there were dinners with friends and weekend trips here and there, but the majority of time was spent in the monotony of a routine I could not find engaging. There's a truth to the saying that your work doesn't define who you are, but damn if it isn't hard to believe otherwise when you're in it. Plus, I think that saying sort of missed the point.

I wasn't worried about being defined as a copywriter, whatever that meant. What I was worried about was being defined as someone who didn't have the courage or gumption or intelligence or whatever was necessary to get out of spending half his waking hours on a task and at a place that he didn't enjoy or find fulfilling. I didn't care if I was or wasn't a writer. I was worried I was someone who let life just sort of happen to them. I was worried about being stuck, just like I'd been in the mud, and not following the instinct to fight my way out. The cabin offered a way to cope with those feelings because it felt like a version of fighting back, of resisting being bored, being stuck, giving up. Even imagining the cabin and its laundry list of projects was a worthwhile distraction from my daily routines. And in early summer, I got good news. I wouldn't just be imagining cabin projects much longer.

After months of bickering and long walks and melting hills, a solution for the slide had been laid out. The old bridge that had once connected the community to the highway over the river east of the slide was getting rebuilt. The plan had its fair share of opponents, but at the end of the day, most folks seemed happy to finally be moving forward. They hoped to open the new route by late summer, which meant I still had a few months to build, prepare, and gather. I spent the time acquiring things for the cabin and making plans for its newest addition, the kitchen.

Until then, the cabin's "kitchen" consisted of a plastic card table, an old rusted-out Coleman stove held together by steak grease and mouse shit, some pots and pans and other essential dishes, a percolator for making coffee, and a few gallons of water sat on the floor. Without the possibility of real plumbing or water hookups, designing the kitchen would require some creative adaptations.

There was no source of water at the cabin. For a chuckle, I had called a few well-drilling companies to find out what it would cost to put in a well. Their answer didn't disappoint. I moved on to other ideas. Certainly, it rained enough at the cabin to make use of a catch system, but hours of research left me convinced that the only way to use rainwater for drinking necessitated filtering and purification techniques that demanded electricity beyond the capacity of AAA batteries, my preferred power source. I continued to lower my expectations until I landed at something just above the current solution, which was single gallons of water refilled at home. The new solution was . . . bigger jugs. At a coffee shop in Seattle, I'd seen a five-gallon jug upended into a simple ceramic dispenser with a basic valve. It was one of those solutions so simple as to feel ingenious. Though I'd still have to bring in the weekend's water, a single jug didn't seem like too big a deal, and it'd be easy to set the whole thing up over a sink. Water was solved. Next, I turned my attention to the rest of the plumbing problem, figuring out where the water went after it left the sink.

On a general level, I understood drains to carry waste liquids to some intentionally designed place of disposal. In the city, I knew that meant sewer lines. In the country, I knew it meant a septic system, but what a septic system actually was I didn't have the foggiest clue. Looking it up, I found the following explanation: "If you are not connected to a sewer system, the liquid wastes from your home go into a septic tank, where most of the solids settle out. The water then goes into a leach field, pipes buried in the ground that have holes in the bottom. The water seeps out of these holes and into the ground." In other words, outside or whatever. Given that the most harmful thing going down the sink would likely be Crest sensitive-gum toothpaste, a full-on septic system was probably a bit of overkill. Perhaps, I thought, I could design something myself that was a bit more in line with the cabin's real-world needs.

Pipes made sense enough to me, as did holes, so I wondered whether I could simply run a pipe from the sink through a hole drilled in the floor and then out into the woods. I'd use biodegradable soap to make sure I wasn't ruining the environment in any cataclysmic way, and at most, I'd be pumping five gallons of water through the thing over a few days at a time, so it didn't seem like I was risking a second mudslide with any drain erosion. There was one problem I did imagine. Over time, little bits of food would inevitably go down the drain and out into the world. The new Seattle rental and its rat problem were fresh on my mind, and it was hard not to picture a gang of wood rats and mice waiting at the end of the pipe like it was a conveyor-belt sushi joint. It seemed only reasonable that eventually they'd get impatient enough to enter the pipe and come on in. Perhaps I could bury the pipe? But then it might just get clogged and back up. Perhaps I could attach a cage at the end to prevent critters from coming in? Maybe rats weren't the only problem. Without a pressurized water source, would there be enough force to flush the food bits out? And, if not, would they just sit and fester, stinking up the pipe and thus the cabin?

These were questions too embarrassing to ask a real person and too specific to search for online. Even trying to formulate the query proved impossible. In the search field, I found myself typing, "Rats in pipe outside no water problem stink," deleted it, then tried again, "Bury water outlet pipe in ground or cage no rats." The results were not promising. Instead of finding a solution, I did what I usually did: lay in bed at night imagining all the ways in which it could go wrong. What was once the hope for a convenient water source inside the cabin was now plaguing me with fear of a cabin that smelled like a stomach and was mostly occupied by vermin.

To distract myself from the pipe puzzle, I focused on the kitchen structure itself. The first consideration was space. At 120 square feet, the cabin wouldn't allow much in the way of big butcher blocks or sprawling islands, but there were some minimum requirements. I needed a small stovetop, enough counter space to salt a steak or chop up some onions, a sink, and room for the water dispenser. Luckily, there were not a lot of options for placement. Three out of four corners were occupied by the stove, the loft ladder, and the cabinet. The futon covered the back wall, and the front wall was more or less taken up by the door, leaving an L-shaped section running from the door to the woodstove available. It was the only corner of the cabin with windows. With a spot picked out, over several visits, a kitchen plan bubbled to life in my head.

A countertop would span the entire area with a sink directly beneath the window that looked out onto the deck. In the corner, the big water jug would sit on a small stand so it emptied directly into the sink but still had room underneath for a few plates and cutlery. On the long side, under the other two windows, a small two-burner propane stove designed for RVs would get set into the counter. Underneath, a shelf would provide plenty of room for the propane tank, a cooler, garbage, and a pile of canned goods and dehydrated hash browns.

I never drew these plans. Instead, I'd find myself imagining the whole thing during quiet moments at work or at home, where I'd lean into a sort of focused, building daydream. I'd think through how the sink would be supported, how I'd build the shelves, what color it should be, if I should stain or paint it, and where I might be able to store the pots and pans. Along the way, I'd test it out, picturing myself standing over the sink, washing a mug and looking out at the frozen peak of Mount Baring through a web of empty winter maple branches. I thought about frying up a steak and scanning the road to find Murphy or a mountain lion wandering up Wit's End. I fantasized about fixing a cup of coffee and standing by the woodstove while the water heated. Visualizing the details was a critical part of the process. It was surprising how a small change could drastically alter the environment of the cabin.

Early on, I'd noticed the cabin fostered an uncommon dedication to keeping things tidy. It was instinctual to store the shoes neatly in the corner rather than tossed in front of the door. I liked it when all the water jugs were carefully arranged. I had a specific preference for how the wood for the stove was stacked, the shape of it. These were all things that I wouldn't have cared

The cabin as seen from the road, shortly after buying it. Rotten plywood serves as a bridge across the muck.

The front of the cabin before any work has taken place. Open deck framing below. The electrical box leads to nothing inside.

Indy pointing out how un-waterproof the rusty roof looks.

The inside of the cabin as I bought it. The left window looks out onto the deck. The right windows look toward the driveway.

The loft after an initial cleaning of the insulation, most of which had fallen out of the ceiling.

Matt, the cheapest plywood available, and my mom's littl red Ranger on the morning of the initial work party.

...st above Sunset Falls, looking over the South Fork Skykomish River toward ...Mount Index on the right. *(Credit: Maddy Porter)*

Looking into the woods at a mesmerizing mix of ferns, hemlocks, Douglas firs, cedars, maples, and alders. *(Credit: Maddy Porter)*

Indy hauling a bucket of rotten wood out of the cabin.

Matt adding cedar decking with the world's most powerful drill plugged into the generator.

Indy and I cleaning things up on the new deck at the end of the first work party. (Credit: Matt Badger)

The little woodstove and its nuclear-shaped vents glowing from a crackling fire.

n early kitchen setup with a Coleman stove, camp chairs, and kerosene lanterns.

Bryan playing guitar out on the deck after a late-morning breakfast.

An unreal sunset seen from the hill above the mudslide. This was taken a fe
years after the slide. The roofs of destroyed cabins can be seen poking throug
the new growth.

Indy using the Dremel to hack away exposed screw ends during construction of the cabin's kitchen.

A close-up of the Boeing shipping crate material salvaged for the kitchen's countertops.

The finished kitchen with gas stove, shelf for beer and cooler storage, and patent-pending bucket plumbing system.

The new bridge constructed to bypass the mudslide near Sunset Falls.

An early-morning target-practice session with the cabin's fine selection of BB guns.

Bryan demonstrating the best way to warm yourself and your coffee at the woodstove.

Quite possibly the most awe-inspiring set of stairs ever created. Note the subtle expansion of tread width. Not pictured: the three or four thousand screws holding it together.

A fresh harvest of salmonberries, which grew like weeds all around the cabin.

A view of Mount Persis from downtown Index in winter.

The cabin illuminated on a very typical foggy gray evening in winter.

BUTTS banner welcomes guests to the outhouse. World's dullest saw also available for impromptu spider battles.

Todd in full pretzel mode beneath the cabin to help replace the rotten rim joist.

Preparing a classic cabin breakfast of leftover rib eye steak bits and dehydrated hash browns.

Kellen, Matt, and I amid the chaos of a full roof replacement. (*Credit: Kate Palmer*)

Slicing up plywood for something or other. Captured just moments before the kickstand sank into the gravel and the bike toppled over. (*Credit: Kate Palmer*)

The patchwork ceiling of sistered joists and salvaged wood, crisscrossed with Christmas lights, pans, and lanterns.

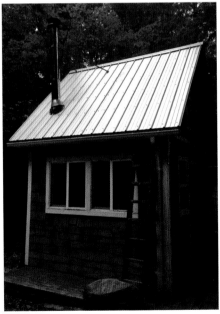

The finished exterior with fresh paint, stain, new shingles, lantern hook, boot scraper, and new roof.

The cabin with its fresh roof, glowing in the dim twilight.

The shelf above the futon, where pancake mix, syrup, books, pu-erh tea, and incense were stored.

Me on a snowy evening, all lights aglow, woodstove roaring nearby. A perfect night.

A fresh dumping of snow after the trees came down
and the new roof was added.

The road out of the Riversites on a beautiful autumn day.

about or noticed back home. I chalked up the phenomenon to
the restricted space. If we're only capable of noticing a finite
number of things about our environment, it makes sense that
a smaller space would allow us to dive deeper into the details.
With the cabin, the details of the place were distilled by its size.
When something was hung in just the right place, or the lamps
burned at that perfect level of glow, or the woodstove was just
starting to burn well, I noticed. It wasn't just the size of the place,
though. It was also a product of the activities. Absorbing the environment was the entire point of being there. There was no cell
service at the cabin, something I'd initially bemoaned knowing
it would hamper my ability to look up building resources while
up there, but it turned out to be a blessing, obviously, to go to a
place and leave the phone in the car, or reserve it exclusively for
playing music. In fact, we made a bit of a tradition out of the
moment when we'd pull off the highway and switch our phones
to airplane mode. It was an intentional act to leave the world
behind for a bit. Among the endless tasks of sourcing firewood
and cooking and cleaning and shooting the BB gun at empty
cans, one of our favorite activities wasn't more complicated than
simply sitting there and looking around. Doing so had made me
hyperaware of the impact of a few lumens of light or an arrangement of blankets. It sounds a bit obsessive, but there was joy to
the act. I imagined it was the same satisfaction that came to folks
who looked after bonsai trees or artists who spent years working
out the details of a painting before revealing the finished piece.
For all these reasons, the design of the kitchen was anything but
hasty. I took my time gathering the kitchen's components.

For the stove, an online search during a particularly slow day at

work led me to a company that specialized in vintage trailer supplies. Among their offerings was a small, stainless steel two-burner
stove with a quirky, *Jetsons*, space-age vibe that seemed to jibe with
the cabin's eclectic character. For the countertop and sink, I made
a habit of swinging by a recycled building materials store on my
way home from work, hoping that something would pop up that
would catch my eye and not empty my wallet. The business oper-
ated by salvaging items from old buildings and homes that were
getting demolished. You could find everything from old wooden
windows and cast-iron bathtubs to Victorian-era doorknobs and
well-worn bowling alley lanes, chopped up into the perfect size for
a DIY coffee table. Most of the best items came at a steep price for
wealthy homeowners who found it easier to pay for character than
earn it. The less desired items, however, were steeply discounted.

On one lucky trip, I ventured outside to browse through
lumber that wasn't decent enough to find its way out of the rain.
Flipping over hunks of railroad ties and old pressure-treated
boards, I came across a massive plank of wood. Nearly seventeen feet long and about a foot and a half wide, it looked like a
butcher block shuffleboard table. The range of color in the wood
was mesmerizing, especially on a section near the end that had
gotten wet, illuminating wooden shades ranging from a deep
rich mahogany to a radiant ocher blond. Down the length of it
were regularly spaced holes, about the size of a golf ball. As far
as I could tell, the holes were the only blemishes on an otherwise beautiful piece of wood. I stood over the plank and imagined preparing a meal, gesturing the motions of chopping up
vegetables and stirring a pot. The width felt about right, and
the menagerie of wood seemed a perfect aesthetic match for the
cabin, already a patchwork of wood tones.

Inside, the cashier filled me in on the history of the boards. They'd been used by Boeing to ship long, delicate airplane parts. Two seventeen-foot planks constructed of mahogany and other hardwoods made up the sides of big crates, held together by bolts that ran through the holes I'd noticed. It was unlikely, I thought when I went back outside after paying, that they were ever loaded into a station wagon for shipment, the board being about a foot longer than my entire car. Fortunately, they had a generous storage policy.

A week later, I returned to the reclaim store with a cordless circular saw in the back seat. The staff were kind enough to help me drag the board outside onto a few sawhorses set up specifically for the breaking down of materials bought too big.

I'd be lying if I said I didn't take immense satisfaction from cutting the soon-to-be countertop in public. I'd spent enough time embarrassed at Home Depot and home-and-hearth stores and lumberyards to feel like I had earned a point or two of pride. I liked being comfortable enough to cut in half a board that was nearly my weight and triple my height. Little did they know it was the first time I'd ever used sawhorses, which always seemed like a waste when there were perfectly good logs or the edge of the deck to use to prop a piece of wood up for a cut. As I blasted through the wood, I made note of how much safer and more comfortable it was to cut something at waist level instead of bent over, the saw running full speed in the exact direction of your kneecap. When the blade severed the last fibers of the countertop, the two halves immediately bucked upward and away from each other, falling backward off their respective sawhorses and clattering to the ground. I made a sort of "Goaugrh!" sound and leaped backward, looking around to see if anyone had noticed. No one was paying attention.

Even cut in half, the boards were now only barely able to fit in the station wagon, stopping about a quarter of an inch shy of the front windshield with all the car's seats reclined and flattened. I jammed my sweatshirt between the boards and the glass and congratulated myself on the responsible, forward-thinking safety precaution that a few millimeters of cotton would provide against 180 pounds of hardwood.

On my way back in to return the sawhorses, I passed by the kitchen materials area, stacked with sinks and appliances and piles of all the knobs and racks and wiring that went along with them. Among the sea of black, white, and stainless steel, there was something different. A tiny, robin's-egg-blue sink, barely big enough to hold a bag of ice. When I picked it up, the sheer weight of it surprised me, a mystery solved by the tag, which indicated its material: cast iron. Apparently, it was also brand-new, despite having been manufactured decades before. It had likely sat, forgotten for who knows how many years, on the back shelf of some store that eventually closed down and liquidated all that remained. Twenty-five dollars later, I was tucking the sink behind my seat for the short drive back home, my arm resting on the cabin's future countertop.

When I got home, I wrestled the wood up the stairs to the house and through the basement door, piling it along with the two-by-fours in a corner where the project's other materials were gathered. And there it remained for a month or more while the summer sped by. There were lots of distractions, days at the lake with friends, concerts, and camping trips. With the improvement in weather came a decrease in stress about the cabin, about rain, about thieves. Summer's cheery disposition lulled me into a state of optimism about things. Or maybe it was the news of the bridge's opening date, set for mid-August. When the fateful week finally arrived, Indy and I made plans to head up on opening weekend. The bridge would be ready Friday. It was Thursday afternoon. We had a day to get the kitchen done.

16

THE KITCHEN (PART 2)

While I waited for Indy to get home, I drew out plans and got everything ready. As basements tend to do, the space had become a depository for all things that wouldn't fit in closets upstairs but were not yet officially bound for Goodwill. I spent the better part of an hour clearing and organizing errant artwork, plastic yard bags full of winter jackets, and old desktop computers that had somehow become nostalgic because their hard drives contained papers written in high school. With a bit of space opened up, I laid a rug over the washer and dryer and carefully laid my tools out on top, like a surgeon would arrange scalpels and bone saws on a metal tray. I plugged the record player into an extension cord from the far side of the basement and cued up a stack of vinyl that seemed like a fitting backdrop for amateur carpentry.

When Indy got home, he joined me in the basement with a cold beer while I started going over the design, the rats interrupting us as they did laps around the ceiling's black plastic. We tried to visualize the size and scope of my crude drawings, taking turns holding the tape measure out so the other person could get a sense of a good countertop height and width. I had taken measurements at the cabin to ensure that our design would center the sink under one window and that the entire contraption wouldn't overhang the door, bump into the wood-stove, or extend too far into precious open floor space. Within those constraints, there were small adjustments that we could potentially make if it seemed necessary. Luckily, the Boeing crate countertops were the perfect width, about seventeen inches, just enough room to squeeze in the sink and the new propane stove. All that was left to do was to figure out the struc-ture that would hold everything up. A structure we both knew would have to be made of two-by-fours.

The cabin was a celebration of two-by-fours. Usually rel-egated to simple structural tasks, the common two-by-four is typically covered up by wall paneling, trim, doors, windows, and insulation. But at the cabin, any real piece of wood was con-sidered beautiful, suitable for tables, chairs, stairs, and kitchen cabinetry. Simply sand the ever-living hell out of the thing to remove the inky stamps left over from the lumber mill, apply a generous coating of wood stain, and you'd have something that looked pretty damn good in a dim cabin with squinted eyes. If poor decisions, lack of experience, and impatience were our brush, two-by-fours were our paint.

With a few adjustments on height, we arrived at a final design and sketched it out fresh. It was the perfect architectural solution, reflective of the cabin's existing aesthetics and our own inability to build anything. What we'd landed on was a sort of boxes-with-legs look that would employ the Boeing shipping crate counter-top and leftover cedar for the lower shelf. I still hadn't figured out what would happen to whatever went into the sink. Nevertheless, I had gotten a stainless steel drain complete with a strainer, expecting to hook it up to some kind of pipe eventually.

While the record player cranked through CCR and Zeppelin and the Rolling Stones, we began ripping up boards with the circular saw and taking turns screwing them together. At some point, a screw punched through a board too far and stripped, spinning in place and refusing to back out despite our best efforts with the drill. Indy, sensing an opportunity, rushed to get his new Dremel out of its box. It was a tool he had no use for, but access to the cabin had gone to his head in the same way it had mine. He wanted the toys and, as such, had bought several items for which he had no conceivable real-world need. They included a new hammer (the largest one the store sold), a variety of cabin work wear items made of things like waxed canvas and full-grain leather, and, most unnecessarily, a chain saw. And, of course, the Dremel, a rotary tool that spun all kinds of attachments at roughly the speed of light. There were little discs made for cutting things, little puffy cylinders that were ideal for polishing tiny items, and sandpaper cylinders perfect for smoothing out hard-to-reach areas.

I watched for nearly forty-five minutes while Indy read the instructions. Every few minutes, he'd add an attachment to the Dremel's end and turn it on cautiously, only to have the bit zip off immediately and soar into some distant, dark corner of the basement. He was going through bits quickly this way.

"Man, you know we can probably just pound that screw

back out, or toss that piece of wood and start over, or just use the hacksaw on it," I suggested for the third or fourth time.

"No, no, no, you'll see. Hold on. I think I got it," he said as he flipped the switch and sent another disc whizzing off the wall and behind the dryer.

It wasn't until he'd gone upstairs to sit through a few You-Tube videos that he got the thing attached and ceremoniously bent down to the screw like King Arthur approaching Excalibur in the stone. Set at maximum speed, the Dremel screamed to life. It sounded like a bee the size of a bear. Tentatively, Indy touched the disc to the edge of the screw and the room erupted in a stunning cascade of golden sparks. I was transfixed. It was beautiful. Indy was not as pleased.

"Gahhh!"

Many of the sparks, each one a tiny bit of molten metal, as it turned out, had sought refuge in and around Indy's face, particularly in his eyes. The screw remained, though it now wore a bright cut on one side.

"That. Was. Amazing," I muttered. And he knew it too. "But maybe safety glasses?"

"Do we have safety glasses?"

"We do not." The safety glasses were at the cabin, where they sat unused next to the chain saw.

A few minutes later, Indy knelt down again wearing a pair of sunglasses that, while probably protecting his eyes, likely obscured his vision in the already dim basement enough to make the entire spectacle twice as dangerous as it was before. Nevertheless, he flicked the switch, the buzz returned, and the shower of sparks was once again born. It was like the Fourth of July. I imagined rats setting out cocktail napkins like adorable little picnic blankets to enjoy the show.

The next hour was a bit of a tangent, albeit an entirely necessary one. We wandered around the basement looking for other things to Dremel the hell out of, one person cutting and the other taking pictures, the competition naturally being to make the larger shower of sparks. When we ran out of old, bent nails in the floor joists and walls, we drove screws through scrap two-by-fours and blasted those away. Eventually, the battery died, and we fell out of its hypnotic display. We flipped the record and got back to work.

Things started to come together. In fact, it was all going better than either of us had expected. Even the nerve-racking cuts through the countertop to fit the sink and stove went smoothly. There was a sense that perhaps we were learning something. Maybe all the YouTube videos and the hours spent wandering Home Depot and the late nights watching *This Old House* were paying off.

I was marking out and making cuts as Indy screwed everything together. When necessary, we'd help each other out, steadying longer boards or holding some joint tight until it could be fastened together. We didn't speak much, and the sounds became a sort of swirl of classic rock beats, the whine of a circular saw, and the percussive thwacks of a battery-powered impact driver. There was a layer of sawdust on everything and plenty more drifting about in the air. It was a beautiful scene. At some point, Indy's girlfriend, Kali, came down to change the laundry and made a comment about how large the new kitchen seemed to be.

"Thanks!" I yelled to her over the sound of Indy driving another screw home.

"No," she said, "I meant, how are you going to get it out of here?"

So high were my spirits about the thing at that point, I would have taken almost anything she had said about the kitchen as a compliment. But I suppose some people just want to ruin things. Technically speaking, we had not expressly considered whether the finished kitchen would fit through the door of the basement—or of the cabin, for that matter. But by now, it was nearly complete. It seemed like a waste to not finish the thing. Besides, we were having too good of a time. The universe didn't seem cruel enough to spring that kind of bummer on such a wholesome project. I assured her things would be fine, and she gave us the sort of look I'd have expected if I said, "Hey, watch this!" and then proceeded to intentionally slam my hand in a car door. As she headed back upstairs, Indy and I buried our fears about the size of the kitchen and the basement door and returned to our carpentry flow state. It was too late to go back now.

When we'd driven the last screw in, we dropped the sink and stove into place and stepped back to admire our work. Certainly, it was overbuilt. There were more two-by-fours supporting the countertop than there were supporting an entire wall of the cabin. It was likely you could have stacked several motorcycles on top of it without incident. But if the cabin ever fell down, perhaps the kitchen would keep things propped up for a while. If there was an earthquake, the shelf beneath the countertop could function as a sort of panic room.

That night, we dug deep through the pile of records and took turns sanding everything. On top, we applied a food-grade mineral oil that made the colors in the mahogany leap out; below, the two-by-fours and cedar were finished with a dark wood stain that matched the richest hues in the countertop. By two in the morning, we were done.

I struggled out of bed for work a few hours later. Luckily, it was Friday. At about noon, I got a text from Indy. It was a picture of the kitchen. He had been applying additional layers of mineral oil throughout the day, unable to inch away from the satisfaction that comes from putting the finishing touches on something you're pretty damn proud of. When I got home, we went down to the basement to admire it again together and mutter reassurances like "Yeah, man, I think this'll be the perfect size" and "Pshhhh, of course it'll fit out the door."

We had plans to leave for the cabin right when I got home from work, but it took us a few hours to run to the grocery store and gather things, all chores we'd meant to do the night before but ran out of time. With all our supplies loaded into my mom's little red Ford Ranger, borrowed again for the task of transporting the kitchen, we walked uneasily back into the basement.

The tension was palpable. It was an old house. Everything about it was narrow, especially the door out of the basement. It also didn't help that the door was a bit crooked and didn't quite open all the way. We both knew there was a damn good chance the kitchen wouldn't pass through, but somehow talking about it or taking measurements to come up with an exit plan at this point felt like bad luck. We didn't want to jinx it, hoping positive vibes and good karma might just shrink us down as we passed over the threshold. It didn't help that the thing probably weighed 250 pounds. It also didn't help that Indy had oiled the ever living hell out of it, ruining any chance of good grips. In the end, we just had to go for it.

Standing at either end, we simply nodded and began. Ever

searching for a decent hold, we started hip-checking the kitchen toward the exit, barking out ideas as we got closer and closer.

"I think we have to rotate it this way," I said as we approached the doorway, which immediately caught on the edge of the countertop.

"I don't think that'll work," he said, twisting and jerking it into another part of the doorjamb.

"Then this way?" Another futile shove proved unsuccessful.

"Ummm. I don't think so."

"Well, hold on."

We were already sweating profusely, darkening shirts now well stained with surplus mineral oil. But we didn't set it down. Once we set it down, we'd be admitting it was a problem. We didn't want a problem. We wanted a miracle. The dance continued with us slowly spinning the whole thing around, flipping it upside down and left side out and right side in and counterclockwise and all the other directions. All our years of changing apartments and houses had made us near experts at fitting things through doorways. We pulled out every move we knew: the McPherson Switch, the Tucson Slide, even the Maricopa Shuffle, a complex corkscrew maneuver originally developed by NASA to get equipment into the Apollo lunar modules. All the while, we grew more and more fatigued. Eventually, we dropped it, both of us blurting out, "LET'S SET IT DOWN!" as it fell in a rash effort to pretend like what was happening was our choice.

"If it's between the kitchen and the house, I'll burn the house down before I take this thing apart," I rasped to Indy, attempting to catch my breath. Hands on his knees, he appeared to nod in agreement. It's possible he was hyperventilating.

After a brief break, we regrouped, considering other options. We thought about taking it up the stairs into the house, but that passage was even narrower than the basement door, and the prospect of losing control of the kitchen at the top of a flight of stairs seemed to be pretty dumb, even for us. Besides, the basement door wasn't all that far from working. We just needed an inch or two. So, we started dismantling the door. First to go was the door itself, removed by popping the pins on the hinges and dragging it away into the yard. But still, no luck. After the door came off, bits of trim from the doorframe were carefully removed. More unsuccessful tries followed. What came next was the highly focused, fury-fueled, not-so-careful removal of bits of the doorframe itself with the business end of a claw hammer, a practice that surely violated the terms of our security deposit. The reward was worth the effort. While I shoved from inside and Indy pulled from outside, a few loose pieces of wood fractured off the frame, and the kitchen was finally birthed into the yard, where the mahogany countertop shone brighter than ever in the golden early-evening light.

Frightened that the house might somehow suck it back in, we immediately carried it down to the truck and swaddled the whole thing in old sleeping bags and blankets before tying it down with an overabundance of ratchet straps. We hastily put the door back together as best we could, vowing to give it more attention after the weekend's cabin visit. Soon, with a few last bags and critical tools loaded, we finally set off for the cabin and the new bridge.

It had been almost eight months since the landslide closed off access to half of the Riversites community, including the cabin. It was a dramatic journey, right down to the last second. A few days before the bridge opened, one unhinged resident threatened to blow up the new bridge because of the disagreements that had festered during the landslide events. True to the neighborhood's character, the threat was brought up and solved by a few people simply going and talking to him. No cops. No bomb squad. He was handled like a dysfunctional family member. Off base, but still one of the gang.

The actual opening day was well documented by retirees wielding decades-old digital cameras. They'd made a bit of a parade out of the event. Folks had marched across, carrying little American flags. Others rode over in the backs of trucks destined for driveways that hadn't had a car in them for over half a year. From the looks of it, there were plenty of tears. When I saw the photos on Facebook, I couldn't help but get a little choked up as well.

It was easy to forget about the struggle the full-timers had been through. The Riversites were not an easy place to live, even when catastrophic mudslides weren't forcing you to hike into your home. In winter, it could dump feet of snow in just a few days. Flooding was common. Power outages were even commoner. You had to protect your garbage from bears. You had to protect yourself from mountain lions and the occasional tweaker. Grocery stores were not close. Hospitals, appointments, friends, family, cell service, all of it was inconveniently located. It was a lot to contend with. Clearly, it was worth it, though. Because when things were going right, the beauty and the peacefulness of the place were an antidote to just about anything. The folks in the photos were getting reconnected to a way of life that was worth fighting for, and there was a part of me that was a little jealous of that fight and the pride that came with it.

By comparison, being cut off from the cabin for a few months was little more than an annoyance. I did not qualify to feel as relieved or joyful as the people who had dealt with the slide day in and day out. On paper, the cabin was nothing more than recreation, even if it meant a hell of a lot more than that to me. Either way, it felt damn good to know that things were getting back to normal.

I drove slowly when I first visited the new bridge, soaking up the views and the sturdiness. Eight bundles of firewood, a wealth of paper towels, a cooler full of steaks and beer, two bags of ice, a bucket of tools, a generator, five gallons of gas, extra sleeping bags, blankets, pillows, a bigger speaker for tunes, extra batteries for when the music died, and—of course—the kitchen. It was an absurd amount of crap, brought in part just for the satisfaction of not having to carry it farther than the eight feet that separated the driveway from the cabin door.

When we arrived, we slid the kitchen out of its blanket crib and ceremoniously brought it inside, easily clearing the cabin's comparatively massive doorframe. In its dedicated corner, the kitchen looked like it had been there all along. The sink lined up perfectly with the window, the countertop slid just beneath the trim on the frames to make the whole thing look built-in, a small miracle considering I had never imagined measuring the height of the windows when planning the design. The stove and sink were set into their nook, a propane tank was attached, and— without a better plan in mind—a bucket was placed under the sink, rendering the sink straining device somewhat unnecessary outside of its aesthetic value.

Stepping back and looking at it, I revisited the work I'd put in to carefully curating each piece. It was hard not to think about the history of the things, which mattered to me, and not because I had some special tie to that sort of sink or that the wood's relationship with Boeing had any connection to my own past. Rather, I liked the improbability of it all. The countertops were elaborate packaging materials, at the far end of a spectrum that started with Scotch tape and Bubble Wrap. By definition, the wood that protected those airplane components was made to be disposable, to work for a while and then get tossed. From the wood's perspective, escaping the trash heap or the burn pile to end up as countertops for a beloved mountain cabin was a miracle of sorts. It was the same for the sink, which had gone decades on a shelf without being chosen, and the two-by-fours, which were meant to end up closed in a wall somewhere, but were now stained display models.

These kinds of thoughts made it easy to be self-reflective, and I wondered how unlikely it was that I was there as well. I thought about all the different versions of life that could have been, how close I might have come to not ending up here with the cabin and the friends to fill it with. It was nice to think that of all the randomness of life, things had a way of going pretty okay sometimes.

The remainder of the visit was one of pure opulence. The fire started early and went late. The beers were consumed with reckless abandon, and our thirst was enhanced with the knowledge that we could simply drive and get more beer the next day. Ironically, it was too hot to warrant doing much cooking inside, though we did prepare the morning coffee via a percolator on the new stove. And we did spend plenty of time staring at the thing, remarking to ourselves how well it fit, pouring water in the sink and watching it collect tidily in the bucket, and turning the gas stove on and off periodically just to remind ourselves that, indeed, it did work. So often, success existed outside of a spectrum, more along the lines of a pass/fail scenario. With fail being expected as the norm, pass felt like a victory of epic proportions.

17

CHRIS

A squared plus B squared equals C squared, right?"

"Yeah, sure, but I don't know that you can just do that. We'd have to know the angle," Matt said, his face only a few inches away from mine.

"I don't think we do, though. We can just measure these and then take the square root."

Matt and I were shoulder to shoulder, cramped together in the dim light of the loft, wrestling with a tape measure and a flashlight and a pencil. I was desperately scribbling every equation I could remember from my sophomore geometry class. Matt was prodding the tape measure against the corner where the floor met the roof, searching for something he could hook the end of the tape to and take another measurement, potentially for the dozenth time. Through the loft window, the result of our efforts was clearly visible, a dozen or so hunks of plywood scattered around the deck below. Each one, a slightly different version of the same triangle. None of them had fit, so we were back up measuring again, trying to figure it out. The triangle we needed, the one between the rafter, the window, and the floor, continued to evade us. It was a forbidden shape.

"Seems like we need the angle. Do you have a graphing calculator?" Matt asked as he whipped the tape against the loft, now trying to free it from someplace it had gotten stuck.

"I haven't even seen a graphing calculator since high school," I said, remembering the days of Mrs. Swartz's class when someone had figured out how to get *Super Mario Bros.* on the graphing calculators and the entire class was lost to it. "But we can find the angle with one of the sine things. It's cosine, sine, and . . . something with a *t*. *Tosine* doesn't sound right."

The weekend's primary goal was finishing out the loft. It had been an easy space to ignore. The cramped, attic-like room was filled with cobwebs, their associated spiders, and the rusty heads of nails long awaiting their final blows. The plywood floors made of old real estate signs were as sturdy as they were caked in dust and mouse droppings—which is to say, extremely sturdy. On the ceiling, pale pink insulation hung loosely between the rafters. At its highest point, there was maybe four and a half feet of room, short enough that attempts at walking around were quickly abandoned for crawling. The best position was lying down, ideal considering that the loft's intended primary function was to be a sleeping area.

Since the road had opened, cabin visits had increased exponentially, as had the contingent of friends interested in coming up. But sleeping arrangements were tight, and more space was needed. The futon was adequate and serviceable for two people, but any more than that and things got complicated. In a few instances, folks had elected to sleep in their cars or out in a hammock tied between the cedar and maple trees that flanked the deck. Sleeping on the floor in front of the futon was technically possible, but so limited was available floor space that you could not lie on the floor and open the door at the same time.

Despite two small windows, one at the top of the ladder and one directly over the door and deck below, there was not much light in the loft. Even at the brightest part of the day, it would have been difficult to comfortably read a book. But the windows offered a big part of the allure of sleeping there. With two available, there was a chance for a cross breeze that would be welcome in all seasons. Having the option to escape the heat for a cool, comfortable place to sleep was plenty of inspiration to do battle with a few spiders and clumps of itchy fiberglass insulation.

A solid cleaning of the floor and a reckoning of errant nails was already complete. The main goal now was to cover up the framing, add insulation where it was missing, and construct a few simple cots. The wall paneling that we were installing, or attempting to install, was the same unspeakably thin plywood that I had used to clad the walls downstairs. It was light. It was cheap. It looked like wood. Perfect cabin material.

The math of the project was killing us, though. In retrospect, it wasn't entirely our fault. Math was the problem. Math is exact, precise, infallible: all words that I would never use to describe the construction of the cabin. The cabin was more like an improv show, lots of people sort of freewheeling around, making things up as they go along, just trying to have a good time and get to the next sketch, get to the next good time. I was just one doofus in a longer line of doofuses who were adding their own DIY flavor to a patchwork of wood and metal. The problem was, with each improvised addition, the problems got more and more complicated, the cuts got weirder and weirder, and the solutions became harder to find. The wall was not a surface on which to apply mathematical theorems. It was more like a scavenger hunt.

We'd dutifully draw out what a panel was supposed to look like, take measurements, transcribe those measurements as best we could onto a piece of wood, make the cut, and then hold it up to find some issue that prevented a proper fit. There'd be a bowed or warped piece of framing, a portion of the wall that wasn't plumb, or an assumption on our part that something was a ninety-degree angle when it wasn't. Carefully, we'd then bring the panel back down, adjust its shape with the circular saw, and return to the loft to realize cutting one section to fit only made another area too short. Circular saw edits made quick work of the pieces, rendering them uselessly small after a few rounds, forcing us to start from scratch. We had done this many times. We were running out of wood.

Having given up on figuring out the right way to do things, Matt and I took another set of measurements, taking into account our past errors, and scuttled backward along the floor, down the ladder, and out onto the deck to cut up another piece. While Matt worked at the circular saw, something caught my attention. There was a disturbance in the trees. The noise matched the movement. It was chaotic, loud, and jerky. Ferns and blackberry bushes shook violently. As they came crashing down, a figure emerged from within, dragging the forest into a maelstrom of sound and smoke. When he reached the bottom of the hill, he cut power to a giant Weedwacker and continued on, stomping out a path led by white sneakers stained lime green from the massacre of chlorophyll. It was when he started yelling that I finally realized . . . this was a neighbor.

"You built your outhouse out of my house!" he bellowed at me and Matt, who had been focused on his cut but was now looking up in wide-eyed confusion.

My mind shot back to the comment Tony had made when we finalized the cabin's sale. "There is one guy who thinks he owns part of the cabin, but it's fine," he'd said. Staring at Weedwacker Man, I thought, *This might be that one guy.*

"Uhhhh. What?" was about all I could muster.

"Your outhouse, that siding came from my house in Kenmore," said the neighbor, wielding a gas-powered Weedwacker in a way I wouldn't have described as nonthreatening.

Terrified of the possible implications for taking another man's siding, especially when you've never met the man, or been to his house, or been to Kenmore, I began retreating in every sense of the word, composing a word salad of *I didn't knows, sorrys,* and *some other guys.* About halfway through a lackluster commitment to immediately tear the outhouse down, I noticed his face slowly warp into a smile.

"Ha! Aw, hell, I don't care," he chortled, setting down his Weedwacker and moving onto the deck.

Rising to shake Chris Rush's big paw of a hand, I felt the tension flow out of my chest like a spilled jar of honey. He was all smiles and compliments about the work done to the cabin. We chatted about ourselves for a bit. Chris was a professor at the University of Washington. As it turned out, he had actually mentored a good friend of mine, a relationship that I heavily leaned into hoping that it would help soften any other neighbor-on-neighbor transgressions that might yet develop. Eventually, the conversation turned back toward the cabin, and all relaxation quickly turned back into fear.

"You know the cabin's on my property, and now the outhouse too," Chris mentioned as if it wasn't a big deal.

Again, I resorted to comments of pure confusion, unsure of where the liability in all of it rested. Sensing my uneasiness, Chris explained.

Years and years ago, he and his wife bought a cabin on Wit's End. The Rushes spent many happy times in their little forest abode and, over time, began to meet other neighbors in the area, including George next door. George had been on Wit's End longer than Chris. In fact, he had been one of the first property owners to try to build anything on the road since it was created back in the '60s. In the late '90s, George decided to build a tiny cabin, just a small place to tinker on and get away from it all. As one of the first people on the road, and without structures to base his guesses on, he approximated the location of his lot, found a flat piece of land, and built what would one day be my cabin, just steps away from what would be Chris and Leslie's place.

Time went by, and George assembled a frame, threw up a roof, and clad the thing in fir siding panels. Then progress stopped. George came less and less frequently. No time. No energy. As Chris watched the cabin crawl toward a crib of neglect, he decided to make George an offer. After all, George owned the lot next to theirs. Grabbing George's lot would give them more space and the bones of a new cabin that would be perfect for their growing family. They threw out a price, and George went for it, selling his lot and the promise of an extra cabin to the Rush family.

Little did either party know, but George's desire to build on flat ground had led him over his own property line and into the next lot. Chris had bought George's lot, but it only contained about 5 percent of the cabin, located primarily on the next lot over. In the years that Chris believed he owned the cabin, many delightful improvements were made. A solid wood door, the one that Indy would later trim to fit the sloping floor, the new windows, the loft, pieced together with scabbed boards and advertising signs, the deck framing, and the Pepto Bismol but Gray Somehow siding, which now adorned the outhouse. Chris had spent dozens of weekends playing with his new side project until one day, Tony showed up, claiming to have bought the lot at auction, after its real owners had abandoned it, thinking the land was vacant and worthless. In the end, Chris had dumped a pile of money into a cabin he didn't own, and now he had to deal with me. From his perspective, I had taken his cabin, built a structure on his property exclusively designed to store poop, then decorated the outside of that outhouse with wood from his own personal residence. It was like a beautiful Greek trag-edy, the stuff of poems. Luckily, Chris thought so too.

When he was done catching me up, I was speechless. I shook my head and started to mumble again about not knowing and being sorry and giving him money or my firstborn or who knows what. Matt stood by loyally, prepared to attack anyone who tried to wrestle the cabin away from us. Chris stopped me before I said anything coherent.

"Ah, don't worry about it," Chris said. "Buy me a beer sometime or something. Hey, have you seen any of the neighbors' places?"

I told him I'd met Murphy and seen his place, but had steered clear of the other cabins. If the Riversites had a décor theme, it would have been NO TRESPASSING signs. Snooping around other people's property, even in a quieter, seemingly abandoned part of the community, had always seemed like a bad idea, but Chris quickly dismissed my worries.

He took us on a tour of Wit's End, pointing out the places he knew and wondering with us about the ones he didn't. There was an older couple who owned the place across from his, but they hadn't been up in years. Brad was across the way, his lot accessible by an incredibly steep rock pathway that he'd constructed to the top of the ridge. There were other cabins where Chris used to know the owners, but time and circumstance had fractured once-tight community relationships. As Murphy had said, the road had once been much busier. He was glad I was around. We ended the march with a walk up toward the top of the ridge, an area I'd wanted to explore but never felt comfortable venturing into since it passed through other properties. Chris put our minds at ease. Exploration was expected, he said. A small trail led us to the top, where we suddenly found ourselves on the lip of the mudslide. Above the chaos for the first time, we got a firsthand look at its scale. Though it hadn't moved much in the dry summer months, it still looked like a chocolate malt, oozing through a shag carpet of moss and ferns.

"Jesus," Chris said. And we nodded in agreement.

We chatted about the impact it had on the community, shared stories about trying to figure out if the road was open, and wondered if it would continue. I asked Chris about all the drama that had been interspersed throughout the slide. He didn't know much about it. It sounded like he'd only followed along every now and then, checking in to see when the bridge would open. Looking back, I wondered if I might have saved myself a lot of grief if I had simply ignored the issue entirely and let the cabin be on its own for a while.

The way back to the cabin was relatively quiet, though Chris pointed out more neighbors along the way. "That one's owned by a schoolteacher; you'll meet her sometime. They'll be back," he figured. "That one was built by an older couple, but then he died, and I think she left it to her kids, but they don't live around here anymore. Not sure what's happening to it. That one was owned by a couple of older ladies; you'll meet them." And the stories continued.

Every cabin on the road seemed to be abandoned, including Chris's, but I realized how quickly the forest could turn a healthy project into a seemingly long-forgotten retreat. A few leaves, a cobweb, a pile of branches. It didn't take much to erase a stay.

We parted ways on the road between our cabins. Chris welcomed me to share his firewood and tools whenever I wanted. I promised to check in on his place whenever I came up. Numbers were traded, hands were shaken, and I apologized one last time for the outhouse, and the siding, and the cabin. It would be months before I saw him again. Like ghosts, the characters of Wit's End came and went, leaving only the traces of their own projects to signify that they were ever there. At times, it made me wonder who wondered who I was.

The meet and greet with Chris was a welcome break from the triangle panel problem, and we returned with fresh minds and good spirits to the measuring tapes and saws. By sheer luck or lessons learned the hard way, the latest piece Matt cut fit almost perfectly, and we smiled as we slammed the thing home with tiny nails that were nearly impossible to hit without crushing your thumb in the process. It was the last piece of paneling to go up. We lay back when it was finished to admire the space transformed. The new wood had brightened the loft up considerably.

The next morning, we slapped together a few makeshift cots using two-by-fours and thin strips of pine. They weren't much, two twin-size platforms that raised you off the ground three or four inches, but it felt like a significant improvement. Atop the cots, bright green sections of foam were added, then new sleeping bags. The finishing touch was a thin strip of lights tucked around the perimeter of the floor and plugged into a portable battery pack I'd recently bought just for the occasion. At night, we flicked the lights on, and the loft glowed to life. Crawling into our sleeping bags, we cracked open both windows and felt the cool breeze shoot through, bringing with it the scent of fir needles and cedar. The acoustics of the loft amplified the sound of the river in the distance. We fell asleep easily, listening to the flow.

18

ANXIETY IN AMBERGRIS

The opening of the bridge in mid-August left me with a little more than a month of warm weather still on the calendar. Summer tends to start and end late in the Pacific Northwest. It's not uncommon to pull your jackets and rain boots out in June and still be reaching for sunscreen well into late September. One year, the air was still thick with wildfire smoke while we gathered Halloween pumpkins. With the promise of more dry weather and the completion of the kitchen and the loft under my belt, I shifted my focus to the cabin's exterior.

Much of the driveway gravel had settled, creating little pockets of loose rock and dips and valleys that would almost certainly get worse with a season of snow and freeze-thaw cycles. It was a problem easily solved by another load of rocks from Cal and a few hours of sweating with a rake and a shovel, just like before. Only this time, I concluded the project with a creative tamping process that involved laying sheets of plywood down on the driveway and backing onto them repeatedly with my car. Whether this actually helped, I have no idea.

Landscaping was more or less taken care of naturally. I was happy to trade a yard of ferns, salmonberry, huckleberry, and native mosses for tulips and Kentucky bluegrass. On a whim, I'd bought a bag of wildflower seed mix that I cast out in handfuls one morning. That afternoon, I watched birds eat through most of it. Much to my surprise, no flowers ever grew. There were some pesky blackberry bushes that were beginning to invade the driveway edges and tended to catch your clothes whenever you got out of the car. A rusty pair of loppers took care of the prickly vines.

The deck had already earned itself a nice patina from nearly a year of rain and snow and leaf muck, which helped it blend in with the cabin. They now looked nearly the same age. The cabin itself, however, was due for some major touch-ups.

The siding was a dull gray, resulting not from paint but weathered cedar shingles, which had been hung on about 60 percent of the cabin. The line where they stopped was about halfway down on the cabin's front wall. After talking to Chris and finding out the property's sordid history of ownership, I realized that the end of the shingles marked the specific moment in time where he found out he didn't own the place. It seemed like the most obvious fix to the cabin and had the benefit of being a nearly idiot-proof task. Put a new shingle next to the old shingle, slam a nail through it. Put a new shingle next to that one, slam a nail through it, and so on and so forth.

On a Thursday evening in early September, I headed into Home Depot with the project's shopping list: a few bundles of cedar shingles and a couple of boxes of nails. It was rare for

me to go into a hardware store with such a small list and clear
picture of the task ahead. Cabin work was often mired in confusing what-ifs. Putting up shingles, however, seemed like a job
that couldn't go sideways in any serious way. Rolling the cartful
of shingles and nails through the parking lot, I realized there
was a problem. These new shingles were a deep reddish brown.
The red-hued, freshly cut cedar was nowhere near the dull gray
that the rest of the cabin had become, so I loaded up the car,
checked the weather forecast on my phone, and headed back
into the store. The coming weekend promised to be nice and
dry up in Index, perfect for painting.

I decided to maintain the weathered-gray look and to have it
cleaned up a bit by painting the trim around the door and windows white, but choosing paint colors was not as simple as grabbing Weathered Gray and White. Just walking into the paint
swatch section at a hardware store is to feel like you've stumbled
into some kind of pixelated acid trip. I'll say it. There are too
many colors. And if it weren't difficult enough to simply pick
one, you also had to acknowledge the paint's name. If you think
the name of a paint color doesn't matter, imagine that person
you couldn't stand from your childhood. Now picture naming
your kid after them. The names were a problem. A certain shade
of gray might have looked nice enough, but was the cabin really
represented by Autumn Fog? Sure, it got foggy sometimes, but
not just in the autumn. And it wasn't foggy all the time, nor was
it autumn all the time. I did like it the most in autumn probably,
when all the trees changed color, but that's not to say the other
seasons weren't good. The swatch stayed in my hand as I picked
through others, each new shade sponsoring a minor existential
crisis about the cabin's identity.

I learned some colors were collaborations between paint companies and the National Trust for Historic Preservation, so you could match your rambler to the color of Woodrow Wilson's childhood home or paint a chair the same shade of blue as some museum in upstate New York. It was like a sort of architectural celebrity endorsement, and I worried that I didn't know enough about a given place to apply its prismatic reputation to the cabin. Perhaps I was overthinking the whole thing, but then I'd pick up another swatch and think, *What in the hell is "Ambergris"?*

After three hours, I had the shingles, the nails, a gallon of "Mushroom Gray" opaque wood stain, a half gallon of "Woodrow Wilson's Childhood Home White" paint (because a little extra class for the trim seemed reasonable), a few paintbrushes, stir sticks, two little red paint buckets, and plenty to say should anyone ever ask me about ambergris—a solid, waxy, flammable substance of a dull gray or blackish color, produced in the digestive system of sperm whales. It could have been a simple trip to Home Depot, but not even shingles were devoid of what-ifs. One minute, you think you're shingling a cabin, the next minute, you've got a fistful of gray paint swatches and are reading about the history of Nantucket whaling.

The next day, I loaded everything into my mom's truck— still on loan—along with an extension ladder—also on loan— between the tailgate and the truck's roof. Though it was nice now, I couldn't help but think of the impending rainy season. It was well beyond time to get a good look at the roof and the possible source of the chimney leak.

Several friends joined me that weekend. We spent the hours listening to music, tearing out blackberry bushes, and bucking up small hunks of wood with the chain saw for the impending woodstove season. The shingles were applied with little trouble, and soon the old paneling was completely covered. It had a patchwork look to it with the mismatched colors, but it was certainly an improvement. While the shingles went up, I ripped off the old breaker box that went nowhere and that clung to the cabin's exterior. In its place, right next to the door, I added a simple hook for hanging a hurricane lamp. When I tested it out at night, the warm glow of lamplight on the cabin's freshly shingled exterior was even better than I imagined it would be. The next morning, more friends stopped by to help out with the task of painting. They hadn't been up since our first foray past the slide, and I was glad they got to see the place in better form under a blue sky and a bit of warm sun. We divided up the paint cans and got to work applying the gray stain.

There are few tasks I loathe more than painting. I dislike the prep work, the putting down of tarps and paint cloths and plastic, and the careful taping around doors and windows, all of which lulls you into a sense that, once you get going, you can really just slap the paint on, not worrying about spilling or coloring beyond the lines. But the tape never really holds, and the tarps or cloths never catch all the spills. If anything, the sense of security that prep work provides only makes you less careful, usually resulting in a larger mess and more frustration. It was inevitable that I would step in the Woodrow Wilson White and stamp little bits of it all over the deck. When we moved the tarps, the speckled white on the cedar decking did not surprise me in the least, but the inevitability of it did little to dampen the quiet rage it induced. Beyond the prep work and the cleanup, I also loathed painting for the sheer discomfort of it. I'd never been a particularly strong person, but I felt athletic enough to be surprised whenever the slow, hot burn of holding a paintbrush or a roller would catch up with me. I would feel exhausted by it. Perhaps worst of all though was how painfully boring I found the task. It was slow, tedious, repetitive work. Suffice it to say, I was thrilled to have the help of friends who made the job go by much quicker.

The last few rows of old shingles were blocked by a pile of scrap wood that had been stacked next to the cabin since the original work party. It had sat there for nearly a year, loosely covered with a tarp and accessed whenever the odd bit of two-by-four or cedar board was needed to complete a project. The pile had accumulated its fair share of grime and gunk despite being partially covered, so I grabbed some gloves and a rake to clear the wood and scrape away the mound of leaves, twigs, and moss that were smashed between the woodpile and the cabin. When I bent down to brush the shingles clean, I saw the board. Below the last row, at the very base of the cabin, was what seemed like a very important structural board that appeared as rotten as the teeth of a dead witch. With great hesitation, I probed one of the ugliest sections with my finger and felt the board give way like cream cheese. Following the board toward the back of the cabin, it only got worse. Entire sections were missing, lost to rot. Toward the front, the damage stopped spreading, but it couldn't have mattered much.

I grabbed a flashlight and anxiously wormed my way under the cabin to get a look at the area from the inside. Pushing through decades of cobwebs, I slowly inched toward the back corner of the cabin on my stomach. The view from underneath wasn't much better. The rotten board was directly beneath the wall and certainly at least partially responsible for holding up the floor and everything above it. With the board effectively rotten beyond existence, that side of the cabin seemed to be teetering on the edge of a sort of structural diving board.

I stared at the problem for a while before pushing myself backward through the dirt, under the deck, and out. Covered with leaves, and likely impregnated by half a dozen spiders, I explained what I'd seen to everyone. They echoed my concern, but we were all dumbfounded as to what was to be done about it. Obviously, we wanted to take out the bad board and put in a good board, typical fix-it stuff, but when the bad thing has the full weight of the cabin on it, how in the hell would you get it out and put in something new?

Figuring more bad news waited for me on the roof, I set up the ladder to check out the leak. There wasn't much to the chimney. Made of stainless steel, eight inches in diameter, it shot through and above the cabin roof about six feet high. To keep water from pouring in the hole around it, Ray had attached a silicone collar, which fit tightly around the base of the chimney pipe and screwed to the top of the roof. This was the first time I had seen Ray's work up close. What had impressed me so much from down below that day had a very different look up close. There was caulk everywhere. The black stuff was studded with pine needles and screws haphazardly packed around the pipe with no discernable pattern. I felt like I was looking into one of those *Magic Eye* illusion posters. If I could just push past the mayhem of it, maybe I could tell where the water was getting in. But I couldn't see it.

Without knowing where the leak originated, I resolved to a sort of nuclear solution, adding three or four more tubes of caulk to the mess and hoping for the best. I piled it on, layer after layer, using a gloved hand to try to smooth the sticky disaster into something cohesive. I didn't stop when I figured the leak was plugged. I stopped when I ran out of caulk. The result was not something that elicited pride. Three different colors of caulk were swirled together with bits of dead leaves, pine needles, crooked screws, and the odd pine cone. Everything about it looked wrong, and I felt foolish and irritated for birthing such a scene into existence.

There was plenty that had been improved at the cabin, and I felt good about most projects. But things like the leak and the rotten foundation were quick to remind me how little I actually knew, how inexperienced I truly was. In the beginning, a total lack of know-how was the punch line of most cabin projects. When things were wrong, they were funny, and our efforts to make them otherwise were the most hilarious of all. Slowly, though, things had changed. I'd learned a few things, or at least learned enough to know the difference between good work and bad work and feel frustrated when things skewed toward the latter. When I bought the place, there was no point of reference for my efforts. I didn't care if a cut was straight. I was just glad to be out in the woods and thrilled to use the circular saw without ripping anyone's arm off. But as I'd gotten more comfortable with the tools and the tasks and the lingo, there was a natural desire to want to improve.

Perhaps it was my Catholic upbringing that spawned the motivational relationship between feeling bad and doing better. Somewhere out there, I imagine there are people who eat plenty of fruit and get enough sleep and don't watch too much TV, and they simply enjoy the process of learning, treating each setback as a welcome lesson, a beautiful part of what it means to be human and evolve. My process was a bit different. Fueled by gas station burritos and sugar-free Red Bull, I found myself staring at sixty or seventy dollars' worth of caulk and roofing screws and feeling the urge to put my head through a wall. This was a good thing, though.

The frustration was a clue that I wanted to be better, both for the cabin and for myself. I wanted to preserve a place that had quickly come to mean a lot to me and the people I cared about, and I wanted to find out how far a newfound interest in building and fixing things went because, in the back of my mind, I had begun to think that it just might be a ticket out of the aimlessness I'd been stuck in for so long. It would have been all too easy to walk away from things, to throw the cabin up on Craigslist and pass it on to the next hapless millennial without a clue. As natural as the frustration when things went wrong and the satisfaction when things went right was the compulsion to travel between those states. At times, it felt like the cabin and I were partners in a sort of joint self-improvement project. When the cabin was all fixed up, maybe I would be too.

19

BARRELS OF FUN

Fall showed up suddenly. It always seemed to.

I loved the fall. I loved the stereotypical things, the crisp air, the mellow days and cool nights. I savored the rustle of walking through dry leaves. I liked the need for sweatshirts, liked having stew on the menu, liked putting boots back on after months in sandals. But most of all, I liked whatever it was about autumn that made me a bit more contemplative, a bit more present. Maybe it was all the deep breathing I did outside, soaking up the combined smells of wet earth and distant woodsmoke from fireplaces and woodstoves fired up for the first time in months. Or maybe it was a reflection of past autumns, which always seemed to carry with them big changes. There were the obvious things, the years of anxiety that came with starting a new year at school, but there were other memories too. It was fall the first time I'd left the country, when I met Matt on a study-abroad trip in China, and later, it was fall in the Southern Hemisphere when Indy and I had taken an epic road trip through the heart of Patagonia. The longest relationships I'd had to date both ended as the leaves fell, and it was fall when my father won an election to serve as a local judge, ending a decade-long stint of work-related travel that often kept him away from home. It was the last fall I had with him. For better or worse, the season always seemed to coincide with new starts, final hurrahs before long goodbyes, resets.

It was fall when I bought the cabin. One year had passed since I'd first gotten lost in the Riversites trying to find Wit's End, and I found myself in a typical state of autumnal reflection. The cabin had certainly changed in big ways. A few hundred hours of work and every spare penny I could grub together had turned it into a respectable little getaway. Other things felt changed too. The time spent in the woods, working on things, learning new skills, getting away from the office and the city and reconnecting with friends without phones or TVs involved had been a balm to a problem I hadn't been able to identify in the years before. Even with the stress of the slide and the continued anxiety of rotten floor joists and leaking chimneys, I found that I was happier than I'd been in a long time. The environment seemed to echo that sense of gratitude. After all, fall at the cabin was stunning.

Alder and maple trees threw down a retro-hued blanket of maroon, gold, burgundy, purple, and marigold, making it feel like you were walking the red carpet of some fancy affair whenever you strolled through the woods. Through the freshly barren branches, views of Mount Baring and Gunn Peak emerged in the distance, each one flocked with the season's first high-altitude snow. In those precious weeks before big rainstorms arrived, the river was low and calm and the water was never clearer, never more emerald. You could see sunken stumps and boulders twenty feet below the surface when the sun was right. During the day, it was just warm enough to work in a T-shirt and shorts. At night, things cooled off enough to beckon palms toward crackling bonfires and heads into woolen caps. Fall was my favorite time to visit.

Indy and I made a special trip up to the cabin to spend an afternoon gathering and burning leaves, a seasonal tradition for Indy on par with most people's sentimentality toward fireworks on the Fourth of July or getting a Christmas tree. It was a smoky affair, but that was sort of the point. Later in the week, you could be sure that when you pulled on a jacket from that day, you'd be hit with the smell and be transported, if only momentarily, back to the cabin, the woods, the fire. We only spent one night, infusing our lungs and our clothes with the burnt memories of autumn, but I returned most weekends throughout the rest of fall to soak up the season, prepare for winter, and break down more firewood to store in the outhouse.

Often I wondered about the outhouse, wondered if it was working, wondered what working would have looked like. I'd never really been confident in the design. And if the design I'd invented wasn't working for some reason, dealing with the collateral damage would have been less than ideal for obvious reasons. The outhouse had started, as most outhouses do, with a pit. The pit was there when I'd bought the place. It was about five feet in diameter and probably four feet deep, about ten feet away from the cabin. The pit occupied the only spot that was flat and didn't have a window looking directly out onto it. It seemed like the beginning of a plan to build an outhouse, or perhaps bury a short person. I'd asked Tony, the tugboat captain and previous owner, if it was indeed for an outhouse. If he said no, I'd maybe think about reporting him to the police for murder. Fortunately, he'd confirmed the outhouse scenario with a texted, "Yep."

Early research made it clear that the creation of an outhouse existed in a sort of gray area as far as certain health-related government departments were concerned. Before that first work party, when the outhouse had been constructed, I called the relevant department and asked who to talk to about building an outhouse. The voices on the other end of the line passed me around until I ended up with a gentleman that sounded perhaps a bit annoyed to be asked about outhouses. It was a fair response to a question that was more or less, "Hey, bud, I've got this here big ol' hole out in my woods. You mind if I poop in it?"

What followed was a long-winded and at times exasperated mumbling of the steps required to permit an "alternative waste system." He seemed keen to mention the potential costs, and he seemed especially keen to mention how much time it would take, both on his part and on my part but especially on his part, to make it happen. He also suggested that the presence of the pit might mean an outhouse used to be there and that I could be grandfathered in to the whole thing, which would save everyone a lot of time and effort. Then came his advice.

"What I *won't* tell you to do," he said, pausing to ensure I knew what the italics meant, "is to simply build your outhouse

using old wood, because the *reality* is the *only* way it'd be a problem is *if* someone complained about it." I could practically feel
the gusts of his exaggerated winking through the phone.

"*I see*," I said, proving I could do italics too. "Well, I'll let you
know *if* I decide to move forward."

"That sounds like a plan," he said, and hung up the phone.

Hiding the operation in plain sight under the veil of old wood
turned out to be the easiest part. The old boards (Chris's boards,
as it had turned out) we took down from inside the cabin became
the outhouse's siding. From the once-swamp-now-driveway,
we'd also found a platform approximately four feet wide and
eight feet long, made from an amalgamation of heavily painted
lumber. The platform fit perfectly as a bridge over the pit and
thus as the outhouse floor. The only thing in the whole outhouse
that ended up being new was the metal on the roof and the toilet
seat, affixed to a simple box inside. In the floor, we blasted a hole
with a Sawzall so things could pass on through. The structure
was relatively simple. The mechanics conjured confusion.

At its most elemental, an outhouse is simply a room above a
hole. It's a place where you can go and get out of the rain and wind
for a second, where you can shut a door and sit down and do your
business without threat of being torn apart by some fearsome
predator, at least until you open the door again. It's privacy, safety,
and, depending on how you set the thing up, maybe a tad bit of
comfort. When I looked up outhouses and composting toilets,
I found legions of supporters who seemed intent on making it
all as complicated as possible. Books were dedicated to the subject, websites were consumed by it. Lots of people appeared to
make their living simply being people who knew a lot about how
outhouses worked. I'd pored over books filled with diagrams of

outhouses with passive ventilation systems, complex sedimentary bases, highly engineered auger mechanics that helped mix things together so they'd break down more uniformly, and multistage setups that separated liquids from wastes. Some were even intent on finding ways to digest doo-doo into fertilizer so you could grow bigger tomatoes. My needs were simpler, my budget smaller, my resources lacking.

I took all the systems in, let them ferment in my mind, and ultimately designed my own, one that seemed to fit the cabin's infrequent use and reflected my understanding of the basic biomechanical processes involved. It was a mega-size version of one of the simplest off-grid setups I'd seen, a bucket with a toilet seat on top. Folks would dump a scoop of sawdust or wood chips in the bucket, go about their business, and then top the waste with more chips. Apparently, it worked great. The part that I didn't like was the part where they then dealt with a full bucket. My revised version upped the bucket size to the biggest bucket I could find, a fifty-five-gallon drum.

The drums were easy to find. Commercial enterprises went through thousands of the things to store all manner of industrial liquids. On the reclaimed market, they'd become especially popular with folks that wanted to use them as rain-catch system containers. On Craigslist, I found a listing with photos that showed great big mountains of drums, thousands of them, all stacked and strapped to one another. It was a barrel supply company. Their plastic fifty-five-gallon drums were only fifty bucks apiece.

On a lunch break from work, I put the address included on the listing into my phone and followed the directions to a nondescript building in Seattle's industrial south end. Parking before an endless wall of barrels exactly like the one I wanted, I walked down the street to find the entrance. I don't know what I expected to find in the front office of a barrel supply company, but I couldn't have underestimated it. I felt like I had stepped back in time. Everything was coated in a layer of black grime. The walls were lined with rusted file cabinets, stacked high with piles of loose paper that looked as if they might have been used as napkins for a few generations of coopers. There wasn't a computer in sight. The concrete floor was splattered with paint and grease and metal shavings. Through the half-open door at the side of the room, I could see guys hustling around conveyor belts while sparks flew in all directions. Before long, someone spotted me.

A younger guy, dressed in a jumpsuit that looked like it had once been blue but was now a watercolor mix of gray and black that matched the oil and grease smudges that covered his face, pushed open the door. He appeared confused, like he was looking at some sort of alien creature. Compared to him, I wasn't far off, dressed as I was in bright orange Chaco sandals, cutoff shorts, and a crimson tank top. Dress for the job you want, not the one you have, they say.

"Hey there, I'm here to buy a fifty-five-gallon plastic barrel."

My reply appeared to only confuse him more. He held up his hand as if to say, "Stay right here," as if to say, "Theoretically, I understand what you're saying, but the request is absurd, so I'm going to assume you have no idea what you're talking about and I'm going to go find someone else to deal with you."

I waited. Another guy arrived that looked nearly identical to the first guy, but maybe ten or twenty years older.

"Can I help you?" he asked. He did not ask it in the way that customer service folks spurt out the phrase robotically. He asked it in the way you might ask a senior citizen struggling in the ball pit at McDonald's.

Now I was confused. Maybe I had missed something. Maybe there was another office. This was clearly the barrel place. Right next to where I had parked, there were maybe two thousand plastic drums exactly like the one I wanted to buy. I could see teams of guys behind these two, literally making barrels as we spoke. The barrels outnumbered us a billion to one.

"Uh, I'm here to buy a barrel? A drum? One of the fifty-five-gallon plastic ones?"

What started as requests had become questions. Was I here to buy a barrel? Was that a reasonable thing to be here to do? Was I crazy?

"Uhhhhhhhh, okay," the new guy said slowly, still clearly concerned. "Ummmmmm, give me one second."

The other guy took off at the first sign of the situation no longer being his problem, and the new guy, whom I deemed to be the main guy, started fishing around in the drawers of industrial metal desks, looking for things. He finally produced a book of receipts with carbon copy tear-outs and a pen and began to fill it out nervously. It was as if the whole place was a front for something or some kind of art installation that had gotten carried away, perhaps one of those flash mobs that had once been so popular had abandoned one of its mobs here and they'd just made the most of it. Or maybe the barrel business wasn't what it was cracked up to be. Maybe they'd been making barrels for decades and still hadn't sold one. From the looks of their inventory outside, that seemed like the most plausible option.

To my utter astonishment, they accepted credit cards. What didn't surprise me was that it was the old manual imprinter kind that made a copy of your card with a great big *KA-CHUNK!* sound. With the paperwork done, the guy led me outside to the fifty-five-gallon-drum mountain surrounding my car. He said, "Like this?," pointing to one of the approximately eight thousand identical barrels. I wondered if there was an answer I could give him that would provide him with immense relief. And as much as I wanted to put an end to his sincere, awkward confusion, I was also deeply tempted to say something like, "What? Of course not! This is way off!" or at least grab him and scream, "What's wrong?! Don't you sell barrels?! Why is this so weird?!" But I didn't. I told him that one looked just great, and as he helped me load it into the back of the station wagon, I imagined him thinking, *Wait till I tell the guys about this.*

The chosen barrel had been added to the truckful of supplies on that first work party weekend, when it was installed in the pit to act as my big bucket. Not wanting to simply fill up a drum and then wonder what to do with it, I had cut big holes in the bottom and filled the ground beneath it with a thick layer of gravel so that it could percolate. Inside the outhouse, a trash can full of cedar sawdust was made available to put your business to bed. My thought was that things would sit for a bit, cozy in their cedar sawdust, until they sort of dried out. That which didn't dry out would find its way down, through the gravel, and into the earth, where it would become dirt itself or get filtered and become bugs or lava or fertilizer or something and eventually help grow plants that would photosynthesize and rain and I had no idea what I was talking about. But the goal, my steadfast hope, was that the holes in the bottom of the barrel would allow things to sort of settle as time went on and that maybe, just maybe, if I was lucky, I'd die or an asteroid would hit the earth before it got full.

With just over a year of use, I decided to check in one morning in late fall to see how things were going. After all, autumn was a time to reflect, to check in on things that weren't always easy to face. Armed with a flashlight and hope, I opened up the door of the outhouse and took a good look down into the pit. Until that point, I had only given the area enough attention to ensure that I wasn't about to sit down onto a rattan chair constructed by black widows. So, when the light hit the bottom of the pit, what I saw surprised me. It didn't look half-bad. Almost tidy, in fact. And it was active. Armies of little bugs were weaving in and out of it all. They seemed delighted, filled with purpose, happy to be busy. Bugs had not figured into my composting plan, but I was thrilled to have them aboard the team.

Less reassuring was the height of the pile they were working on. Despite their efforts against my own, the barrel was certainly filling. Judging by the line where the pile stopped, I was at about 20 percent capacity. I did the math in my head. Assuming I continued visiting with the same frequency, shirking the responsibilities of regular adult life as often as possible, it meant that the barrel would be full in six more years. In other words, I would have to sell the cabin in six years. Maybe, with some careful planning and a diet higher in fiber, or cheese, or whichever food blocked you up a bit in lieu of rib eyes, Caesar salad, chili, and dehydrated hash browns, I could stretch it out a bit. At least for now, though, things were working.

20

GLORY IN STAIRS

When Bryan came up to visit in early December, the charm of autumn was long gone, replaced by a frozen stillness that only comes from multiple days of single-digit temperatures, the forecast for the entirety of Bryan's visit.

He'd come back to soak up some cabin time and get his hands dusty with a few projects. At our respective jobs, we'd fallen into a pattern of meeting up online and chatting about our respective escapes, the cabin for me and a sailboat-turned-tiny-home for him. Looking back, I'm not proud to admit that the negative effect of these conversations on my productivity was catastrophic. A pack of chupacabras let loose into the office would have been less of a distraction than conversations about cabin projects. To my employers of this era, I apologize.

There were times when it was nice to work alone. I enjoyed the solitude that came from one-person jobs like sanding boards, putting bits of trim around a door or window, even painting. It was easy when working alone to fall into a rhythm that allowed your mind to wander in a way that felt like meditation. But for more complicated projects, I always tried to corral someone to lend a hand. Besides, it was hard to blame anyone for bad cuts and misplaced tools when you were by yourself.

It was good working with Bryan, in part because his knowledge of woodworking and carpentry had been evolving right alongside my own. When we got together, we'd share newly acquired skills and techniques, but mostly, we'd commiserate over how hard and confusing so many things were. So many projects required a descent into bottomless rabbit holes of minutiae. From that place, I'd often find things hilarious or puzzling or enraging. Things like the thickness of plywood (why make something exactly 23/32 of an inch?) or the cure time for a certain paint would have me in stitches laughing or wanting to punch a hole in the wall. Relaying those stories to most people would usually end up with a mumbling, "Ah, you just had to be there," postamble. Through his own experiences and our endless online chatting, though, Bryan was often in that rabbit hole with me. He was there with me in other ways too, stuck in a job as a writer that wasn't what he'd imagined it would be. We were both glad to be away from our desks for a long weekend, gripping drills and hammers instead of mice and keyboards. The plan for that weekend? Build some stairs.

The loft had reached a state of refinement that made it as habitable as the rest of the cabin. The average spider count was down to single digits during any given survey, and most of the sharp, protruding nails had been beaten into submission after colliding with heads, shoulders, knees, and toes. Matt and I had done the painstaking work of covering 98 percent of the walls and ceiling with thin plywood panels. The remaining 2 percent was made up of gaps. It's not that the loft ceiling was all that complicated, but inaccurate cuts compound as you add each piece that fits "pretty good." The last piece was a complex triangle that took us hours to fabricate. It fit, more or less, but it also had to, because we'd simply run out of wood. In addition to the wall paneling, we'd constructed a few simple cots to raise up off the floor a few inches. The gain in elevation wasn't much. The cots were more symbolic. Bugs and spiders and dirt on the floor, people just above. A good cleaning and a few nights in the loft cemented the loft as the de facto sleeping area.

The main problem was getting up there. Since I'd bought the cabin, a homemade ladder of exceptional crudeness was the only way to access the loft. The feet were uneven, forcing it to always lean, threatening collapse or a rapid slide away from the wall at any given moment. The rungs were too close together, creating a nerve-racking maze for your feet whenever you attempted to descend. And even though the loft floor was only eight or so feet off the ground, the ladder was not tall enough to reach it. Instead, it merely provided a wobbly boost before a core-testing scramble to make it all the way up or down.

The hope was to replace the ladder with a set of stairs. Certainly, a new ladder would have been simpler, and improving on the current model would have been almost impossible not to achieve. But I wanted stairs for a few reasons. Stairs would make it easier to get up, especially when carrying something. As it was, we'd usually stand at the bottom of the ladder and launch our bags and pillows and jackets up into the loft from the ground.

When things had to come back down, we'd toss them on the futon, a practice that had more than once endangered mugs, lanterns, and eyeglasses that were set on a small table adjacent to the futon. Stairs also felt a bit more impressive, a bit classier maybe. And finally, I wanted stairs for the task of building them. I'd reached a point, carpenter-ically speaking, when a ladder felt like it would be a bit too easy to make. Building a good set of stairs carried with it a host of new challenges, especially given the cabin's unique character.

According to code books and the experts, a normal set of stairs was three feet wide. The height of each stair was ideally seven inches, and the tread, the part you stepped on, was usually about eleven inches deep. Stairs that conformed to these criteria at the cabin would have taken up more than a third of the interior space before bursting through the wall and ending somewhere out on the middle of the deck. Standard stairs were not an option. We had to get creative. That was the fun of it, though.

Bryan and I spent the first night of his visit drinking pu-erh tea (an earthy, fermented black tea that had become a bit of a cabin tradition) and sketching out designs on paper. Stairs were tricky. They involved angles. Angles were tricky. Stairs also demanded a high degree of accuracy. It is amazing how easily our bodies adapt to a flight of steps, navigating what is more or less a copy-paste of muscle movement. Good stairs allow for a mindless ascension. For us, that meant figuring out, for a given angle, exactly where the stairs would start and end and how each of them could be made to be exactly the same size, all while still providing a suitable surface to stand on. In the weeks leading up to the visit, I'd obsessed over framing books and watched countless videos on YouTube about building stairs. Much of that knowledge felt like a distant memory once we were there, in the cabin, racking our brains against the math of it all. Electing for a more direct approach, we ditched the calculators and graph paper and ended up drawing outlines of the stairs directly on the wall, stretching a tape measure across the plywood to get a feel for where they would land on the floor, trying to imagine how they'd get secured in place. We taped off different stair tread sizes on the floor and stood in them to get a sense of the size. We drank more tea. We started over a few times. Slowly, rough numbers became more specific. By the end of the evening, we felt like we had sort of a plan.

The stairs would start off narrow, to minimize their impact on precious open floor space. Besides, once you were near the ground, the assurance of a large step felt fairly unnecessary. It was up high where you wanted a wide place to land your foot with confidence. As such, our plan called for stairs that would get progressively wider, maxing out at the full width of the hole that led to the loft once you were at the top. From the ground, they'd appear to curve a bit. Form and function. Check and check. To experienced carpenters, the task would have likely been an absolute cinch, but we felt like engineering gods when we drew up the final plans. And the fun hadn't even started yet. We still got to build them. The anticipation tinted our efforts to fall asleep with a nervous excitement. We couldn't wait to wake up, couldn't wait to break out the tools and defy the frigid December morning with boiling cups of coffee. Even if we screwed them up (highly likely), at least we weren't trudging into an office, meeting online, and merely talking about the act. Here, we were doing the thing that we only ever talked about wanting to do. The self-awareness to know we were in the good moment made that moment all the better.

Dawn broke over the Cascades into a shockingly bright, cold day. The sun seemed nearly blue. Outside, everything was covered in a layer of hazy white frost. We took our time getting ready, stoking the fire a few times while we made a hearty breakfast of ham steaks, fried eggs, and hash browns, all covered with healthy shakes from a giant bottle of Tabasco that had been a staple at the cabin since the beginning. By the time we started to gear up with thicker socks and extra sweatshirts, we were on the second percolator of oil-thick coffee. I headed outside to unload the wood while Bryan got the generator going to top off batteries for the circular saw and the drills. While they charged, we grabbed our steaming mugs and went over our precious plans one more time.

After the first cut, the plans were added to the woodstove, the previous night's work soon drifting away in a plume of smoke that wandered aimlessly through the frozen forest. Apparently, we'd gotten something wrong about the angle and how one cut would affect the way the stairs hit the floor and how the height of the stair tread itself needed to be taken into account for the height of the stair overall and blah blah blah blah. We began improvising. We were better at that anyway. Years later, we'd come up with a term for this style of carpentry: *jazz*. Jazz was what happened when you recognized that a complete lack of mathematical proficiency is what had driven you to a liberal arts degree. Jazz was woodworking done by trial and error. Jazz was overbuilding something to compensate for a lack of confidence in your abilities, the materials, gravity, physics, and so on. We were more comfortable with jazz. It was better than math, which

I never trusted at the cabin. What I did trust was taking a look at a thing, measuring the hell out of it, giving a cut my best shot, and holding it up. If it fit well enough, I'd blast a million screws into the thing and move on. If it was too sloppy, if the gap was too big, if it was too wobbly, then I'd try to learn why and start over. It was only a matter of time before mistakes got smaller and smaller.

Miraculously, it started to come together. Ever afraid of worst-case scenarios and failing structural pieces, we spent a few hours driving screws through the stairs into anything a screw might grip. We screwed them to the floor, the walls, and the loft joists. Still not satisfied, we added bits of wood simply for the purposes of adding more screws to the thing. With every fastener added, we gripped the stairs and gave them a good shake to see what effect it had had, always deciding, "Yeah, that definitely helped." In most cases, the stairs stayed still while the cabin notably swayed around it. It was hard to tell if that was a good sign or not.

As each tread was added, we took turns testing it out, getting the sense of it, making minor adjustments to the width and underlying supports. The process was not unlike cooking, adding a bit here and there, tasting as we went, modifying things as necessary. When we were done, we took a step back and admired our work. The area surrounding the deck was covered in sawdust and scraps of wood. Considering our complete lack of plans, we'd wasted astonishingly little. That was one benefit of learning this way—we got good at reusing things. We'd have run out of wood long ago if we hadn't.

To the average person, the stairs were at most a rustic amalgamation of standard lumber, suitable for a tree house or chicken coop. The stamps from the mill were still easily visible on the sides of the board. The screws weren't uniformly spaced out. The screws didn't all match. Some of the screws were nails. We weren't picky. Despite how crude they were, we couldn't have been prouder. They fit. They worked. They were damn strong. And perhaps what felt more important than anything was the knowledge that, placed in any other cabin, they would not have fit. If they had been built by anyone else, they would not look the same. And at the core, even though we'd eschewed the plans and the math, we'd created something that still followed the essential principles that made them right and good. They were consistent, they were comfortable, they were solid, all the things stairs should be. Yet they were also somehow infinitely unique, and the feeling of our tangible creation, compared to the tasks that typically dictated our day-to-day, bred in us a feeling of deep, deep contentment.

21

THERAPY

I t came on faster than we'd expected. Or maybe the cold had prevented us from being able to feel them, the mushrooms. To be fair, it was probably two degrees outside. I had no thermometer at the cabin to verify such information, but I had checked the forecast before coming up. Every night showed single-digit temperatures. Bryan and I built stairs that first night. The following night was a little different. They were prepared in their usual fashion.

Weeks before, back in Seattle, I took the bag of dried mushrooms out of the freezer, where they were nestled in a large Ziploc bag. I'd gotten out the coffee grinder, the one we didn't use for coffee, and transformed the contents into a powder with a few pulsing whirs. I remembered to crack the lid open slowly, remembered to do so because I'd found out the hard way that the dust tends to billow out into your face otherwise. It had happened before. It was not enjoyable. Once powdered, the mushrooms were stored in an airtight glass container, ready for transport. At the cabin, the powder was combined with hot water and a small dose from a packet of brown gravy mix. The resulting concoction, a hearty stew that promised to alter minds.

We drank our portions and sat with the typical nervous energy, wondering what places this trip would take us. What followed were the usual practices. Repetitive trips to the outhouse, setting things up responsibly, preparing kindling for a later fire, filling water bottles. Pockets were emptied of valuable items like wallets, keys, and phones and then filled with even more valuable items—flashlights, lighters, perhaps a snack or two for the long walk ahead.

It wasn't bad to take mushrooms inside the cabin. It was incredible even, but it was impossible to ignore the draw of the outside, the unknown, the natural world, the adventure, the exploration, even if the mercury was hovering near zero. We'd adapt. We would be like gnomes tramping through our frozen kingdom. Everything would be crystal clear, hilarious, new, and yet somehow familiar. More than familiar. It would be timeless. We would be timeless.

"You don't think it's too cold, do you?" one of us asked.

"Nah, we'll bundle up. It'll be fine."

We put on what seemed like the appropriate amount of coats and hats, which turned out to be all of them, coupled with thick boots and socks to match. Fully kitted, we departed, leaving the cabin unlocked. The chances of someone breaking in were minimal compared to the chances of us losing the keys on some ill-conceived romp through the forest. Out the driveway, we turned right onto Wit's End, past the old Cherokee Chief covered in brambles that belonged to who knows who. We went over the hill at the top of the road, past Chris's quiet cabin, past the old ladies' former getaway, recently trashed in the wake of a fallen tree. We had tried to help with a tarp. It was beyond help. No one had seen them for years.

It was quiet in the way that only extreme cold can be quiet. Not the muffled hush of snowy surroundings. It was a metallic silence, sounds bouncing thinly off frozen trees, twigs, rocks, mosses. There was no bass, only treble. It was as if even the sounds themselves were too cold to come out, holding their echoes in for warmth. The sky was clear, and the moon was full. The stars, almost too bright to look at directly. The smell of smoke was heavy in the air. Everyone in the Riversites was likely huddled around their woodstoves. Smart.

"Huh, it is, like, really cold out," I said to Bryan as we turned off Wit's End and onto the main road.

"Yeah, it really is."

The pace quickened.

"Um, do you think it's like . . . Is it too cold out?" Bryan asked, slowing down.

"Yeah, it might be."

We stopped.

"Should we be out here?"

"No, we should not."

This was a problem. We were in trouble. Of course it was too cold. Jesus Christ. We had on thin jackets. What kind of a plan was this? It was colder than space. So stupid. Back to the cabin quickly. We had to go quickly now. The hill was steep. Had it always been this steep? Must get back to the cabin. Don't look at the reflective eyes. Not a good time to see the cat's eyes. Far too cold. Everything was frozen. Would the trees explode? There were the eyes. Faster now. Was it too cold for trees to explode? At least we weren't too high. We made the responsible decision. Inside the cabin, we'd make a fire. Things would be safe. Things would be warm. Good choices. It would all be over soon.

Inside. Inside. We were inside. But things weren't better. Hadn't the cabin been warm when we left? It felt the same as outside, possibly colder somehow. Fire. We had to make a fire.

"Are you okay?"

"I am not okay."

"We have to make a fire."

We decided Bryan would make a fire and I would light the lamps. Big fire and little fire. A good call. Bryan squatted in front of the woodstove, which had held a glowing bed of coals only forty-five minutes before. Or had it been longer? It was impossible to know. It must have been longer. We'd spent too much time putting on jackets.

I hadn't lit the lamps. I'd gotten distracted. Had only managed to perch on the stairs, watching Bryan from above. My foot jangled with a nervous energy, like jingle bells on a sleigh. There was only anticipation for the next moment. Anticipation for anything. I was just trying to get through each second. Each second was a success. I still had my mind. I still had my mind. *I'm still sitting here. I'm fine. I still have my mind.*

"How's that going, man?" I offered out loud, but possibly to myself.

Bryan turned to me, his eyes leaping out of his skull. "I am barely grasping at the edges of reality."

It was the funniest thing ever said. We roiled. We kettle

corned, exploding with laughter, scattered on the floor, crying, crawling around, looking for our sanity under the futon. Oh, look, a lime. We would die in this cabin. It would be hilarious.

Bryan retreated to the stairs, wiping the tears from his eyes, working on the laughter stuck in his maw, holding his face in his hands while I positioned myself in front of the woodstove. Things were up to me now.

All the required components were there. Paper, lighter, kindling, stove. It was all there, laid out in perfect little piles. We'd set it up this way exactly for this reason. This was the T-ball of making a fire. It was a wonder the thing hadn't started itself already. With confidence, I picked up a slip of paper, torn from the weekly savings leaflet of the Red Apple in Sultan, and held it. In my brain, a ragtag group had been left in charge of all motor function while primary, secondary, and tertiary teams were dealing with the chaos that was unfolding in my hippocampus. Brain cells were getting called back from vacations. Managers had been woken up. No one was not working to make sense of the short-circuited chaos coursing through my mind. In the control room of my hands, there was only Gene. Gene was new, and this wasn't his department. He was the assistant to the secretary who regulated my sodium level. This was way out of his league.

While Bryan held on to the stairs and the edges of the universe, I bombarded Gene with requests to crumple the paper. In turn, he frantically rummaged through binders of information. There was nose-picking and flipping people off. He flew through sections on drawing and button-pushing until, at last, crumple!

Clumsily at first, my fingers began curling. The paper was bending more than crumpling, but it was a start. More fingers twitched to life, and hand met hand. Finally! Crumpling! It was happening! With practice, I crumpled faster. Gene was on his game now. There would be promotions, champagne. Erica in metabolism would surely screw him now! Haha!

Putting the paper in the woodstove presented its own host of problems. The hole was about the size of a postcard, but may as well have been a Cheerio. With practice came success. The woodstove was filling with paper. We were crumpling. Gene was on it.

Thanks to the rehearsal with paper, putting the kindling in was far easier. Things were going well. I dared not turn around and look at Bryan. I felt that if I stopped focusing on the wood-stove, I would be lost forever. Sanity was a room only reach-able through the door that was this fire. If I didn't light it, there would be no coming back.

I picked up the lighter, and my mind teetered. There was consideration for an internal dialogue about the philosophical nature of flame and light, but I pushed it aside. What exactly were sparks made of? Not now, damn it. What would the op-posite of a lighter be? Gene! I demanded he take over. It was a Hail Mary, but it worked. Click. Spark. Gas. Yes.

A timid flame caught the edge of the crumpled paper. It grew, and out of the frozen stillness, a purr crescendoed into a roar. The wood was catching. The chimney was drafting. Fire was born. I fell back, limbs scattering to the floor like Jenga pieces. Bryan was amazed. I was amazed. Now, there would only be fun. Warmth equated to safety. With warmth, we could drop the mooring lines of our minds and drift. And so we did.

A time lapse of what followed would have shown the frenetic behavior of two men browsing the unvisited corners of their own realities. We feverishly changed positions, endlessly debating the merits of sitting on stair number four versus stair number five. We evaluated whether the underside of the loft ceiling made the cabin feel more like a boat or a pumpkin. After careful arguments on both sides, it was clear that we were, indeed, on the inside of a giant pumpkin. We fiddled and rearranged every item that wasn't too heavy to move. Hours were spent dictating the placement of lights, the frequency of incense, and the genre of music. We curated our experience with ceaseless energy, finding limitless joy in the position of a sponge, the tilt of a mug, and the alignment of a blanket. Nothing bored us. We were only curious, and the smallest of discoveries felt like a treasure of unimaginable size.

Taking mushrooms is a bit like skydiving. You'd prepare for the moment for weeks, building up the courage to take an epic plunge, relinquishing all control. At the door, it'd be all nerves and stomach bubbles, but you'd come too far. There was a reason you were here; you had to trust the judgment of your past self. Jumping out, the experience would begin as a sort of logarithmic chaos, things going faster and faster until it couldn't seem to speed up anymore. Then suddenly, the chute would open, and your world would slam into a stunning, graceful, floating descent. And the view, and the clarity, seemed to go on forever.

I went to a therapist once. She had an office in a strip mall–type industrial complex not far from where I lived. I walked to my first and only appointment, hoping to use a bit of exercise to prepare mentally for the task at hand. When I arrived, she offered a comfortable couch in a cozy enough room, and we got to talking. Most of that appointment was background, explaining the process, asking about my goals, the usual stuff, from what I've heard. I'd convinced myself of having an open mind about the whole affair, but I knew when I left that day that I wouldn't be back. Lots about it didn't feel right. The person was a stranger, the room was unfamiliar, the exchange of money was awkward. I felt like a sort of emotional dairy cow showing up to get milked. I'd wished that it felt right or that I'd gone enough to realize that it could feel right, but it didn't and I didn't.

The first time I did mushrooms wasn't too far from Index, long before I'd come to own the cabin. I'd spent the night at an A-frame and tried some with an old friend. It was revelatory.

The clarity was always welcome, though the experience certainly wasn't, and isn't, for everyone. The way up could be challenging, sometimes overwhelmingly so, but to me, it always felt like an appropriate exchange. The brand of madness that made us howl with laughter trying to start a fire was just part of the process. Sometimes, if you want to really clean the house, you have to move all the furniture around first. I considered myself lucky to be part of the population that felt like they could reap the benefits. Since that first time, years before the cabin, I'd returned to them now and again. And always, always, they offered something: acceptance of failed relationships, comfort about my father's passing, reminders to celebrate a love for myself and a deep appreciation for the people around me. Like the cabin, it seemed the mushrooms had a way of knocking loose and providing what we needed, even if we didn't know we needed it, even if sometimes all we needed was a night filled with laughter.

If there were any constants for those journeys, it was the company and the setting, both of which were always curated to be of the highest order. We took them in small groups of only our closest friends. We took them and watched the Milky Way over the Pacific Ocean. We camped out and swung in hammocks beside backcountry alpine lakes at dusk. We brought our guitars and made music in desert canyons, surrounded by the smell of flowering sage. It made sense that we'd take them to the cabin. The cabin brought things out of people. Routinely, it felt like a place for therapy. Even without the mushrooms, we went there and said the things that were otherwise too hard or too silly or too uncomfortable to say. The cabin seemed to make room for the thoughts that we rarely had time to dwell on.

All too often, an early Sunday drive back to the city after a weekend on Wit's End felt like the morning after New Year's resolutions kicked in. We left the cabin feeling confident about calling our parents more often, confronting our partners, quitting our jobs, and pursuing our passions. Always, it was positive. The cabin was like a passive emotional hype man, reducing the clutter of our own self-doubts and making room to feel like we could do anything. And so it was, visiting the cabin naturally became a bit addictive, the way exercise and vegetables and decent nights of sleep can become, if you allow. Every time we went, we felt surer about who we were, what we wanted out of life, and what we needed to do to get there. So we kept going.

It was never clear to me what made it that place. You could chalk it up to outside factors. Sure, lots of cabin weekends involved drinking or a few joints or something else. But all those things existed at parties and get-togethers back home and didn't yield the same kind of spiritual release that the cabin did. And it was common to go there and have nothing more than soup and tea. Maybe the propane tank hooked up to the stove was always leaking and we just didn't know it. I had other suspicions, though.

The cabin's close quarters, the lack of cell service, the immersion in the woods, all of it combined to make a place where it seemed like the outside world didn't exist. Like all of existence had been distilled into this tiny place, where complex thoughts and ideas and emotions were easily laid out and examined. The sheer simplicity of the cabin made it so that everything seemed a bit simpler by comparison.

On the rare occasion when the power would go out back home, I remember the shock of quietness that came when the world was devoid of the hum of refrigerators and furnaces and computer fans and washing machines and dryers and dishwashers and garbage disposals and on and on and on. At the risk of sounding too much like a person that has a collection of aluminum foil hats, spending enough time in the woods makes you aware that even something as simple as a light bulb often has a buzzing, unnatural intensity about it that wears on you. The cabin, with its bucket plumbing system and ice-powered refrigeration and total lack of Wi-Fi or cell signals and laptops, was like a vacuum among the rest of the twenty-first century. In that space, the mind wandered, relaxed, repositioned itself. I read once that people typically check their phones once every ten minutes. The lack of everything at Wit's End gave room for our minds to explore spaces that took more than ten minutes to get to. The size too was critical.

If you stood in the middle of the cabin, within one step, you could stoke the fire, grab a drink from the cooler, hand someone an extra blanket, fill a hurricane lamp, load the BB gun, pick a book off the shelf above the futon, wash dishes, fix a cup of coffee, get something out of your bag, or look out the window to see if the weather was getting any better. Like the distraction of the phone, I became aware of how easily the connections we make with people are pulled apart by completely innocuous tasks. Conversations get cut short while someone runs to the kitchen. We get distracted looking for things in other rooms. People branch off to have separate conversations from the group. The cabin didn't allow for divergence. You were locked into a space with your own thoughts and the people closest to you. By virtue of that environment, cabin invitations were not random. Being cooped up with someone you didn't get along with would be a nightmare. The result was a roster of visits only made by close friends and family. By virtue of that history, the cabin became steeped in happy memories that only reinforced its seemingly magical reputation.

Friends would escape to the cabin to heal after a breakup, or to bring a new partner, but only when they felt the relationship really meant something. Yos-wa and Sarah made it their de facto Thanksgiving destination. If folks were visiting from out of town, a trip to the cabin was a critical part of their stay. Following a long reporting stint in Turkey covering the war in Syria, Bryan flew up to decompress at the only place he knew where it would be easy to do so, the cabin. When people texted me about potentially getting up there, it was often phrased as a "need."

Taking the time to set things up, to get the hurricane lamps just right, to get the fire really roaring, to make the perfect meal and keep the incense burning all night. All of it felt like the necessary and final steps of a pilgrimage to a place that fostered the vulnerability people needed to say or think or feel whatever they really needed to at that time in their lives. It was a sacred space for people, and it gave the projects I worked on there a greater degree of meaning, and it made me want to create more spaces that could offer people an escape when nothing else could. I couldn't take credit for the experiences people had there, but I felt a mix of pride and responsibility to share it. It seemed everyone could use some time away at the cabin.

In time, the mushrooms ran their course. Teams returned to their usual stations. Exhaustion clocked in along with sensibility as we decided to start drinking water, checked to make sure we had plenty of wood for the night, and gradually became more still, more silent. Our thoughts went from a boil, to a simmer, to a steam, to a lingering warmth, and slowly, we began talking about the night, reliving the best moments, wishing it had never ended while secretly being glad to come down, to be done, to return to a state of automatic body functions, absolute motor control, and thoughts that came at us under the speed limit.

Late into the night, we talked and took turns congratulating each other on the recent stair build, sitting on them and remarking how strong they were, how well they fit the space. We talked about how much more satisfying it was to build these than even our best days in the office. We walked up and down, up and down, all night, just to feel their sturdiness. Certainly, we'd talked about it before, but that night, we couldn't help but wonder what it would take to switch careers. We joked more about the proposition of us building cabins in the woods as our job, as if building a set of stairs gave us the skills to build a place from the ground up. But still, it was a hell of a fantasy to think through. Only sometimes, they didn't feel entirely like jokes. Sometimes, those conversations felt like they might be about doing something so good it had a gravity to it that would inevitably pull us in, impossible to avoid.

Before long, we each made our way up the stairs to the simple cots Matt and I had constructed out of nothing more than two-by-fours and remnant cedar planks, topped with lime-green memory foam and teal sleeping bags. The cots were positioned in an L-shape so we could both put our heads next to the open window. With my contacts removed, I could barely make out the shapes of branches, still in the frozen night. It was too cold for wind. We cracked the window the width of a pencil and let the icy air slip in. We were well protected now, deep in our sleeping bags. Despite the freeze, I could still smell the pine trees. There was life somewhere out there. In the distance, I heard the train roll over the river.

22

MIKE

I rode the satisfaction of the stairs through the holidays, visiting the cabin as often as possible with friends to show them off and enjoy the place surrounded by deep, powdery snow, which had shown up in full force. The previous, unusually warm winter had been more mud than powder. I was happy to be back on track, though the white stuff came with its own set of challenges. While the main road was plowed, Wit's End was not. Often, that meant parking at the bottom of the hill and trudging through knee-high white in order to reach the cabin. More often than not, the brief and inconvenient adventure was the perfect appetizer to a weekend away.

When friends and I would arrive, someone would get to work shoveling snow off the deck and clearing the steps that led to a crude firepit we'd cobbled together below the deck. Simultaneously, fires would get started in the cabin and in the firepit, and we'd spend the evening transitioning between them, enjoying the crackle of sparks and cinder in stereo.

Shortly after New Year's, I headed up for a quick overnight. A week of warmer weather had likely done enough melting to allow driving all the way up to the cabin. It was an opportunity to replenish the heavier supplies (wood, water, beer, etc.) before more snow arrived. We'd learned the hard way to leave the extra beer in the cooler in case it froze and exploded. When I came over the top of Wit's End, a shock of color startled me. FOR SALE, the sign said.

Wit's End had its fair share of places that seemed abandoned, but none as fully as the one that was adjacent to me, on the driveway side of the cabin. If you weren't looking carefully, it was easy to miss, so thoroughly covered with moss and leaves and branches as it was. I'd asked Murphy and Chris about it and they knew nothing. It predated their own time, which meant that for at least a decade no one had made much use of it. From the looks of things, it had been forgotten for much longer than that.

I'd circled the place a few times myself. Enough to know that the door was locked or stuck in place, that the foundation was made up of crumbling cinder blocks and old car batteries, and that those materials were, unsurprisingly, not doing the best job of keeping the place from slowly falling over, sinking into the moss. The entire cabin was leaning heavily to one side. Attempts to get a peek of the interior of the place through the windows were thwarted by faded curtains with a daisy pattern.

I'd come to thoroughly enjoy the relative peace on Wit's End. Usually, I had the entire road to myself. Lot lines didn't matter when a forgotten forest surrounded you, and I appreciated the illusion of grander ownership and privacy that the low population allowed. In many ways, the abandoned cabins felt like an insurance policy against the potential for lousy neighbors, noise, and riffraff, though I often wondered about the people that owned those places. Maybe they'd moved away with intentions of coming back for the warmer months. Maybe they'd passed and left the cabins to a younger generation who didn't care about spending time in the woods, searching for cell service, pooping in a hole. Maybe they'd had a few kids and the momentum of life had carried them in other directions. But why keep the place if you weren't visiting?

The answer, I thought, was that these places were just too easy to hold on to. Property taxes were less than a few tanks of gas, and the road dues that we paid every year for snow removal were loosely enforced and rarely expensive. For just a few hundred bucks a year, folks could hang on to the dream of an escape in the woods. Never mind the fact that their cabin was disintegrating. Most of it would probably still be there whenever they wanted to revive the fantasy. The cabins were like gym memberships that start on a New Year's resolution, get used a few times, and then simply suck money out of a bank account because of the possibility that maybe, just maybe, next week you'll be gripping kettlebells again. But the new bridge built after the mudslide had changed the formula a bit. Road dues now included a "special assessment," which made membership into the tiny cabin club a bit more significant, economically at least. I guessed whoever owned the mossy cabin decided that was about enough. They were never coming back to go over the new bridge.

If there was a glimmer of hope, it was the price. They wanted

$8,500 for the place—$1,000 more than I had paid for mine. I chuckled thinking of the idiot who would spend that kind of money on what was essentially a cabin-shaped booby trap. Maybe there was a Jet Ski inside I didn't know about. When I got home, I found it on a real estate website. There weren't any pictures of the inside, though they didn't pull any punches with pictures of the outside, which clearly evidenced the cabin's main problem—namely, that it was indistinguishable in form and function from the rotten logs that sat next to it. A week later, it was marked SOLD!

In early February, I returned to Wit's End. There was rain in the forecast, and I wanted to see if the last gallon or so of caulk that I'd added to the roof had improved the chimney leak at all. I had little optimism about the roof and less about my new potential neighbor. For all its seclusion, the cabin wasn't always a place of pure peace and quiet. You could hear cars rolling over the loose gravel on the road below. One neighbor several hundred yards away had rather vocal dogs who seemed scared of the dark. Then there was the common chorus of rural life, the chain saws and hammers and Weedwackers and leaf blowers. Even though these sounds came from distant corners of the Riversites, they usually felt much closer, especially in winter, when the acoustic diffusion of leafy maples and salmonberry was lost. There were times when a quiet moment with a coffee out on the deck would get interrupted by a loud truck or the percussive thwack of an impact driver, but the interruptions were typically short-lived and tolerable, mostly because they were far enough away.

You could not have fit a basketball court between my cabin and the moss house. To folks living in the city, that may not seem like a big deal, but in the middle of the woods, where your eyes and ears pick up the sound of an owl landing on a branch seventy yards down the road, you're going to notice someone at the end of the driveway. Part of the problem, of course, was that whoever bought the place was going to need to do some serious work. What with the severe leaning problem and foundation made of car batteries, the moss cabin was about as turnkey as a barn fire. Perhaps if it had been the cabin of, say, Teddy Roosevelt, a team of carpenters and archaeologists and historic preservationists and botanists and engineers could have come in and done something, using cranes and tweezers and scaffolding to shore it up and make it back into what it once was, which was likely never any good to begin with. But the historic preservation squad seemed an unlikely new neighbor. More than likely, it was someone who was going to tear the thing down and build something new. It was a process that would certainly add a lot of hubbub to my hubbub.

Fearing the worst, I'd begun to fantasize that whoever bought the place would visit rarely, maybe only on weekdays. I hoped that they didn't have a family, or pets, or friends. I prayed that their primary hobbies were reading, knitting, and muscle relaxers. What I certainly didn't want was someone like me, who was visiting frequently, making a hell of a lot of noise, building outhouses on other people's property. I would have hated it if I moved in next to myself. I certainly wasn't proud of these thoughts, of my desire to have a neighbor who was more like a benevolent ghost than a person. And of course, I'd make every effort to be the sort of neighbor that Chris and Murphy had been to me. But damn, I did like being alone up there.

In the decade or so that I'd lived in Seattle after moving

there for college, I'd changed houses more than a dozen times. Roommates would need to leave, couples would break up, landlords would sell houses, apartment complexes would get torn down. There was always some reason. Over the years, I'd had a fair share of good neighbors who'd offer a beer or lend a hand to move a sofa. I'd had bad ones who'd scream at you about parking spaces or throw your laundry in the trash if you didn't get it out of the washing machine fast enough. And I'd had plenty that I simply never met. It seemed the default for city neighbors was to simply nod in acknowledgment when you passed on the street or in the hallway, but to mostly pretend that you didn't know one another, even though the only things that separated the most intimate parts of your lives were two sheets of drywall and a couple of two-by-fours. None of these relationships had ever given me much stress, though, because in reality, I knew I'd probably be moving again soon. Long term, it didn't seem to matter much. I didn't intend to leave the cabin anytime soon, though. Whoever moved in now, they mattered.

Needless to say, I was anxious as I pulled up Wit's End. Worried about what I might find. Worried about the neighbor. Worried about the leak. And when I remembered it, I was worried about the rotten joist I'd discovered only a few weeks before. Rolling over the hill's crest, I looked down at the cabin and saw, sure enough, a new vehicle, a black Jeep. It wasn't at the moss cabin, though. It was in my driveway. A stone's throw away, beside the real estate sign, stood a man and a shovel and a pile of gravel and a trailer.

I coasted to the bottom of the hill and rolled down my window at the entrance to the cabin's driveway, where the man met me with a smile and a wave.

"Are you here?" he said, gesturing toward his car and my cabin.

"Uh, yeah, that's me. How's it going, man? You must be the new owner. I'm Patrick."

"Hey there, I'm Mike."

He looked to be in his late thirties, maybe early forties. He worked in Federal Way at a warehouse about an hour and a half away. He had bought the place to live in full-time. He was going to fix it up. His dad was going to help. He was going to live in the trailer until the house was done. He'd parked in my driveway while he made his own. He felt bad. He'd move right away.

We played Tetris with our cars until I was backed into the cabin. I told Mike he was more than welcome to park in front of me while he finished spreading the gravel that would soon become his own parking spot. When the cars were arranged, we met between them and kept up the conversation. He couldn't stop grinning. He was thrilled to be up.

Mike and I talked for nearly an hour. I caught him up on all the neighborhood news I knew of, regaled him with tales of the slide, filled him in on the plowing situation, or the lack thereof on Wit's End, told him about the cigarette butts I'd sometimes found on the porch. In turn, he caught me up on his plans to revive the cabin, which he prefaced with a strong laugh about how unlikely such a project was to succeed. He had a folksy way about him that reminded me of my dad a bit. He ended most of his sentences with the phrase *and stuff*. I liked him immediately.

He asked if he could come check out the inside of the cabin. I said he'd be more than welcome. When we stepped inside, the smell of piñon incense and butcher-block oil wafted out. Everything was tidy, the hardwood countertop nearly glowing in the fading evening light. It looked really good inside, and

I felt a warm rush of pride grow in my throat as Mike took the tour; and by "took the tour," I mean he stood in the middle and slowly spun around. He peppered me with compliments about the woodstove and the kitchen, asked what I was doing for water, and chuckled at my embarrassment over the sink-drain-bucket solution, which I'd come to accept as permanent. We chatted about the options for rainwater harvesting and generators and solar power, none of which I had any clue about up until a year before. What came as an unlikely relief was our shared confusion about things like wells and filtering rainwater and bringing electricity up the road. Mike seemed like a guy who knew what he was doing. It was nice to hear he was unsure about a few things too.

Back outside, we said our goodbyes. I told Mike he was welcome to park at the cabin whenever he needed. He told me he'd be happy to loan me any tools he had. We shook hands and parted ways. I stood on the deck and watched him wander down the driveway. Four steps beyond, he picked his shovel up and went back to work. Considering we were still inside voices away from each other, the goodbye felt a little overly formal in retrospect. If I had any notion of a mutually respected invisible wall of privacy, Mike quickly dissolved it, making periodic chitchat as I unloaded the car. Often, still talking to me from his driveway while I was inside the cabin dropping things into the cooler. I could hear him fine. The rest of the weekend went like that, Mike and I engaged in separate cabin projects, a Frisbee toss away from each other, occasionally talking about this or that. Most of the time, he'd start up first.

I learned more about his plans, which involved combating the severe slope of the property with a series of terraced levels that would include gardens, extra sheds for storing things, a firepit area, and an outdoor shower that would be in direct view of my deck. It seemed like a big list that was unlikely to come to fruition anytime soon, so I tabled my apprehension about the scale of the project and my fears about a front-row seat to his shower.

At the end of that first night, we took advantage of the mild winter afternoon to sit on the edge of the deck and drink a few beers together, talking about his hopes to spend the weekends fishing up in the mountain lakes, or hiking, or hunting. Before long, it was dark, and the early patterns of rain could be heard through the canopy overhead. We said goodbye again in case we didn't see each other the next day, which seemed unlikely. We also exchanged numbers.

"Happy to check on the place if you ever need me to . . . and stuff," said Mike as he slid his phone back into his pocket. "And of course, if I ever see anything up here, I'll let you know."

"Actually," I said, "that might be really great."

I thought of all the times I had lain awake at night worried about the cabin, worried about tweakers and mudslides and windstorms and snow loads. Always, always the anxiety would last until I crested the hill on Wit's End and saw the place was fine. In a way, the worry had been a necessary evil. Because often, it pulled me back. Once I was there, of course, it didn't take long to remember how truly good it was to be there. The anxiety was like a trick to force me into a habit of cabin visits that were clearly benefiting my mental health in all kinds of ways. After a week or two or three under the fluorescent lights of my office, getting back to the cabin felt almost medically necessary, so much so that I often thought back to a time when doctors would prescribe "clear country air" to address the ailments of folks living in industrialized cities. I wondered how many people would still benefit from a prescription for cabin time instead of a bottle of pills.

In so many ways, the cabin had started as an experiment. I had wondered if I'd use it, if I'd be able to work on it successfully, if friends would visit, if I'd even enjoy being there. I had the answers to those questions now, but other challenges had surfaced almost immediately. I'd never expected to worry about the thing as much as I did when I was away from it. Surely, the slide had exacerbated that anxiety, but I didn't imagine it going away anytime soon. Mike's offer was an invitation to alleviate much of that worry, and I could not have been more grateful for it. He could build his damn shower wherever he wanted. I'd help him.

I found myself peeking out the window to see what he was up to while I made dinner. I watched him put the finishing touches on his driveway in the rain with a headlamp and a rake. As soon as he was done, he moved his Jeep to the fresh pad of gravel and then hopped out, disappearing into the trailer. I turned my attention to the woodstove, which sizzled with the drips of a leak I had clearly not fixed. If anything, it seemed like it might have been worse.

The next morning, I got out the ladder I'd stowed behind the cabin in the certainty that my caulk fix would not be sufficient. Mike's Jeep was gone. I had the place to myself again. With me up the ladder went an arsenal of potential fixes. The collection included a special tape I'd seen on infomercials where they blow a bowling ball through a boat and then use the tape to seal it up, no problem. It wasn't the only tape I got. There were several that promised similar results. I got them all, along with more screws to fasten around the silicone flashing that surrounded the chimney. My previous caulk job had absorbed a new col-lection of pine needles and leaves and bits of moss. It was even more impossible to tell what the hell was going on up there, much less where a tiny but persistent leak was originating from.

The plan was to return the ladder, and the truck I used to haul it with, back to my mother at the end of the weekend. It felt like a last chance to solve the leak, so I threw everything I had at the thing. For a radius of about two feet, everything around the chim-ney was now tape or caulk or watertight screws with little silicone washers on them. It was purely a guessing game. Surely at some point in a metamorphosis from roof made of metal to roof made fully of tape, the leak would be controlled. But this certainty did little to give me confidence in the work I was doing at that mo-ment. At no point in the process did I have the thought, *That'll do it.* It was more like I was going through the motions, letting the cabin know that I recognized the problem still existed and I was doing what I could to fix it, even if what I was doing was clearly not really helping. The leak certainly wouldn't patch itself. Any amount of effort seemed better than nothing, even if at the end of the day I felt a bit like I was standing on the ground jumping in the hopes of taking flight.

Mike came back later that day, retiring immediately to his trailer. The rain resumed as the sun went down, and I sat on the edge of the futon staring at the top of the stovepipe, waiting for the inevitable disappointment that would surely come in the form of a drop of water. But nothing came. It rained on and I continued checking the pipe and the woodstove. There was not a dribble, not a hint of moisture. Up in the loft, I ran my hand along the top side of the plywood where the chimney ran through. It was cold, but dry. A few times, I thought I heard a hiss on the woodstove or caught the fall of a drop out of the corner of my eye, but they must have been mild hallucinations. It rained all night. In the morning, things were still dry inside.

There's an uneasy satisfaction that comes from working a broken thing and having it be fixed without knowing how you fixed it. Once you jiggle a strand of Christmas lights back to life, you never really trust them again, even if their return to illumination is a welcome sight. Clearly, something I'd done had deterred the rain's entry point into the cabin, but who knew if I'd just diverted it to some other area that was less visible? An unknown leak in the wall was a far worse outcome than a known leak that I could catch in a bucket. The rotten piece of the foundation was a perfect example. Who knows how long wet leaves and moss and dirt had been piled against it, holding in moisture until it became dirt itself? Simple ignorance had turned a problem fixable with a rake and shovel into one that would require saws and planning and pressure-treated lumber.

When I packed up, I still returned the bucket to the wood-stove in case the leak broke through. A week later, when I came back up to see how things looked, there were two surprises: the bucket was bone-dry, and Mike's cabin was completely gone. As he explained to me over a beer, it had just sort of fallen over while he and his dad were attempting fixes to the foundation. By the sound of it, there was no eruptive crash to the ground but rather a more pronounced lean and then a quiet collapse, like the place was sighing its last breath. Mike's new plan was to "take these broken bits," by which he meant the remains of his entire cabin, and "go ahead and add them to this ditch I'm making to sort of fill it up and make it level . . . and stuff."

The ditch he was talking about was man-made. Mike had

created a retaining wall downhill from his parking area, and now it needed to be filled to bring it up to something approaching level. The remnants of the cabin would provide a grand head start. There was something poetic about the cabin getting buried like that. For who knows how many years, the forest had slowly gone about the process of reclamation via rot. Without getting too existential, I supposed the cabin was always on its way to becoming dirt that would one day feed new trees that might be used to create new cabins and on and on and around and around. Mike simply sped the process up. Less poetic was the possibility that he had also used the foundational car batteries as ditch filler. I appreciated that he seemed to take it all in stride. Granted, he still had the small trailer to live in. Maybe he was glad the process of renovation was no longer a consideration. He could start fresh, build from the ground up, and create his own little escape in the woods.

23

RID OF ROT

Winter elapsed into spring. I'd get up to the cabin every few weeks to check in on the place, have a fire, see Mike's progress, bumble around the woods with friends. Small projects popped up here and there. In an effort to reduce the number of spiders in the outhouse, Indy and I constructed a wood-storage box with a hinged lid out of scrap lumber and plywood. It kept the wood dry and the spiders at bay, which was the goal, but certainly had its faults. The hinged lid, for one thing, was so heavy, it nearly required two people to lift. We'd also made it too deep to reach the bottom. To this day, there's likely an unreachable layer of dry wood in that box.

With every completed cabin project came a greater detachment from my job, from my desire to somehow make it something that I connected with. Slowly, it was becoming nothing more than a resource, a place to go so that I could afford more wood, more screws, more tools, and have health insurance for those times when projects didn't exactly go as planned. I found myself heavily involved in an affair of purpose, finding more confidence and self-esteem at the end of a measuring tape than I did buried in an overloaded inbox. When June came around, a naive hope for drier weather made me start thinking about one of the larger tasks still on the checklist: fixing the foundation.

I was certainly no engineer, but it seemed you wanted only a few things out of a foundation. You wanted it to be level, flat, and for it not to move, ideally ever. The cabin's foundation came up a hair short on these criteria. In places, a hair meant quite a few inches. Sometime before I had taken ownership, the concrete holding up the corner closest to the driveway had settled. The blocks had simply sunk into the ground, causing the floor to gradually slope downward from one corner to the other. It's strange to think of a cabin literally bending, but that was the deal. It was the reason the door had to be cut at such an odd angle. The slope was significant enough that things tended to roll. On more than one occasion, I found myself on the ground fishing out a couple of limes or a can of soup from beneath the corner kitchen cabinet. You could feel it too when you walked. It was nothing dramatic. But, especially if you'd had a few whiskeys, it was common to end up at the sink when you were aiming for the door.

The good news was, in the years I'd been there, the slant hadn't changed. Whatever had caused the sinking was either over or well stalled. Once I'd adapted, the problem was easy enough to ignore. It was maybe more than that. It was maybe even something I loved about the place, just like the bad cuts, the bent nails, the stripped screws. Each scar recalled vivid memories that, upon reflection at the very least and often in the moment, were usually filled with laughter and good times.

The perfect edges and well-driven screws delivered no memories. Though I hadn't contributed to it, the slant was a part of the cabin's character. That being said, I recognized there existed a line between quirk and collapse.

In other places, the foundation wasn't a bit short. Rather, it didn't exist. When I'd discovered the rotten rim joist, a term it took me at least three weeks to discover, on the opposite side of the cabin, unlike the sunken blocks, it seemed like a problem that was definitely ongoing, the rot spreading like wildfire. As it was, the joist was far gone enough that the cabin may as well have been supported by sheet cake. Along with a dozen or so other joists, the rim joist helped make up the entire structural base of the cabin. Because it was on the perimeter, or rim, it was especially crucial because it sat directly beneath one of the cabin's four walls. For months, I'd eyed the mushy wood with equal parts suspicion and fear, and I caught myself stepping more gingerly on that side of the cabin.

The problem, as usual, was that I had no idea how to fix it. How does one take out a board that is supposedly bearing the full weight of the cabin, and then slip a new board in? I pictured kneeling next to the cabin, a new joist in one hand, performing a sleight of hand exchange, Indiana Jones–style, swapping out the rot for not in the blink of an eye. More likely, fix-it fantasies involved using the car jack for my Subaru to raise up the cabin and replace the joist like a flat tire, but I had no idea if the car jack was strong enough. How much did cabins weigh, after all? Did the cabin weigh more than the car? Maybe I was overthinking things. Maybe it was easy. Maybe it was as simple as just ripping out what had become wood gunk and tossing a new piece of pressure-treated lumber in its place.

As usual, the answers to these questions were sought in an anxiety-fueled research frenzy. I'd spend the majority of my free time buried in YouTube videos and building code books trying to understand how all the pieces got put together. Admittedly, there was an energy to those quests that I enjoyed. The compulsion brought about focus, curiosity, and the satisfying growing pains associated with learning new things. It wasn't just learning for the fun of it. It was learning for a purpose. There was an end goal. Somewhere out there was the answer. If I worked hard enough, I'd come out the other side with new skills and a cabin that'd hopefully stay out of the forest murk for a few more years.

The process was slow, but stumbling around was also one of the keys to my education. In my quest to learn the name for a rim joist, I'd learned about the difference between joists and beams, top plates, sill plates, headers, jack studs, and king studs. I'd discovered the most common terms for lots of structural members, poring over the exploded anatomies of house framing until I could name each component from memory. In most cases, what I saw of those diagrams and illustrations resembled parts of the cabin, but the pieces never quite matched. The cabin's reality felt like the blurry memory of one of those drawings, the gaps filled in with squinted eyes and dim lighting. Building from memory is essentially what I was doing, reading books and watching videos until I felt like I had a good image in my mind, and then going off into the woods, working from recall. More often than not, I had to come back and peek at the drawings over a few weekends. Sometimes, it helped to bring a guide. For the foundation, that meant Todd.

Todd was a friend from a previous copywriting gig. We shared an interest in writing, though he was admittedly far more

proficient at it. He was a playwright and often penned short stories for Seattle's hippest zines. Before that, he'd had a litany of
past employers, ranging from selling supplements at a vitamin
store to turning a shovel on an organic farm in Montana. Somewhere in between, he had found himself on the crew of a home-
remodeling company. His experience wearing a tool belt made
him a minor god in my eyes. When I asked him to help out, he
seemed calm and confident about the project in a way that set
me at ease. I described the problem and offered my attempts at
ideas for solutions. Things sounded fairly straightforward from
his perspective, so we made plans to head up the second weekend of June, giving me a week to prepare. I'd made Todd well
aware of my inadequacies as a builder. It seemed like the least I
could do was go up early to take a few measurements and snap a
few pictures so we could go over the plan with some hard data.

On a rare weekday visit, I pulled up to the cabin having
packed nothing more than a premade sandwich from the deli in
Sultan, a notebook, and a measuring tape. I swept the deck clear
of needles and leaves before sitting down to eat, letting my legs
dangle over the edge while I stared out at Mount Baring and
Gunn Peak. The sun was out, and things felt optimistic. Maybe
the joist would be easy to repair. Maybe I was about to realize
that things weren't so bad after all.

I finished the sandwich and unlocked the cabin, tossing the
wrapper in the garbage can just inside the door. The scent of
cedar and sage incense still hung in the air from my visit a few
weeks before. It was an olfactory invitation to come in, settle
down, crack open a book, and stay awhile. But I resisted. There
was work to do.

Back outside, I knelt and brushed away the dead leaves accumulated against the cabin's foundation and used the flashlight on my cell phone to get a better look at the rim joist. Even in full daylight, the forest canopy made it seem like dusk down at ground level. The rim joist seemed unchanged. A gentle finger prod produced an easy hole. I pushed with my fist and found no greater resistance, replacing the small hole with a much larger one. Running down the joist toward the front of the cabin, things firmed up, and by the time I got to the front edge, the board actually seemed to be dry and strong. Toward the back of the cabin, the rot ran all the way. At the corner, the joist simply disappeared. I jotted down the required measurements and took a few videos of my finger probing the softest bits. The measuring tape zipped itself back in as I walked around the rear of the cabin to see if I could poke my head underneath and gauge the health of the other rim joists.

When I grabbed the rear joist to pull myself under the cabin, it cracked and chipped away. It too was rotten. Half of the cabin's exterior joists were complete trash. It was a wonder the thing was standing at all. A check of the rest of the foundation, though, resulted in good news. Things seemed quite solid even if none of it matched. The clearly salvaged wood in varying shades of stain and paint, all bearing the holes of nails long since removed, were not pretty, but they were intact.

Reporting the state of things back to Todd, I expected him to have concerns. To my surprise and instant relief, the rotten joist sounded like an easy repair. Together, we went over the materials list, which included new pressure-treated lumber to replace the joists, galvanized brackets to tie things into the existing support system, stainless steel screws that would hold it all together and never rust, and an extra jack to lift things up if necessary.

It wasn't until he'd lain down in the muck of leaves and wet moss in the pouring rain that Todd saw the true scope of the work. He confirmed my suspicions: there was almost nothing conventional about the foundation. The joists were all different sizes, spaced out at seemingly random intervals. Some were pressure treated while others seemed protected from the elements only by a lazy paint job. It seemed fitting for a weekend of work at the level of worms that it should be raining, and not some usual misty, scattered-shower nonsense but intentional, flood-inducing, biblical torrents of water, made all the worse by the fact that we were on the side of the cabin where the rain came shooting off the roof, missing the gutters that had been bent away by heavy snow loads just as Murphy said they would be. Somehow, it was June.

We divided the work, one of us outside and one of us underneath the cabin where the clearance was only large enough to belly crawl. There was no choice but to be right in the mess of it all, covered in mud and cold and muck and wet. On paper, it was the least pleasant type of work, but the absurdity of the task made it wonderfully hilarious. We were bog men, slithering around with impact drivers and bottle jacks and circular saws. The harder it rained, the harder we laughed, and the laughter kept us warm and comfortable.

We added support to the good joists beneath the cabin and ripped out the old stuff before using the car jack (apparently, not a terrible idea) to lift things up a bit so we could slide new pieces in place. For all its seeming complexity, the job was really just a series of simple tasks, and I was thrilled that my own idea of a fix was more or less exactly what needed to be done. It took us a few hours before we were able to stand back and admire our work. Where rot once reigned, new wood stood. I was relieved and happy to check the foundation off the list.

Todd started cleaning up while I stomped into the cabin confidently and got busy setting things up, performing what had become a ritual of bringing the interior of the cabin to life. I got the fire going, waiting until the little woodstove began puffing energetically before I turned my attention to the hurricane lamps, which were topped off with fresh kerosene, lit, and placed in their usual homes: one lamp on the cabinet in the corner, one on the little table next to the futon, under the stairs, another to roam between the TV tray that served as a coffee table and the hook outside beside the door. When I heard a subtle shift in tone from the woodstove, I told Todd to add another piece of wood and adjust the damper down a quarter turn. While he did, I lit a piece of piñon incense and put it in its ceremonial place, the chimney of a tiny ceramic replica cabin I'd ham-fisted together during a pottery class with my sister. Placing the incense in the tiny cabin's chimney made it look like it had its own little woodstove going inside.

As things began warming up, we took turns changing in the loft, bringing our wet clothes down to hang as near to the woodstove as possible without lighting them on fire. It wasn't long before they were steaming, turning the cabin into a sort of makeshift sauna. I got up to let out some of the heat and make good on a promise to Todd for a traditional cabin dinner of rib eyes, Caesar salad, and as much beer and whiskey as he could care to have.

We spent the remainder of the evening eating, drinking, and splitting a story on my uncle's old typewriter, taking turns at the keys, improvising a narrative that was as unconventional and ridiculous as the cabin's foundation. It was a silly night, one that neither of us was likely to encounter in our day-to-day routines. As usual, the cabin was exactly what we needed.

Todd's visit that night was his first, and it felt good to show it off to someone new. Nearly two years after buying it, I'd stopped bringing things up to add to the cabin, all the little nooks and crannies having been filled in, and enough visits had been logged that setting things up meant a particular set of practices, a certain arrangement of amenities. All in all, things were well dialed.

In the woodstove corner, a small firewood holder with a leather sling kept hunks of dry alder and maple tidy. On the windowsills above the kitchen, hot sauce, tea, a few knives, a bottle opener, and other essentials filled the space. Behind the water jug, in the upper corner of the cabin above the kitchen, we'd squeezed in a fallen alder branch and decked it out with bits of moss so it looked like it was growing right through the cabin. On the wall above the couch, a green shelf held everything from beloved books and cribbage sets to pancake mix. The cabinet was a repository for essentials, paper towels, whiskey, batteries, extra toilet paper. Rarely was there something we needed that the cabinet didn't provide. On the ceiling, tiny Christmas lights were strung around the room and powered by a rechargeable battery pack. Also from the ceiling was a small, polka-dotted paper lantern that glowed a subtle moonish blue. In all sorts of places were bits of moss, colorful rocks, interesting pieces of wood that we'd grown fond of on some hike, each one bearing the memory of some good time gone by.

Every atom of the cabin carried with it some meaning. The bowls and plates were all from my sister, who'd become a bit of a pottery master. The mugs were from cafés and diners visited on past road trips. The moccasins I kept under the stairs had been my father's. The photo of a goat and a mountain, atop the shelf above the futon, was from a famed Seattle muralist who just happened to be a close friend of my brother's and had once been my counselor at summer camp. Everywhere you looked, the people and places that I loved most were reflected in elemental tchotchkes. Gathering them had been a slow process.

Back in Seattle, I moved a lot, bouncing between rental houses and apartments. They were fine places, but none of them felt like home; none felt significant. Slowly, it made sense to start bringing the things that meant the most to me to the cabin. Like a squirrel gathering nuts for the winter, I gathered the brightest tokens of my life at Wit's End. In time, the meaning of them began to act like the core ingredients of a tincture, imbuing the rest of the cabin with their significance. It wasn't long before the meaningless items bought out of necessity, the pots and pans, the futon, the rug, the TV tray, began to cultivate their own connection to those of us who frequented the cabin. The hurricane lamps became sacred, the creaky futon beloved, the pink tiles beneath the woodstove always remembered. The depth and magnetism of meaning in that place was like a living thing, infusing everything and everyone that entered. In that way, the cabin had the power to resurrect, to take a plastic TV tray and give it the significance of an heirloom dining table, to transform a dollar-store paper lantern into a one-of-a-kind work of art, to carve out crummy plywood paneling into a journal of past adventures. To take an aimless kid and revive in him a sense of purpose, to show him that there was a lot of good out there if he just took the chance to go find it, to risk discomfort, to gamble a bit on the belief that things can improve. Everything I gave the cabin came back as something more than it once was, and I couldn't help but wonder what else it might provide.

24

TRUSTING IN TREES

Summer arrived in full swing, and I found myself pulled away from Wit's End by circumstance and other adventures. A new relationship had blossomed into something I wasn't entirely ready for or expecting. Her name was Kate.

We'd met at the bar in downtown Seattle where Indy worked. I'd brought her to the cabin on our third date. Some would say following a relative stranger to an off-grid cabin in the woods with no cell reception is a bad idea. I was thankful she thought it sounded perfect. We spent the night sitting by the fire and taking dark walks through the woods to look at the stars. Maybe it was the levity of going into something without any expectations, but our bond grew quickly into something larger. We'd been together for six months. After a month, we'd started making plans for an epic trip. In August, I quit my job. We had one-way tickets to Southeast Asia.

It wasn't as if we weren't coming back. The very loose idea

was to bum around for a while, scuba diving and eating weird fruit and riding mopeds in the jungle. When it felt like time to come home or when we ran out of money, we'd turn around. My hope for the trip was to get away from the desk and the mindless copywriting assignments and put a pen to paper regarding something I felt a bit more connected to. I'd started writing about the cabin and sending bits and pieces to Bryan, who'd been doing a similar experiment describing the general mischief surrounding the rabble-rouser marina in Oakland, where he lived on a sailboat.

My biggest qualm about leaving had nothing to do with the anxiety of international travel or of leaving friends or family, although those things would be hard. I feared for the cabin and worried how my own anxiety regarding its welfare would play out from several thousand miles away. Having fixed the rim joist with Todd and seemingly quelled the leak with one of many, many applications of caulk and waterproof tape, it seemed that the cabin was in a good place to fend for itself. Plus, Mike was around now, so I had a direct line to someone on the ground. But none of that stopped me from making one last trip up to batten down the hatches before I left.

When I got to Wit's End, a few weeks before boarding a flight for Vietnam, I realized I wasn't exactly sure what I could do to prep the place for a few months of abandonment. I added extra wood chips to the outhouse, did a deep clean, made sure all the windows were secure, and opened the curtains to show would-be intruders that the only thing inside to steal was some expired chili and a handful of Bukowski books. I moved the cookstove's propane tank to the outhouse, thinking if it was going to explode for no apparent reason, I'd rather have it happen in the outhouse, and raked away the new accumulation of leaves from around the perimeter of the deck and siding. As I puttered around, it was clear that I'd really come up not to prep the cabin but to say goodbye to a place that had come to feel like a home. As excited as I was to get away, I knew the distance would be difficult. Sitting on the deck, thinking about all of this, a voice brought me back to reality.

"Hey there!"

I turned around and saw Andy coming down the driveway, beer in hand, covered head to toe in sawdust. I'd heard the ever-present drone of chain saws since I'd arrived that afternoon. Now it was clear where the work was happening.

I'd met Andy earlier that summer. He'd bought his property the year before I had, but circumstances hadn't allowed us to meet until recently. I couldn't be sure of his age, which I'd guessed at various times to be somewhere between thirty and sixty. He had a timeless optimism about him that I always found refreshing. He and Mike and I had become easy friends, and I enjoyed the camaraderie of our little community on the forgotten road in the woods. Each of us was eking out a bit of a dream here and there, though it was clear from the tight construction, sharp lines, and seamless joints on Andy's cabin that he was far more experienced. It didn't surprise me when I found out he worked as a carpenter.

Andy had the last lots on Wit's End, where the road terminated in a big gravel turnaround. There were three parcels to his name, which extended out from the turnaround like spokes on a wheel. A tiny, seasonal creek ran through the back half of each lot. Beyond, there was nothing but national forest. He was on the frontier of the Riversites, was usually the first to see wildlife, was the one who pointed out the barred owl that had taken up residence in a cedar just beyond Murphy's place. Now, he was hammering out the edges of his territory, removing a couple of massive maple trees with the help of a few professionals.

"Man, it's awesome," he said. "It just totally opened things up down there. The sun is just pouring in, man. You should think about taking some of these things down," he added, gesturing toward the web of branches over the cabin.

Up until that point, I had never really considered the trees as anything more than an aesthetic boon to the property. I appreciated them for the shade they provided in the summer and the colorful leaves they dropped in the fall. They didn't cause any trouble beyond the occasional dropped branch. Besides, half the point of having a cabin in the woods was the woods. Removing the trees felt like a step in the wrong direction. But, according to Andy, the trees were a problem. At least, some of them were. Beckoning me to the end of the driveway, he pointed to the maple and the two alders that crowded the edges of the deck.

"See that huge branch? And see how this alder's leaning toward that other one, and how they're both sort of bending over your cabin?" he said. "One big storm and those could all come down on you."

"Huh" was about all I could come up with.

If Andy's goal had been to generate a new source of cabin anxiety in me, mission accomplished. I'd become an expert at worrying about the cabin, and it wasn't hard to imagine the devastation that the trees would wreak if they came down. A toppled maple would surely piledrive the place into a heap of matchsticks. We agreed I should have his arborists come take a look. Fifteen minutes later, two new people were standing in my driveway. Seeming more like general guys than trained arborists, they did appear to own chain saws and ropes and other tree-professional-type things, so I craned my neck and heard them out. They agreed with Andy. The trees were not good.

"Seven fifty to take the three of these down and clear the road. More if you want 'em turned into rounds and stacked," said one of the guys.

"You really think they need to come down?"

"Listen, son. It's not a question of whether they come down, it's a question of how and when."

Sensing he had just hit a home run in the taking-down-trees-marketing department, he and his partner turned and headed back to Andy's, calling out, "You've got our number!" before they disappeared around the bend. I kept staring at the highest branches, watching them sway in a gentle breeze drifting down from the Cascades, the most basic parts of my brain trying to convince me that if they hadn't fallen yet, why would they fall now? Right?

Tempted as I was, $750 was a big chunk of change. I'd saved dutifully for the trip with Kate. That amount of money represented a lot of lost adventures. Deciding to tempt fate, I held off making the call. Instead, before I left, I gave the whole place an extra solid going-over with a few nubs of incense. A few weeks later, I found myself on a deserted beach looking out at the South China Sea, watching the moon rise over crashing waves. The cabin seemed impossibly far away. To my relief, something about the distance made it easier not to worry about.

Our time away went by quickly. We sweated through the end of summer in Vietnam, cruised on motorbikes through the northern hills of Thailand, and went bowling barefoot in Laos. In Indonesia, we met up with my mom and sister for a few weeks. We'd been gone a few months by that point, and it was good to see them, though it made me homesick. When they left, we started making plans for our own return home, stopping in New Zealand on the way. It was a bucket-list destination for both of us, and we were happy to check it off. I'll never forget the relief that came from stepping off the plane from Indonesia and into an environment with a relative humidity of less than a billion. The weather in Southeast Asia hadn't agreed with me. New Zealand, with all its mountains and forests, felt far more like home.

To cut costs, we spent the first part of our trip participating in a work-exchange program at a massive sheep ranch outside of Christchurch. The idea was, we'd help out on the farm for a few hours each day, and they'd let us stay there for free and feed us if we behaved. It was a cheap way to experience the country and get to know a few locals. Most of the time, though, we were on our own.

The gentlemen who owned the place had tasked us with painting and renovating a century-old schoolhouse on the farthest reaches of the property, where it was tucked away in its own private cove. There was a spring for water, but no electricity, and an outhouse for a toilet. We spent a few weeks in the sun, scraping old paint from the exterior siding, fixing rotten boards, patching holes in the roof. We'd wake up with the sunrise, drink our coffee on the beach, and work until the heat of the afternoon implored us to take naps in the shade. At night, we'd rinse off the day's sweat in the ocean and dry off next to a fire in the sand. It was as close to an idyllic life as I could have imagined, and all I could think about was getting back to the cabin, getting back to building, making this rhythm a central part of life and not just a feature of my time off.

Putting distance between myself and the office job I'd left offered clarity on a thought that had been brewing for some time, that building was maybe more than a new hobby. I'd decided that when we got back, I'd make it a priority to explore changing careers. The idea sounded daunting, starting completely over at the age of thirty-two. In many ways, the previous ten years of writing felt like a waste. I didn't regret the good stories, the ones that took me abroad, the ones that seemed to make a difference to the people they were about, the ones that allowed me to write in a way that felt honest and necessary. What I did regret was the rest of the time, grinding it out, hoping my feelings about the less-inspiring work would change when I knew it was unlikely. I'd stuck with it for as long as I had because, in reality, the job was not that bad. Perhaps that was the most dangerous part about it—that it was fine. What wasn't fine was the constant sense that I was missing out on the chance for something a bit more. It was a curiosity that manifested itself in all sorts of ways, depression, anger, frustration, laziness, and boredom to name a few. Once I decided that it wasn't for me and that I'd start figuring out how to make a move, the optimistic shift I felt about the future reaffirmed suspicions I'd had for years.

We got home just in time for Christmas, just in time to enjoy the holidays before we faced the prospect of having nowhere to live, no money, and no jobs. In early January, we moved onto a tired old houseboat from the '70s in Seattle's Lake Union. It was the cheapest short-term place we could find. Neither of us wanted to go back to our old gigs, managing bars for Kate and copywriting for me, but the demand for a steady paycheck limited our choices and soon, we were back to the grind. Fortunately, we had the cabin to escape to.

It was just after New Year's that I made my first return trip. When I came over the top of Wit's End, I feared the worst. I hadn't had the courage to text Mike once during my absence to check in. Instead, I'd just sort of hoped for a no-news-is-good-news situation. When I crested the hill, I was relieved to see that the cabin sat seemingly undisturbed.

I parked on the road just beyond Mike's place and walked into the driveway, fishing a rake out from behind a curtain of cobwebs to take care of the thick layer of leaves and branches that covered the deck and the driveway. When things were clear, I backed in and got out my keys. The door opened easily. When I stuck my head in, the familiar scent of piñon incense, moss, cedar, and smoke greeted me as potently as ever. Everything was okay. I was home again.

It wasn't until the light of the next morning that I noticed the fallen tree. About fifteen feet beyond the deck, a massive maple had toppled over. It was nearly three feet in diameter. Who knows how tall it had been. The area where it had crashed to the forest floor was littered with exploded pieces of wood the size of beer kegs. While walking among the chaos, I heard the door of Mike's trailer open. He came out and greeted me and immediately recounted what had happened.

"Yeah, and so that happened just after you left for the summer," he said. "I was just cooking dinner, and I heard an explosion and stuff. I came out, and that thing had just given up, I guess. It wasn't windy or anything."

I stared at the hulking remnants in disbelief, imagining the catastrophic effect it would have had on the cabin if it'd fallen the other way. Then I looked back up at the trees Andy's guys had identified as problems. They'd have to go. The following Monday, I called up a local tree-removal company first thing in the morning.

"Hello. Can I help you?"

"Yes, I'm calling about a few maple trees and an alder tree I'd like removed."

"Okay, and how tall are they?"

I'd never been good with guesstimating these things. How does one estimate the height of a tree? Stand next to it and then imagine fifty of myself stacked up to get it in units of five feet, eleven inches?

"Um, maybe a thousand feet?"

"What?"

"Is that too high? A hundred feet? Twenty feet?"

"I'll just put down eighty."

I made a mental note that eighty feet was a reasonable answer. Going into cabin ownership without any knowledge had taught me to remember tidbits like this. If you can spice up total ignorance with a few real-world facts, a few slang words, a few tools of the trade, it's remarkable how much credibility it buys. We talked for a bit longer before she told me that no work could be done in the winter.

"The trees are simply too brittle when the temperatures are this low. It's not safe. Give us a call in the spring and we can schedule an appointment."

I hung up the phone and marinated in the knowledge that the trees hovering over the cabin, constantly freezing and thawing, constantly taking on more weight through rain and snow and ice, were not kind of in danger of falling over, they were so likely to fall over on their own that arborists weren't even bothering to come out and cut them down.

For the rest of the winter, visits were tinged with the fear of those trees. At night, while the woodstove puffed away and snow tumbled off cedar branches in powdery cascades, I sat terrified of every creak, every moan, every hint of a breeze. Nightmares of wooden bombs exploding in the loft, impaling friends with mossy, sap-smeared spears, occupied my dreams. Every trip that didn't end in chaos felt like a miracle. But even that didn't stop me from returning. The cabin was a dangerous but necessary addiction. Back home, I counted the days until spring.

25

THE ROOF'S LAST STAND

Winter was a hard return to stark realities. Kate and I had gone from summertime moonlit swims in a private cove in New Zealand to frigid nights walking down an icy dock to use the bathroom. We'd spent a month on that decrepit houseboat. Outside, it snowed with unusually high frequency for Seattle. Slowly, things improved. We both got jobs. We moved to a nicer boat with a bathroom and a Nintendo 64 and then to a very nice garage that had been converted into a studio apartment. We were getting back on our feet in baby steps, and although we'd ended up back in the same types of jobs we'd escaped, there was at least a plan now.

Unable to make the great leap into home ownership on our own, we'd decided to join our friends Matt and Dayna to buy a house together, pooling our limited resources to guarantee cheap rent and instant access to friends that were more like family. The choice to live together as a little community was a testament to the bond we shared and the belief that when life got hard, good friends made things a lot easier. We liked hanging out. We wanted to make it as easy as possible to do so. The fact that we were too poor to do anything else was merely coincidence. Plus, Matt had a tendency to make very good chili and usually too much of it. We'd be downstairs with our bowls ready.

The other part of the plan was a consideration that maybe, just maybe, with a modest mortgage divided up between all of us, monthly costs might be beaten down far enough to allow me to quit my job and do a bit of building. When I got back from the trip that winter, when I returned to the same job, I found myself online again having more earnest versions of the same conversations I'd always had with Bryan. He was bored. I was bored. We wanted to work on cabins. That was the basic story. Over and over and over again, we'd play out the fantasy of rising every day to throw some wood together in the fresh air. We traded sketches of designs for new cabins, talked at length about future projects, and tried to imagine a scenario where we could build things in the woods every day without being entirely irresponsible.

In late winter, the conversations took a turn toward seriousness when one of the abandoned cabins went up for sale on Wit's End. It was small, like my cabin, but in fairly good shape. There was no outhouse to be found and the parking was limited, but it was decent enough. It sold in a week for nearly $30,000. The main obstacle to our cabin-building fantasy was always the same, that the costs simply didn't add up. We assumed that cabins like mine sold for little more than their worth in materials, not four times that amount. Unbeknownst to us, the market had significantly improved, and suddenly, the math started to make sense. If we could get a cheap-enough lot, we'd quit our jobs and build a place from scratch to either sell or rent out. More importantly, we'd fast-track a possible career change directly to the version that we fantasized about. Instead of spending years earning credit on a real construction crew in the hope of one day building cabins, we'd just go straight to figuring it out on our own, out in the woods. All we had to do was find cheap property. Maybe it would take months or years, but we were fine to wait while we set up the pieces and saved our pennies for land and lumber.

Buying the house with Matt and Dayna was a key to the puzzle of living with less and saving more. To speed up the process, I took on second jobs, doing freelance copywriting in the evenings after spending my days doing the exact same thing for a tech company just outside of Seattle. It was grinding work. Often, I was at my computer for sixteen hours a day. Most weekends were lost to writing e-books and email templates and blogs and social media posts. But knowing that the money was going toward a way out made it all a bit more palatable. Plus, in the meantime, I was taking every opportunity possible to get up to the cabin and practice.

On the first truly warm spring day, which didn't come until late May, I stepped away from the keyboard for a trip to Wit's End with Kate. It'd been raining constantly for weeks. We celebrated the sun with a choice to head up on my old bike, a 1976 Honda CB550. I loved that bike. Despite the oil leaks and the questionable electronics, it was a joy to ride and nearly as fun just to look at. It was a beautiful bike, all candy blue and chrome and leather. Rarely did I feel cool in life. If I ever did, it was usually because I was riding that bike.

We took the long way, through the farmlands and river valleys of Fall City, Carnation, and Duvall, thick with the green starts of new crops. We took back roads to follow the southern banks of the Skykomish and finally crossed the river to join with U.S. 2 in Sultan and continue on toward Index. Where the road grew tight from the crowding of massive evergreens, we could feel the dip in temperature from their shadows. Where sunlight pierced the forest floor, we could see steam rising up from the sodden duff.

I parked the bike on the deck so the kickstand wouldn't sink into the driveway's soft gravel and we sat down to tuck into sandwiches and soda waters we'd packed while the bike's engine cooled, clicking and popping and dribbling oil behind us. The day was almost too perfect, everything working out. We'd been almost too lucky so far, suspiciously lucky, which didn't bode well for the task ahead.

The bike ride was only part of the inspiration for the day's visit. There was a project in mind. On a trip up a few weeks prior, during the rain, I'd noticed a new leak. This time, however, it was higher up, above the chimney nearer the peak of the roof. Even though I'd been offered the free use of ladders owned by Mike, by Murphy, and by Andy, none of them were tall enough to reach the very top of the cabin. Creativity demanded another solution. Kate was that solution. We went over the plan.

Outfitted with a roll of metallic duct tape, she would climb to the top of the old loft ladder, which barely reached the lowest edge of the roof. Before she went up, I'd create a harness out of some spare rope, and by "harness," I mean I'd wrap the rope around her waist and secure it with thirty or forty square knots. At the top of the ladder, Kate would toss the loose end of the rope over the ridge of the cabin. Waiting on the other side, I'd catch it and proceed to pull, dragging her up the roof to the ridge, where she would hold on for dear life with one hand and apply as much tape as possible to the area's seams and screws with the other. The fact that a plan like this made sense to her rather than sounding like a rock-solid way to fall off a roof and break your neck is one of the many reasons I loved her. Ten minutes after she set foot on the ladder, we were racing down the highway, her right hand held aloft with a comically large amalgamation of blood-soaked paper towels and duct tape. It took eight stitches to close up her index finger.

To be fair, the plan had worked. She'd gotten to the top of the ladder, I'd dragged her up to the ridge, and she applied nearly half a roll of the metallic tape to just about everything she could reach. When she was done, I slowly lowered her until her feet were safely on the ladder. It wasn't until she was a few steps down that it happened. A bit of discarded tape had gotten caught at the edge of the roof. She noticed it as she was climbing down and, as casually as one might brush away a fly, flicked her hand to knock it free from the roof. In doing so, her finger had caught the metal roof's rust-encrusted edge and made quick work of her finger.

We used up half a roll of paper towels and the remaining metal tape to contain the aftermath. Getting her helmet on took a bit of teamwork, but soon we were on our way. Her throbbing stump of Brawny raised aloft, we made the usually forty-minute trip to Monroe and the emergency room in just over twenty.

When the doctor asked what happened, we offhandedly mentioned working on a roof, not including the part that involved dragging her around like a baited worm. On the way home, eight new stitches in her finger, she couldn't stop laughing at the absurdity of it all.

A few weeks later, we returned to the cabin. Kate's finger was healing nicely. The new leak, however, had not healed at all. I stood outside on a drizzly early-summer morning and stared at the roof. It looked absurd. There was caulk and bits of tape everywhere. Half of it was pure rust. Most of the edges were bent out of shape from heavy branch thwacks. There was only one real solution.

For a few years, the frustration of failed roof fixes and chimney leaks had formed itself into a tight little cocoon somewhere deep in my mind. Now, the metamorphosis was nearly complete. What was coming out the other side was raw, unfiltered determination. I was going to take the caulk off, remove the screws, rip up the tape. I'd take out the chimney and tear away the rubber boot that surrounded it. I'd strip the metal, scrape away whatever was underneath, go back down to wood, to wherever things were finally okay, and then I'd start over. I was done patching the thing. Enough already. I'd replace the whole thing.

26

BLOWING THE TOP OFF

n July, arborists came to take down the two alders and the maple that were leaning—apparently quite precariously—over the cabin. It was a different crew from Andy's fellas, whose number rang as disconnected when I tried them. When I met the lead arborist for an estimate, he had stood with me on Wit's End and used a laser pointer to show off different parts of the tree. Both alders had multiple spots where a common fungus had started to take over. "These areas," he'd said, lasering between darkish blobs on the bark, "are the weakest points on these trees. It's really only a matter of time before the rot grows enough to cause the tree to break apart." The maple was deemed healthy and unlikely to fall toward the cabin if it did fall. The maple would stay.

It took a few weeks after the initial evaluation to schedule them to come up and do the work. When the day arrived, I was stuck at the office, experiencing the type of nervousness not unlike that which bubbles up when someone you love is undergoing a medical procedure. Even though taking the trees down was commonplace, I couldn't help but expect the worst. I worried some unseen area of rot would destabilize the tree and someone would get hurt, or the cabin would get clobbered, or Mike's place would get clobbered, or anything would get clobbered other than salmonberries and ferns. That evening, I got a grainy photo from the arborist's long-outdated cell phone. Things had gone just fine. There looked to be a mountain of wood, heaped in giant rounds beside the driveway. Everything was covered in sawdust. I grieved for the trees briefly and then felt a rush of relief. The nights of anxiety about getting impaled while I slept were over.

I'd waited to start on the roof until after the trees were down. In the slight chance that the cabin had been destroyed by a hunk of trunk, I knew the sting would be that much sharper if it had happened to a brand-new roof. Besides, I wanted time to plan. I wanted the roof to be perfect. For two months, whenever I had a spare moment, I dedicated myself to learning about all things roofing, about the structural components, the rafters, the collar ties, and the ridge beams. I read about the hardware, about hurricane ties and mending plates that were all meant to help strengthen connections between framing members. I dove into reviews of roofing-specific underlayments, membranes, adhesives, and fasteners. I compared the benefits of asphalt shingles to metal panels. I watched countless videos of metal roofers carefully snipping and bending bits of steel into the perfect bit of flashing to keep water out of tight valleys and spots where the pitch of the roof changed. Some videos became favorites, and I found myself watching them over and over. I felt like I was studying for a critical exam, one that wouldn't allow calculators or cell service.

Before the big weekend, I made the hour-and-a-half drive down to Chehalis to see my mom and borrow her truck, the little red Ranger that had become somewhat of a mascot for bigger cabin work weekends, along with her big extension ladder. Back in Seattle, I began gathering the supplies: a few sheets of plywood, considering that there might be several sections of rotten wood underneath everything; two rolls of heavy-duty ice-and-water membrane, which was like a giant roll of rubber tape that provided protection to the sheathing in the event water got under the metal panels; the metal panels, made of corrugated steel; a giant box of special roofing screws that had little silicone washers, which prevented water from following the screws into their holes; four tubes of caulk; and a new silicone boot to go around the chimney. The extension ladder, the roofing supplies, and just about every tool I owned filled the bed of the truck. The cab was full too. A good friend, Kellen, was joining me. He'd been a founding member of the initial big work party, was responsible for nailing up most of the interior wall cladding downstairs, and was excited to get up to the mountains for a bit of work on a warm, sunny day. On the way up, we stopped at the Fred Meyer in Monroe and filled in the rest of the truck bed with cases of beer, bags of ice, steaks, bags of chips, eggs, sausages, hot sauce, and a few bananas to maintain appearances.

Arriving at the cabin, we set about the typical tasks of loading the cooler with ice and beer and perishables. We replenished the water jug on the ceramic dispenser and checked the level on the propane tank. I swept the deck and pushed back the line of spiders in the outhouse with the broom. Inside, we organized our bags and restocked the cabinet with dry goods. I'd expected to be nervous during those last-minute chores, expected to find comfort in the idea of aborting the whole project altogether, expected to consider ultimately choosing to stick with a manageable leak rather than risk a completely destroyed roof. But I didn't. Instead, there was only a simmering excitement to be out in the sun, doing right by the cabin, exercising the skills I'd practiced and studied, creating something tangible, making something better, making it last.

We unloaded the tools and organized the materials at the far end of the driveway to make room in the truck bed for the old roofing. With the ladder extended to its maximum height and Kellen's foot on the lowest rung to keep things steady in the soft gravel, I ascended, rungs in one hand and a drill in the other. First to come down were the support arms that held the chimney erect, followed by the silicone boot at the base of the chimney, the removal of which required a bit of digging around. Years of failed fixes had resulted in a sedimentary amalgamation of screws and caulk and waterproof tape that did not exactly pop off. What came as a surprise was the satisfaction I took from rooting around in it, each layer a memory of some previous attempted leak repair and the cabin visit that accompanied it. It's rare to find nostalgia in silicone, but I took it where I could get it. Relying on more persistence than precision, the sticky, screwy mess eventually gave up and revealed the roof below. I slid the boot up over the chimney and tossed it aside before twisting the chimney free and carrying it down.

There was a momentary, but critical, break for snacks before I swapped my drill for a hammer and pry bar and headed back up. I climbed to the top of the ladder until I reached the ridge, covered in a narrow band of rusted steel. It had likely been a few decades since the roofing was put on, affixed to the plywood below with big flatheaded nails. Wind and rain and time had certainly taken their toll. Up close, I could see that many of the nails were popped out, almost certainly allowing water to sneak in underneath. I set the teeth of my pry bar beneath the head of one that looked like it was still holding fast and jerked up. It pulled out as if sunk in a stick of butter. The next one, I removed with my fingers. Thirty seconds later, the rusted ridge cap was clattering to the ground. I was off to the races.

It didn't take long to gain a bit of confidence on the roof, which was far too steep to walk on. Working systematically, I began pulling up each panel's nails, sliding the panel to the edge of the roof for Kellen to grab and stack in the driveway. There was a danger here. The panels didn't weigh much, maybe twenty pounds or so, but they were big, unwieldy things, about the size and shape of a twin bed. It didn't help that, as Kate's finger had recently found out, the edges were an efficient first step toward the sorts of ailments that resulted in lockjaw. If a panel were to slide off the roof into an unsuspecting person, it was sure to cause some damage. Kellen seemed aware of the possibilities of decapitation. He took his job seriously. He had gloves on. He was responsible, professional even. The gloves did not impact his ability to toss beers up.

Before long, there was only one section of metal left. Decades of rust and gunk and moss had created a sort of glue that held three panels together. I'd removed every nail I could find, but the panel was still hesitant to shake free. Without any better ideas in mind, I straddled the top of the cabin like a rodeo cowboy, grabbed hold of the monstrosity, and went to town shaking the bejesus out of it. The rippling metal sounded like thunder. I shook harder. Clouds of rust dust leaped from the old, shrieking panels, but it would not let go. It was as if the old roof were fighting for its life, begging for one more season, promising a winter without leaks. But I knew that roof was a lying son of a bitch. Gripping it with both hands at the risk of tossing myself off the roof, I refortified myself with the rage of past leaky seasons and gave it everything I had, until it slipped from my hand and swung down, pivoting on that one miraculous nail before getting overwhelmed by angle and momentum and plunging off the roof with a horrendous shriek, ripping the gutter off as it went. It seemed to take whole minutes for the sound of it to end. I looked at Kellen and yelled, "Got it!" There was certainly no turning back now.

There are basically four layers to a roof. The bottom layer is made up of rafters. Like studs in a wall, the rafters give the roof the majority of its structural integrity. On top of the rafters comes sheathing, usually plywood, that provides a solid, uniform surface for the roof. Atop the sheathing is some sort of waterproofing material—often a thick, felt paper or a rubberized material that comes in big, heavy rolls. There was scant evidence that the cabin ever had this critical component. Traces of what looked like felt paper clung to the plywood here and there, but for the most part, the old wood was bare and, as you'd expect, plagued with rot.

Wherever water had made it through the old, rusted metal, the plywood had turned black with mildew and decay. Of course I found black spots around the chimney, and near the ridge, where Kate had tried to fix the leak before ending up in the emergency room. But that was only the beginning. The roof's plywood was polka-dotted with water damage. I'd spent years trying to battle what I thought was one or two leaks. Little did I know, the roofing had been failing more or less everywhere, and for a long time. The weaknesses Ray and I had introduced around the chimney were a fraction of the overall problem. If anything, the chimney hole and resulting leak had provided a critical clue, a warning light that the roof needed serious attention.

I began the surgical extraction of rotten plywood while Kellen gathered all the old metal and bad wood into a tidy pile next to the truck. After a piece of old plywood was removed, I'd shout down measurements for new pieces so Kellen could cut and toss them up. We fell into a casual rhythm that way, and slowly, the roof began to come back to life.

It took until late afternoon to get all the rot removed and the new plywood down. With the alder trees gone, the high sun fell directly on the cabin. It had gotten hot. This was mainly a problem because I'd chosen to go overkill with the next part. Instead of traditional roofing paper, I'd opted for a super-sticky, ultra-heavy roll of a sort of rubberized membrane. On the top, it felt like the surface of one of those cheap inflatable boats people buy in the heat of summer to toss their kids in, the kind with the flimsy screw-together paddles and some extreme name like Eagle 3000. The bottom of the membrane appeared to be straight tar. As the mercury rose, this tar tended to liquefy and become not just sticky but damn-near magnetic.

The membrane was three feet wide. A strip about ten feet long, as wide as the roof, weighed as much as a few sacks of potatoes. In ideal conditions, you'd cut a sheet the length of the roof, carry it up, and roll it on in a neat, wrinkle-free strip. In reality, I'd be tangled in the thing long before I got near the ladder. Trying to cut it was nearly impossible. The blade simply gathered the black muck as I forced it through. It was weapons-grade adhesive. I worried about getting tangled up in it permanently, like some kind of human flytrap.

By the time I got to the top of the ladder, my shirt, hands, calves, and shoes were all attached to the sheet I was carrying. Most enraging were the spots where the adhesive found bare skin. Two more trips up the ladder and I would have been smooth as the day I was born. I abandoned the plan to strategically and systematically roll out the membrane, instead opting to lunge at the roof in a desperate attempt to get the whole mess away from me.

Luckily, the stickiness was hungry for a new victim. Slowly, I liberated myself and got the sheet stuck down, working out the wrinkles as best I could. Whoever replaced the roof next would have to remove all the plywood. It would never separate from this stuff voluntarily. Back down in the driveway, I took a step back and evaluated the first strip. It was in a U-shape and full of wrinkles, but it was on. In time, it got a bit easier. I wondered if perhaps the goo was like a virus. Once I was covered in it, the adhesive recognized me as one of its own and sought other things to cling to.

Matt, Dayna, Amy, and Kate showed up to lend Kellen and me a hand. Matt jumped at the chance to help me stretch the strips over the plywood and smooth out the wrinkles as we stuck them down. To have two people on the roof wasn't exactly safe. Even among close friends, I'd say it's not common to share a ladder, but we made it work. To reach a distant area, one of us would lean way over, gloved hand outstretched, while the other person would lean an equal amount, but in the opposite direction. It didn't take us long to get good at it, performing a sort of poor man's Cirque du Soleil performance but with more grunting.

Having a second set of hands to work the wrinkles proved invaluable, and when we got to the shaded side of the roof, things vastly improved. We learned to keep the roll out of the sun. We learned how to cut a strip and then reroll it to make it easier to apply. On the backside of the cabin, there wasn't a wrinkle to be found. By the time the final piece was applied, the light was beginning to fade. We decided to call it a day, opting to let the tools lie where they were and do a full cleanup the following day, hopefully in the shadow of a new roof.

We tossed some logs in the firepit outside and got to work building up a few embers to cook dinner. I'd recently brought up an old cooking grate from a Weber grill and was pleased to find that it fit perfectly atop the edge of the clay firepit. The rest of the night was spent stuffing our guts with tacos, tossing a few cards around, and swatting at mosquitoes that made it past heavy layers of Repel-brand lemon-eucalyptus bug spray, our preferred repellent. The day's efforts brought bedtime earlier than usual.

Breakfast was big. There were sizzling ham steaks all around, coupled with plenty of eggs, hash browns, and sausage. We took our time getting ready, going over the next phase of the plan, familiarizing ourselves with the materials, the metal, the screws, charging the drill batteries, visiting the outhouse, having seconds of hash browns, visiting the outhouse again. After setting a third percolator of coffee on the stove, Matt and I grabbed the drills and a mountain of screws and headed onto the roof. Down below, Kellen got to work gathering the metal while Kate and Dayna were occupied working out the form of a new driftwood bench.

With the membrane on, the next step was to install horizontal strips of wood across the roof that we'd attach the metal to. The strips provided an air gap so that the metal was less likely to rust. The unexpected side benefit was their application as a new foothold for Matt and me, allowing us to leave the ladder behind and mountain goat about the roof with reckless abandon. We got good at scrambling. What we were not good at was keeping things from falling off the roof. Below, it rained screws.

Each metal panel, about three feet wide by twelve feet long, was held to the roof with small, self-tapping screws specifically designed for the task at hand. *Self-tapping* meant they didn't need a pilot hole to find purchase and pull themselves through the metal and into the wood below. This was all theoretical, of course, and potentially mostly marketing. Describing the screws as "self-tapping" was like describing me at ten years old as "self-room-cleaning." In most cases, it took a few seconds of ramped-up drill speed and solid, consistent pressure for the point of the screw to burrow a little hole and start to grab. Ideally, we would have held the screw with one hand and the drill with the other to help guide it along. But most of the time, our death grip on the ladder or one of the horizontal wooden strips made it a one-handed operation. Over and over, we'd place a screw on the drill, praying that friction alone would hold it in place, take a deep breath, and reach out. Gingerly, so as not to knock free the screw's grip on the bit, we'd position the tip on the surface of the metal and squeeze the drill's trigger, gently at first, then gradually increasing the speed and pressure. If we were lucky, this constantly straining, breath-holding, vein-popping maneuver would result in a driven screw. Usually, it resulted in an expletive and a screw lazily rolling off the roof into the driveway. Periodically, Kellen would replenish us with more screws. Slowly, the pile of panels in the driveway made their way onto the roof, the cabin taking well to the look of new metal.

That evening, I stood on the ladder alone with a Sawzall, staring at a holeless, freshly covered roof. It was perfect. The metal was slick and strong. The screws were in neat little rows, an unnecessary but immensely satisfying detail we'd worked hard to achieve. I imagined you could have turned the whole thing upside down and it would have floated. But it wasn't done. I had to ruin it to finish it. The chimney hole required resurrection. Three years earlier, I'd stood in the driveway and watched with horror as Ray drove the Sawzall through the roof and popped his head out in a cloud of sawdust and metal shavings. At that point, I didn't feel comfortable screwing up a hole. Now I was wrapping up a complete reroofing. Maybe it was the shiny new metal, but it was hard not to reflect.

Despite the increased skill and confidence, I wasn't looking forward to turbo-stabbing the place with a high-powered Sawzall, a tool that is the mechanical manifestation of anxiety. Sometimes it was hard to tell if the blade was oscillating or if the world was shaking around it. Out of respect for its chaotic personality, I took my time, carefully marking out the hole's shape with a thick Sharpie and then drilling a pilot hole in the center to have an open place to get the Sawzall started. I'd bought a new blade for the task, hoping a keen edge would equate to less mayhem.

The Sawzall buzzed to life with its usual terror, eclipsing the sound of the generator it was plugged into below. With utter care, I guided the blurred teeth through the metal and along the thick black line. If someone were to ask me how long I can hold my breath while simultaneously tensing my entire body, I would tell them at least as long as it takes to cut a chimney hole out of a roof. If the blade had been dull, I might have passed out before the last bits of metal were severed. As the disc of metal fell through and clattered to the cabin floor below, I felt myself gasp for air. The first gulp shot right back out as an immense sigh of relief. The hole was reborn. It looked clean. It looked right.

Matt and Kellen fed the chimney back to me, and I slotted it into the bracket attached to the loft floor, giving it a hard twist to lock it together. I couldn't help but remember the struggle I'd gone through just to find out how that pipe connection worked. It took me weeks to figure out. Next came the bright orange silicone collar that bridged the gap between the hole in the roof and the chimney pipe itself. It was a bad connection with the old collar that led to the original chimney leak. This time, I was methodical. First, a layer of sealant in tight, thick, concentric rings. Then the boot, set into the sealant so that it squeezed out neatly in all directions. Next, screws were driven through the boot's flange, every half inch, resembling the rivets and fasteners that hold airplane wings together, which was exactly the level of strength I was striving for. On top of the screws, multiple layers of roofing sealant, molded by hand to create a seamless transition between the roof and the boot. I spent a few hours carefully sealing the whole thing up and attaching the metal arms that supported the chimney at its otherwise wobbly top. Just before dark, I slapped on the rain cap at the top and climbed down. Even though it was August, even though it was at least eighty degrees, we tossed some paper in the woodstove and lit a small fire so we could take in the full scene in the driveway.

Bright red sparks bubbled out of the chimney like popcorn, then drifted away in a puff of light gray smoke, the bright metal roof reflecting every photon of the day's dying light. Compared to the dark, evergreen forest that framed it, the roof appeared to be nearly glowing. On paper, we'd done little more than reroof a shed, but from the grins we wore on our faces, it was clear a lot more had been achieved. I realized then, in a strange way, the cabin was done.

I wasn't there at the beginning, when George had looked for flat ground and started building a little cabin on someone else's land. I wasn't there when Chris bought the cabin and added his own touches, the windows, the deck framing. I had not built the cabin, but I did feel like I'd finished it. Based on the condition of the place when I'd found it, I doubted anyone had ever stayed in the place before my time. There was a good chance the first night of the work party was the first time someone had spent the night there.

I was eternally grateful for the boosted efforts of those who came before me. The cabin arrived in my life like a paint-by-number drawing, all the lines present, just waiting for someone to come along with the patience and care to fill things in. Anything less and it might have been too overwhelming. Anything more and there might not have been enough to spark an all-consuming curiosity. When I bought the cabin, I didn't know how a foundation worked or how a roof went on. But now, I'd learned enough to fix up both and everything in between.

The history of the place had a lot to do with what I found so inviting about building in the first place. Sure, I liked the tools, liked being outside, liked the physicality of it, liked the little puzzles, the smells, the camaraderie of building buddies, but there was more. I often thought about George, placing that first concrete block, the one that would eventually sink into the ground. How many times had I lain on my stomach to pull a can of soup out from the kitchen because of his efforts? How many nights had we all spent laughing, crying, singing, learning in the space that occupied the 120 square feet above that hunk of rock and sand and gravel? There was no way for him to know what he was beginning on that day in the woods. What the cabin had come to mean to me made me think back on the improbability of it all, but it also made me intently aware of my own efforts to add to the place, to create something that someone else might fall in love with ten, twenty, thirty years from now. Building things slowed down time, translated efforts into results that reverberated for decades. At a desk, I'd compose an email that was sent to thousands. At most, the pinnacle of engagement would be thirty seconds of someone's time. More often, it was just a thing to delete. But there was a chance when I screwed a tread onto a set of stairs that it was just the first act of a lifetime that could span entire generations of friends and families who might step there, on their way up to sleep in the loft, on their way down after changing from a rainy romp in the woods. The act of building carried with it benefits that often felt nearly tectonic in scale, and it mesmerized me.

As I packed up my tools, I couldn't help but notice the look of them. They'd taken a beating. The drills were freckled with siding stain and covered in scratches and scrapes, as was the circular saw, its black grip worn to a dull charcoal gray. I had endless half-empty boxes of screws of all different shapes, sizes, and colors. Each one was capable of triggering memories of projects that made the place a little better, made me a little happier. I'd acquired three or four extension cords, a few boxes filled with different drill bits and attachments. My tool bucket had become an unwieldy, overflowing bouquet of chrome and steel and rubberized grips. Nothing looked new. But they didn't look worn out. Rather, they looked broken in, warmed up, ready for a lot more.

It would have been nice to celebrate the roof late into the night, but it was Sunday. People had to get home, back to work. We'd save the celebration for the next visit, hopefully paired with a bit of rain. It'd be nice to watch it roll off the metal. Instead, we loaded up the old roofing materials, bound for salvage suppliers and the dump, and pulled out of the Riversites at sunset. On the way home, we stopped for burgers and milkshakes at the drive-in in Startup. The parking lot was crowded with families and friends headed back to the city after a weekend in the mountains. It was always like this in summer. Looking out into the parking lot, I took note of the cargo. There were trucks full of ATVs, and folks pulling boats. There were a half dozen RVs and vanlifers and plenty of Subarus loaded with backpacking gear or climbing rope, all evidence of their respective weekend's activities. Then there was the truck with a fat roll of old roofing, its ass end hanging three feet beyond the tailgate, like a giant rusted cigar, surrounded by tools and leftover groceries. I wondered if people were jealous. They had to be. I would have been.

27

THE GUN

F all came and went. I found myself working more and more, trying to save for a hypothetical building project neither Bryan nor I were sure was even possible. The biggest downside was trading cabin weekends for a few extra days composing email templates and Google ads for cash. When winter arrived, I needed a break. There was a lot of snow in the forecast. It seemed like a good time to get away.

The night before I left, I texted Mike to find out how the roads were. Though community dues paid for plowing, it only applied to the main road. If Wit's End needed plowing, it would be up to Mike, Andy, Murphy, Chris, and me to schedule it and pay for it. When I'd brought up the subject on prior visits, no one seemed too bothered by it. Worst-case scenario, we parked at the bottom of the hill and walked up. I was always prepared for the hike, but it was nice to find out how things were looking from Mike beforehand and plan the shopping trip accordingly. If we had to hike uphill, it made more sense to pack a bottle of whiskey than a case of beer. The road, it turned out, was overwhelmed. It'd be a whiskey night.

As Indy and I gathered steaks and coffee and other essentials at the Fred Meyer in Monroe, it dawned on me that a simple sled, pulled by a rope, would make any load a lot easier to haul, and if we had to get down the hill to make another trip, a sled wouldn't be the worst way to return to the car. Luckily, there was a sporting goods store that shared a parking lot with the Fred Meyer, so we loaded up the groceries and drove over. No sense exerting ourselves when there was an uphill hike looming on the horizon.

Inside, we found the recent snowfall had cleared the racks of nearly every type of sled, leaving only cheap plastic discs in either red or blue for $9.99. We got one of each and started looking for rope. Meandering around the store, we ended up near the gun case, a glass display full of oiled steel. Regardless of your stance on guns, I think it's fair to say that they are at least a subject of interest to most people. I had no interest in owning a gun, but it was damn hard not to stop by and check them out. In the display case were dozens: Lugers I recognized from my love of World War II movies; tiny handguns that looked like the ones James Bond used; big, modern things I could picture in the hands of RoboCop; and, shining in the corner, a pair of Colt Peacemakers, giant revolvers with silver barrels and ivory handles. They looked like the epitome of spaghetti western sheriff guns. That's when we noticed. Every gun in the case was a BB gun.

"Hello? Anyone working the gun case?! Help!"

Indy couldn't take his eyes off it, the ivory-handled Peace-maker. It wasn't even fake ivory. The handle was just off-white. Inspired by ivory. That's what it was.

"Which one are you looking at?" said Dave of the Monroe Big 5 Sporting Goods store.

"The Colt Peacemaker."

"This one?" he asked, pointing to a different one with a blue barrel.

"Do we look like idiots? Who buys a gun with a blue barrel? It doesn't even have the ivory handle!" I didn't say this to Dave, but I tried to make the same message clear with a little chuckle.

"Uh, heh, he-he, no. The one with the silver barrel and the ivory handle." Obviously.

Dave took it out unceremoniously, which I vowed to never forgive him for, and let us hold it.

"Oh, it's heavy," Indy said, his eyes lighting up like Gollum in sight of the ring. And indeed it was. He handed it over to me, and I marveled at the weight. It could not have felt more like a real gun, a statement that doesn't mean much considering the sum total of my gun experience was once touching Joel Elder's dad's shotgun in fifth grade on a dare.

"That's the price, then?" I asked Dave.

"Yup, this one's at $129.99."

"Huh."

I handed the gun back, and Dave returned it to the case. Indy and I retreated to the fishing aisle to discuss.

"It's pretty expensive," I said. It seemed especially expensive because it was so incredibly unnecessary. Not that any BB gun is necessary, but we already had a BB gun at the cabin. The plastic rifle model had been an early addition, and we used it plenty, plinking away at empty cans strung up from vine maple that grew about twenty yards from the cabin. The activity was a frequent accompaniment to our morning coffee. It was a good way to wake up.

"I want that gun," Indy replied, seemingly set on it. I sensed an opportunity.

"You should buy it, man." Clearly, we both wanted it. But maybe I could persuade Indy to take on the full financial responsibility while I merely benefited from the joy that would come along with keeping it at the cabin, where I was certain it would live. He took a moment to let the wheels turn in his head a bit more before finally giving up.

"Ah, I don't need it. Let's go."

Morosely, we walked to the counter with our rope and our sleds. I could only think of the gun. While the cashier rang up our items, I barely whispered to Indy, more of a moan really, "I'll throw in forty bucks."

"And we'll take that gun," Indy said, though it was more of a shout, a call to Dave, wherever he'd gone.

With great enthusiasm, we returned to the gun case and forced Dave to sort through a ring of maybe twelve thousand keys to undo the lock again, a task he clearly hated. Soon, we were back at the counter, now piled with sleds, rope, a gun, and enough BBs to take down a herd of elephants, all the necessary components for a sort of dipshit's biathlon.

Turning to Indy, I said, "We're going to need an alibi." Dave, now at the register, was not amused.

Halfway out to the car, Indy began ripping the thing out of its cardboard box.

"Jesus Christ, man, you can't just be handling guns out here in the parking lot," I said, nervously glancing around.

"Oh, relax, it's Monroe. Half these people are carrying guns already." Standing in a parking lot full of jacked-up trucks and NRA bumper stickers, I couldn't argue.

We loaded the sleds and rope back in the car and pulled out onto the highway. Indy had the new steel in his lap, eyeing it with a childlike amusement, involuntary giggles escaping from beneath his layers of Carhartt and Filson Tin Cloth. He was dressed like he had just trundled down from his gold claim to pick up hardtack and bolts of fabric. The cabin, an opportunity for him to occupy his truest form. While he twirled the barrel around and practiced pulling the hammer back, I found it hard to keep my eyes on the road.

As the road curved through Sultan and Gold Bar, the branches of dark evergreens started to appear more and more bent with the weight of the latest dumping of snow. From what I could tell on the Facebook page reports prior to leaving, the Riversites had received nearly two feet. I was looking forward to it. On a normal day, the decrepit cabins, charred meth RVs, rusted-out abandoned cars, and mud-covered road could look downright depressing. On a snowy day, everything was fresh and good.

Turning off the highway, we found that the road into the Riversites had been recently plowed. We made our way slowly past frozen stands of hemlock and cedar, crept by the rock face whose never-ending drips had earned it the nickname the "Car Wash," and admired the icicles that had become of its spouts. When we dropped down to the turnoff for the cabin, I saw that even Wit's End had been plowed out of neighborly generosity. We wouldn't need the sleds for anything responsible.

Anxious to get started on an afternoon that would surely be lodged in the best parts of our memories, we furiously shoveled the driveway clear, parked the car, and got to work. Beers were thrust into snowbanks, gloves were donned, and snowshoes gifted to me by my late uncle were strapped on tight. Indy loaded the Peacemaker to maximum BB capacity and slipped a fresh CO_2 cylinder into its handle. By the time we were ready to head out and romp through the snow, Mike had stirred from his trailer and come out to say hello. It was a testament to his character that, upon seeing us with a couple of sleds, beers packed into our pockets, and a gun in our hands, he had no questions as to what we were up to. Rather, he gave us a big smile and told us to have fun. Before we parted ways, I held up the Colt Peacemaker for him to see.

"Check it out, man! Colt Peacemaker!"

"Oh, wow. Nice, bud! That's the same one I have!"

I knew Mike carried a gun from time to time. He told me on several occasions that he'd made a habit of walking the road most mornings with his gun at his side. It was a sort of safety-patrol-induced exercise regimen. Thinking of his walks always made me feel good, like the cabin had its own security detail. The fact that he was doing it with a Colt Peacemaker made me feel even better. But I had to come clean with him. I couldn't have him thinking we were on the same level.

"Yeah, but this is just a BB gun," I admitted.

"Oh, so's mine!" Mike replied cheerfully.

And with that, we set off to do our part protecting the neighborhood, because sometimes the cabin wasn't a place to hone our skills. Sometimes it wasn't a thing to worry about. Sometimes it was just a place where we could go and forget about everything beyond the thrills that could be had with a plastic sled and a BB gun and a good friend. Sometimes it was a place we went to bank experiences we knew would come out the other side of time as nostalgia. Sometimes the only agenda item was whatever. Always, it was perfect.

28

A GOOD GOODBYE

A few months later, Bryan and I put down an impossibly low offer on an empty lot in the Riversites. The owners accepted almost immediately. In May, we quit our jobs and started pulling out ferns in the woods just down the road from Wit's End, clearing an area so we could build a new cabin from the ground up.

That summer, we worked every daylight hour to create something grander than either of us could have imagined. It had great big exposed beams and cathedral ceilings, stained glass windows, and pine trim, charred using a Japanese wood preservation technique called *shou sugi ban*. There was a hot shower, a toilet that incinerated human waste at a thousand degrees, even a refrigerator. Though we'd originally hoped to finish in August, it was nearly a year after we started that I found myself out near the highway, sinking a FOR SALE sign into the ground.

Selling the new cabin wasn't always the plan. We thought

maybe we could rent it out or save it for friends and family to use. I think in many ways, the notion that we could quit our jobs and build a cabin seemed so far-fetched in the first place that we never really considered what we'd do when we got to the end. By the time we were finished, our struggling bank accounts made it clear what needed to be done. So we let it go, in the hopes that doing so might permit us to do the whole thing again someday.

For the cabin on Wit's End, that year had been the ultimate test. Bryan and I lived there full-time while we built just down the road. What had once been little more than a hut of nightmares became a real, honest-to-goodness home. It offered us warmth and shelter during massive winter storms, kept the mosquitoes at bay in spring and summer, and provided the perfect place to warm up when the first chill of autumn set in. Even the outhouse played along, never quite getting full, like some sort of strange biblical miracle.

When the new cabin sold, I immediately grew anxious for what would come next. By no means a master, I had come a long way from the place I was years before, testing drills out by slamming holes in the closet of a rental house. Looking around the cabin on Wit's End, it was impossible not to account the full aggregate of mistakes that had been made and adapted to: the gaps in the wall paneling, the ever-sloping floor, the deck board that had rotted away because the space between them was, as Murphy had said, too narrow. There were problems everywhere, but now that I knew how to take care of them, I couldn't seem to commit to the work.

The truth was, when I saw the jagged edge of a bad cut made by a dull blade in the hands of a close friend, it offered a fond memory. I knew how every nail, every bit of trim, every screw had come to be in that place. On one of the walls, there were still dirty boot marks clearly visible on the wood where we'd all carelessly tromped around on the plywood before nailing it in place on that first work weekend. Etched in carelessness, the footprints were now evidence of a grand time I'd never forget. I wanted to build, but I couldn't reconstruct the cabin. Stuck between a desire to do more and an inability to ruin something that was, for all its faults, already perfect, I realized the only way forward was to create a completely new place and fall in love again. With a heavy heart, I decided to sell the cabin on Wit's End.

The decision came fast. When the pandemic hit, prices on escapes out of the city skyrocketed. Apparently, telling the entire world to get away from one another made a little cabin out in the woods an especially alluring thing. Two days after a chat with a real estate agent in the area, the listing was up online. The next night, I accepted an offer. In hindsight, I'm glad it happened so fast. If it had been drawn out, if I had to consider dropping the price, if anything had not gone smoothly, I'm sure the pangs of regret would have caught up with me and I would have kept the place.

In the end, Wit's End became far more than a cabin to me. It was a mentor and a martyr, offering me the opportunity to learn new skills even if it meant a few bruises got left in the process. Were it not for the cabin, discovering a passion for building was entirely unlikely. I reflect often on where I might be if I hadn't made the irresponsible decision to buy the place. Maybe I would have found something else—hot-air balloon operator or glassblowing or falconry. Or maybe I'd have given

up and resigned myself to a career and a routine that wasn't fulfilling. One thing was clear: that little place had fundamentally
changed the course of my life. The summer after I sold Wit's
End, Bryan and I returned to the Riversites to build another
cabin. This one we kept. In between builds, I returned to my
day job, now as a carpenter.

At first, when people asked me what this book was about,
I told them it was a story of the misadventures that happened
when I bought a derelict shack in an underdog neighborhood and
did my best to make it a special place. I shied away from the part
about my own discoveries of purpose that led to a new career
and a life that feels, on the whole, a lot more rewarding. I think
I shied away from that part of the story because there was never
a real aha moment. There was not an instance where everything
changed. If it were a movie, there'd be no point when the music
swells and your eyes fill up with tears and you know everything
is going to be all right. Perhaps it would make for a better story if
there were such a moment, but if there's a lesson in all of this, for
me at least, it's that those moments are unimaginably rare in life
and, as such, they're a hard and often hopeless thing to chase after.

What's not rare is the quiet, persistent voice that nags us
into wondering what else might be possible, what change might
be a bit better for us in the long run. This story is about what
happens when we give that voice room to grow. It reminds me
of the water thing.

There's no name for it, it being a sort of sacred social pact that
happens when good friends gather around cold water. It happened often at the cabin, down at our favorite river spot. We'd
walk there and take in the view at all times of the year. In the
heat of summer, swimming was assumed. But often, we'd make

the trek down in fall or early spring when the water was extra cold and the clouds ensured there'd be no warming sun. At the water's edge, someone would voice the idea of jumping in. There'd be smiles, of course. A joke. It sounded awful. The shock of the cold water would be overwhelming. There weren't towels. There were never towels. There was never sense to it. But experience had taught us that there was more than the freezing water.

We knew that when we shot to the surface and let out a "Whoop!" and began scrambling back to shore, that when we got to the rock and pulled ourselves out and stood there with our blood pumping at full throttle and the cold stone under our feet and the snowy mountains over our heads, we knew that that moment would without a doubt be the best part of our day, our week. We knew it wouldn't be forgotten, a permanent footnote seared into our memory. And we'd stand there, laughing, screaming, and smiling in the sacred knowledge that we knew what the really good stuff was and that it was always, always worth jumping in, always worth it to wonder, to take chances, to brave a bit of cold in the hopes that you'll come out the other side somehow, unbelievably, all the warmer.

When I last left Wit's End, Kate waited in the driveway while I looked over the place a final time, a nub of incense smoking away atop the woodstove. Certainly, there were good things on the horizon. I'd used the proceeds from the sale of the cabin to buy property on Washington's Olympic Peninsula. It was five acres, filled with towering cedar, Douglas fir, hemlock, maple, and madrone. There was a big meadow where elk tended to bed down in the summer, and where the property sloped away down the hill, you could see for miles over the cobalt-blue water of Hood Canal.

For a while, I had entertained the idea of creating a replica cabin at the new property, even took pictures of every inch of the place to make sure I'd get all the details correct, right down to the colors of faded paint on the loft floor. Ultimately, though, the impetus of moving on was to create something new, to fall in love again and challenge myself to go beyond what was comfortable. That's where the good stuff was, after all. Granted, some things would be the same. I'd been careful to arrange for certain amenities to be excluded from the sale. The woodstove, for example, the heart of the place, was now packed away and awaiting its future home. But other things stayed, like the old cabinet, the robin's-egg-blue sink, and the kitchen, where I left a note, a hurricane lamp, and a bit of incense for the new owner.

Dear Newcomer,

I was seventeen when I left the house where I grew up to move to college. It took me ten years to find another place that felt like home. This was my first cabin.

It was purchased on a whim, the day after I saw it. At the time, it was just a shell of what it is now. There was no flooring, no deck, no driveway, no stove. Friends and I poured ourselves into making this our home away from home. In the process of doing so, more laughter, tears, and memories went into this place than I will ever be able to account for.

We ate fat rib eye steaks cooked on an old Coleman camp stove, shoveled countless loads of gravel around the driveway, and shot BB guns with our morning coffee. We picked salmonberries and fiddleheads in the spring and sat around campfires in the fall. We cooled our feet in the river every summer, and we waited greedily for the first snowfall every winter.

This was our clubhouse, our escape, our retreat. It was the base camp for so many unexpected adventures and will be forever remembered as the setting for so many favorite stories.

On the surface, it might not be much, a ten-by-twelve room with a bucket for plumbing. But I hope that you're buying this place because you see in it what I did back then. You see that when the oil lamps are just right, and you've got something good warming on the stove, and you've put your feet up next to a crackling woodstove, when you've got everything just the way you like it, at that moment, the outside world disappears for a bit, and you'll swear the sparks coming out of the chimney are pure magic.

This is what the cabin gave me and the people that I love. I'm thrilled it's someone else's turn now. Enjoy!

You'll see that I left you with a little gift, some piñon incense and an oil lamp. I used each of these every time I visited the cabin. I encourage you to try them on a cold winter night to cozy up the place after you've shoveled the driveway clear of snow. Use them on balmy summer evenings to light the deck and keep the mosquitoes away. Use them with friends. Use them when alone. Use them whenever you need to feel like you've escaped somewhere else, just for a night. I promise, they'll make this little cabin come alive.

Cheers,
Patrick

ACKNOWLEDGMENTS

A huge thanks to Farley Chase for thinking this idea had legs and patiently walking me through the journey of bringing it to life. Many beers are owed to Marc Resnick for his support and enthusiasm and advice throughout the editing process. Also, kudos to the entire editorial team at St. Martin's who waded through and fixed a tangled manuscript. (I have a tendency to throw out punctuation like it's hard candy at a small-town parade.)

I feel like the acknowledgment sections of real books are filled with thanks to the countless people who assisted with research efforts, the librarians and professors and subject matter experts who gave credibility to an idea so that it could become a book. *CABIN* was the culmination of almost a decade of field research, so it seems fitting to take this opportunity to thank the team for some of its most inspired data-gathering sessions.

To Matt for slogging through the geometry of cladding the loft and for building the cots and draining the driveway, but mostly for the countless hours spent holed up in that cabin playing music and laughing. Wit's End was a playground for a friendship I am eternally grateful for.

To Dayna for roof assistance and bench project management and for so many hilarious nights with Matt and me. It is an honor to share with you the knowledge that if a grape tasted a chip, it would be ashamed of itself.

To James for help with that other stair project that ultimately ended in us tearing it all out and building a ladder instead. It was the right choice.

To Indy for so, so many trips, for the tradition of Twisted Teas and dust burritos, for the kitchen, for the disc sled BB gun decathlon, and for that terrible firewood holder that's probably still up there annoying people. I will never forget that night in the red light of our headlamps in the loft, laughing so hard I was worried I might have a stroke.

To Kellen for the roof help and the inside wall sheathing and the late-night sing-alongs.

To Amy, even though I'm not sure she ever really helped with anything. Why is that, Amy?

To Dan for the wood box roof, for the evening when you found the hammer, but mostly for always bringing the magic. And to Alex, for being exactly the sort of friend the cabin always welcomed.

To Todd for crawling around in the muck with me to fix the foundation and for all the writing help.

To Kiersten and Kali and Malia and Yos-wa and Sarah and Dan and Zach and Casey and Casey and Kelsey and Husted for your incredible friendship and so many good memories at the cabin. I love you all.

To Bryan for the stairs and for Jean Claude's after-market center console, for the spice racks and the tables, for also quitting, for giving me the confidence to do any of this, for joining me in all of it.

To Kelly for chopping wood better than anyone has ever chopped wood, for going to the outhouse to fart, and for supporting all the cabin projects. I know it's a lot but clearly worth it, right? Right?

To Martin for what will forever be one of the best weekends up there, with that one playlist, when for a few hours we thought we'd all move to Turkey.

To Lewis and Sam and Ben and Jill and Nicki and Ron and Brian and Maddy and Trevor and Logan and Jayln for years of enthusiasm for all of this and for visits to the mountains that always left me feeling proud and lucky to have you as family.

To Kate for the outhouse shelves and the roof tape. Sorry about your finger. Above all, thank you for believing the cabin was an appropriate third date, for loving the place as hard as I did, for giving me the support that's made it possible for me to keep pursuing projects in the woods.

To Marge who will never read this book because she's an illiterate dog but deserves all the praise in the world anyway.

And most of all, thank you to my mother. Directly or indirectly, everything I am grateful for in this life is because of you, and there is a lot. Dad would be proud.

P.S. Friggin' huge shout-out to the following: Cheez-Its, Rainier Beer, bagged ice, hurricane lamps, Hungry Jack original dehydrated hash browns (and the far more rare Hungry Jack cheesy dehydrated hash browns), Fritos, spiders, the Umarex Colt

Peacemaker Revolver single action army six-shooter .177 caliber air pistol BB gun, Nalley jalapeño hot chili, salmonberries, owls, Subaru all-wheel drive, Bluetooth speakers, the band Bon Iver, the Monroe Fred Meyer and the Monroe Lowe's, the practice of talking about going for a hike tomorrow but never actually doing it, chain saws, three-inch deck screws, gravel, Fresh Express bagged Caesar salad (the supreme variety, not the regular), Sears, Roebuck & Co. potbellied stoves, IKEA futons, the star cluster Pleiades, piñon incense, dry socks, the Whistling Post Saloon, Gore-Tex, Repel lemon-eucalyptus bug spray, rib eye steaks, headlamps, AAA batteries, five-gallon buckets, limes, ibuprofen, propane, and paper towels.

ABOUT THE AUTHOR

Kate Palmer

Patrick Hutchison is a writer and builder from the Pacific Northwest. His work has appeared in *Outside*, *Wired*, *Vice*, *Seattle* magazine, and *Seattle Weekly*. He grew up in Washington State's rainy southwest corner, eventually moving to Seattle to attend the University of Washington. Working on the cabin described in this book inspired him to leave copywriting to pursue carpentry. He now finds himself most often in the woods, working on tiny homes, cabins, and tree houses. When he isn't building, you'll find him at his home in Tacoma, Washington, where he lives with his wife, Kate, and their black Lab, Marge. *CABIN* is his first book.